*The Domestic
Context
of American
Foreign Policy*

A SERIES OF BOOKS IN INTERNATIONAL RELATIONS
Bruce M. Russett, *Editor*

The Domestic Context of American Foreign Policy

Barry B. Hughes
CASE WESTERN RESERVE UNIVERSITY

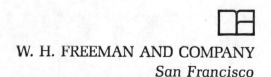

W. H. FREEMAN AND COMPANY
San Francisco

Library of Congress Cataloging in Publication Data

Hughes, Barry, 1945–
    The domestic context of American foreign policy.

    Includes bibliographical references and index.
    1. United States—Foreign relations—1945–
I. Title.
JX1417.H83   327.73   77-17472
ISBN 0-7167-0040-9
ISBN 0-7167-0039-5 pbk.

Printed in the United States of America

1 2 3 4 5 6 7 8 9

To Marilyn and My Parents

Contents

Preface

This book was begun in the summer of 1971 when I first taught a course in American foreign policy. There was no shortage of books and articles describing U.S. foreign policy since World War II, and a great many works also analyzed the process by which foreign policy is made. Throughout the preparation for and teaching of the course, however, I found it very difficult to uncover adequate analyses of the domestic context of foreign policy. Foreign policy studies overwhelmingly focus on the international environment of U.S. policy and on the governmental decision-making institutions and process. Books describing the process of policy making invariably devote only one chapter or part of one chapter to public opinion and interest groups. In much of the work that does examine the domestic context of foreign policy, authors appear compelled to "take a stand" and to tell us whether or not the public controls foreign policy. Many of these books and articles vacillate, however, presenting considerable evidence on the weakness of the public input and then trying to salvage some role for the public in their conclusions.

This book does focus primarily on the domestic context of policy and does not take a stand. It began with the assumption that if good scholars found it so difficult to agree among themselves and *with* themselves, the relationship between public and policy must be complex and variable. What we need to discover are the circumstances under which the public and, more importantly, various groups within the public have greater or lesser influence in the policy process. A second assumption of this book was that in the investigation of the complex relationship between the public and policy a great deal of data on public opinion, interest groups, and political parties must be presented.

In 1971 (and even as of this writing), one of the most directly relevant works in the literature was Gabriel Almond's *The American People and Foreign Policy*, a great tribute to a now 26-year-old study. Ideally this book should be an update and extension of that study, and that was my original intention. Much has changed since 1950, however, and as a result this is a different kind of work. This book draws heavily on a now-massive volume of survey data and on voting data, both of which were much harder for Almond to obtain. It also relies on recently elaborated analytic models of the policy process. Instead of Almond's discussion of the American character, of the instability of public moods, and of the psychological impact of the cold war, I include reviews of public attitudes, over time, on various foreign policy issues, analysis of intrapublic opinion differences, a study of congressional voting on foreign policy, and discussion of rational actor decision making. The fairly considerable amount of information in this study and its analytic framework should make it useful to the current generation of political scientists.

A number of people made it difficult to finish this book. Foremost among them were Mike Mesarovic and Marilyn Hughes. I thank them both, especially Marilyn, for giving me more interesting things to do than sit at a desk and write. Others have contributed considerably to the effort. Davis Bobrow encouraged and supported me in the initial phases of this work. Kathleen Francovic and Bruce Russett generously took time to read and comment on the entire book in preliminary draft. Frank Sorauf provided very useful feedback on the congressional party voting analysis. Richard Lamb was patient and supportive throughout the process of the final revision, and his confidence in the work has been very gratifying. The problems that remain are mine, not theirs. Evelyn Rogers never lost her good spirits throughout the typing and retyping of at least two complete drafts, and the final typing by Wanda A. Reeves was invaluable.

Barry B. Hughes
October 1977

The Domestic
Context
of American
Foreign Policy

1

Introduction

Two questions frame this study of American foreign policy. First, what do the American public and groups within the public think about various aspects of the United States' foreign policy? Second, how much does it matter what they think? The two questions obviously can be posed and answered separately. The American people may have fairly clear opinions about what our foreign policy is and should be, yet rarely have any significant input into the process of making foreign policy. Or there may be several important channels through which significant numbers of the public can influence foreign policy, while, by and large, the American public has remained uninformed about and uninterested in foreign policy.

Although the focus of the book will remain on the public as a whole and on subgroups within the public, the second question—what does it matter what the public thinks?—requires a broader excursion into the study of foreign policy. Public opinion polls will tell us what the public thinks, will provide a record of the recent history of that thought, and will indicate the degree of homogeneity or heterogeneity in public thinking. However, the polls will not give us any information concerning the relationship between public opinion and actual foreign policy decisions made by those in elected and appointed positions. We will therefore look more broadly at the process of making foreign policy and at the output of the process when it proves desirable.

Models of Foreign Policy Making

Three major groups of factors work jointly to determine foreign policy for any nation.[1] First, the external environment, particularly the strengths and policies of other nations, places constraints on what policy can be made and accounts for the situations and events that elicit foreign policy. Second, various groups exist within nations that work actively for particular foreign policies, since many groups are advantaged or disadvantaged by every foreign policy decision. The domestic setting of foreign policy—containing such groups, and providing the economic, military, and other resources of the nation—can be a powerful determinant of foreign policy. Finally, those persons who actually make foreign policy decisions, as well as the institutions within which they do so, have their own independent impact on the final policy product. Decision makers may act in accordance with their own goals and values even when these significantly differ with many goals held by the general populace. Decision makers may also misperceive public sentiment and/or the external situation, as a result of institutional and human limitations.

The three sets of factors—external, domestic, and decision making—do not, however, constitute anything near an adequate representation or model of the foreign policy process. First, as a model the representation is too simple: Further subdivision and specification of the elements are necessary. Second, it does not show us the pattern of interactions among the elements of the foreign policy process. For instance, while the first two factors (the external environment and the domestic setting) do affect the making of foreign policy, they do it *through* the decision-making process, rather than independently.

A better model of the elements determining foreign policy can be seen in Figure 1.1. The same three basic elements are elaborated somewhat. The domestic setting and the decision-making process

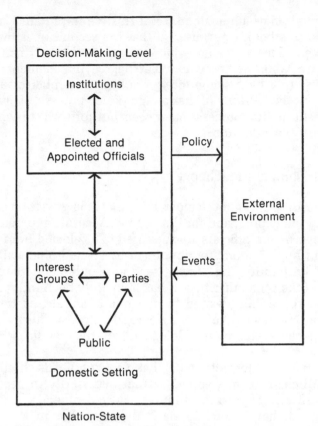

FIGURE 1.1
A GENERAL FOREIGN POLICY MODEL

combine as two elements of the total nation-state or country. The policy of the country affects the external environment, which in turn affects the country. The domestic setting was divided into the general public, and smaller interest groups and parties, while the decision-making element was separated into institutions and elected and appointed officials. In the figure, the arrow between the decision-making element and the domestic setting shows the potential for two-way influence, as do most other model arrows. The decision-making process can affect the domestic setting, and that setting can in turn affect the process; for instance, Americans tend to support foreign policy once it is made, even if they originally favored some other policy.

The foreign policy model of Figure 1.1 still does not tell us the relative importance of the three major elements in the making of foreign policy, much less the importance of the newly introduced subelements. Some understanding of relative importance must, of course, be this book's purpose, so that the second question noted above (What does it matter what the public thinks?) can be answered. We want to know to what degree the elements of the domestic setting help shape foreign policy. A number of different "theories" of the working of the foreign policy process, as well as of the domestic policy process, have been put forward, to which we should turn our attention.

Classical Democratic Theory

A standard description of democracy is that it is government of the people, by the people, and for the people. According to democratic theory, government officials are supposed to be elected from (of) the public and by the public (or appointed by elected officials), and to work for the public. The phrase "for the people" is perhaps more ambiguous than the other two. It has frequently been interpreted to mean that the policy desired by the public should be translated directly into policy by the public's elected officials. This means that officials become "instructed delegates" of the people who elect them.

An alternative interpretation is that elected officials should make policy on behalf of the people, but not necessarily in accordance with specifically expressed opinions. Elected officials, it is sometimes argued, have more specialized knowledge in the area in which they are making policy than the public and hence can better interpret than the public itself what is in the interest of the public. This version of the democratic model can be labeled "Burkean," in honor of its eloquent advocate of the nineteenth century, Edmund Burke. Burke informed his constituents that[2]

> I did not obey your instructions. No. I conformed to the instructions of truth and nature, and maintained your interest, against your opinions, with a constancy that became me. A representative worthy of you ought to be a person of stability. I am not to look to the flash of the day. I know you chose me, in my place, along with others, to be a pillar of the state, and not a weathercock on the top of the edifice, exalted for my levity and versality and of no use but to indicate the shiftings of every fashionable gale.

Whatever the exact form of the representation process, classical democratic theory suggests a version of our foreign policy process model (see Figure 1.1) in which the relationship between the domestic setting and the decision-making level is largely one-directional, from the public to the government. The public elects officials with the assistance of public-based interest groups and parties; through the mechanisms of election and, as importantly, of postelection influence with elected officials through interest groups and parties, the public controls the making of foreign policy. The elected and appointed officials interact with the institutions of the American policy system. For instance, the separations of powers among congressional, executive, and judicial institutions is important in the shaping of foreign policy, especially because the democratic model is concerned with preventing the accrual of power within a few hands and the thwarting of public will or good.

Critics have directed two kinds of attacks toward the democratic model. First, many have questioned its accuracy as a portrayal of the way in which policy *is actually made*. We will discuss below some of the alternative forms of the foreign policy model that scholars have put forward to describe the foreign policy process. Second, quite a number of people reject the democratic model, and in particular the "instructed delegate" version of the model, as a prescription for the procedures by which foreign policy *should be made*. It has not been at all incompatible with general support for the American political machinery, as Walter Lippmann has shown,[3] to argue for a reduction in the influence by the public over foreign policy. Lippmann's argument was that the public is too poorly informed and too emotional about foreign policy to direct it successfully. Implicit in Lippmann's argument, of course, is the assumption that the public has influenced foreign policy considerably, that is, the assumption that some version of the democratic model is descriptively correct.

It is important that the reader maintain the prescriptive/descriptive distinction. Those who accept the democratic model as a reasonably accurate description of how policy is in fact made disagree as to whether the democratic procedure is satisfactory. Thomas Bailey cites and evaluates many examples of the importance of public sentiment:[4]

> In 1803 a rising tide of Western resentment over the closure of the Mississippi prodded President Jefferson into a course that led to the purchase of Louisiana. In 1809, with public opinion so hostile that the very foundations of government trembled, Jefferson was forced to bring about a repeal of the embargo on shipping. In 1854 an enraged North halted the pro-Southern President Pierce in his design to wrest Cuba from the palsied grasp of Spain. In 1893 an aroused nation compelled Cleveland

> to abandon his plans to restore the dusky Hawaiian queen to her throne. In 1898 the war-mad masses forced the nation into an unnecessary clash with Spain, in spite of McKinley, Mark Hanna, and Big Business. . . . In 1921 a determined citizenry insisted upon the Washington Disarmament Conference, for which a lackadaisical President Harding received more than his just share of praise. In 1928 an organized and inspired public kicked Secretary Kellogg into immortality by forcing him to negotiate the Kellogg-Briand pact.

Overall, Bailey's sentiment is that public participation has been a desirable phenomenon.[5] Although he accepted Bailey's description of American public opinion as frequently important in shaping foreign policy, Walter Lippmann strongly denounced that participation:[6]

> The unhappy truth is that the prevailing public opinion has been destructively wrong at the critical junctures. The people have imposed a veto upon the judgements of informed and responsible officials. They have compelled the governments, which usually knew what would have been wiser, or what was necessary, or more expedient, to be too late with too little, or too long with too much, too pacifist in peace and too bellicose in war, too neutralist or appeasing in negotiation or too intransigent. Mass opinion has acquired mounting power in this century. It has shown itself to be a dangerous master of decisions when the stakes are life and death.

Many political philosophers, including John Locke, Alexis de Tocqueville, and Carl Friedrich, have agreed democratic procedures can work in domestic decisions but are inappropriate or dangerous in foreign affairs.[7]

The alternative foreign policy models discussed below are basically descriptive, but normative evaluations by those who write about them are inevitable. One political scientist has identified three basic descriptive models of foreign policy decision making: rational actor, organizational process, and bureaucratic political.[8] Each of these gives a somewhat different view of the relationship between decision-making elements of the model and the societal elements. Thus they all merit some attention.

The Rational Actor Model

The rational actor model bears some similarity to the Burkean version of the democratic model. The rational model portrays the decision-making process as one in which primary decision makers (e.g., the president and his close advisors), when faced with a problem, define the general values and objectives they hold, list the alternatives available to them, examine the consequences of each alternative, evaluate the consequences, and make a decision. Those describing this model frequently point to the behavior of the executive committee organized by President Kennedy during the 1962 Cuban missile crisis as illustrative of rational decision making. When the Soviet missiles were discovered to be in Cuba, Kennedy organized the approximately thirteen-member committee. That group did in fact list its alternatives, debate them at length, and choose one.

When those making the decisions are elected by the general public, or appointed by those who are, and when (as most rational model theorists assume), the policy evaluation criteria center on what is "best" for the country and not just what is best for the decision makers, then the rational and Burkean models have much in common. The rational model in the abstract, however, applies just as well to elites that have not been elected, and for whom criteria other than the "good of the country" prevail. In fact the criteria could center on the good of the decision makers or a small class of the population. Moreover, the rational actor model generally assumes a very small decision-making group, generally within the executive branch of government and unlike the one that Edmund Burke's colleagues in the British Parliament would have recommended. Finally, the rational actor model assumes that the coterie of decision makers dominates the institutional structures, rather than being significantly constrained by them. Thus the overall image is that shown in Figure 1.2.

The rational actor model frequently pervades the thinking of those who come to the study of foreign policy from the study of decision making by individuals or by fairly small groups. Most individuals and some groups do go through the steps of establishing and evaluating alternatives when faced with an important decision—it is considered a mark of "good" decision making to do so, and most readers probably associate this rational actor model with a good procedure for governmental decision making. Commentators on the political scene and even political scientists who should know better also frequently adopt the rational actor model when analyzing the decisions made by a foreign country about which little is known. For instance, the Soviet Union's decisions are frequently discussed as if only one person or a small group at most participated in the decision process. Many other students of politics argue that the rational actor cannot adequately describe procedures in a large government of a complex society. Moreover, they frequently argue that it should not.

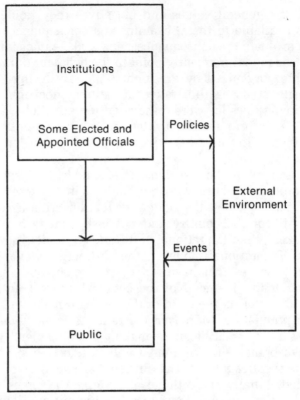

FIGURE 1.2
THE RATIONAL ACTOR MODEL

Organizational-Institutional Models

For many years, political science as a discipline was in large part dominated by a rather more complex model of governmental decision making. The study of politics was at that time frequently the study of institutions. According to the prevailing model, you could tell a great deal about foreign or domestic policy in any country by looking at the constitutional structure of government. In the United States, perhaps the fundamental factor to understand was the division of powers, first between the federal and state governments, and second among congressional, judicial, and executive branches of the federal government. Naturally, not everything of importance can be identified from only *formal* organizations—no organization chart shows all of the real power relationships, and the informal organization must also be—and was—given the attention of scholars.

The clear implication of the institutional model was that the institutions dominated individuals, that roles shaped policy preferences perhaps more than did idiosyncratic variables. It was more important, in understanding a country's foreign policy, to look at the institutions and the external environment than to look at the specific elected or appointed decision makers. Figure 1.3 portrays the model. Frequently tied to the institutional perspective was a historic one. If a scholar looked, for instance, at the role that Britain played for centuries as a balancer of rivalries on the continent, it certainly appeared that such policies were largely independent of the personalities involved and rather determined by the British system of government and the situation posed by the British geo-

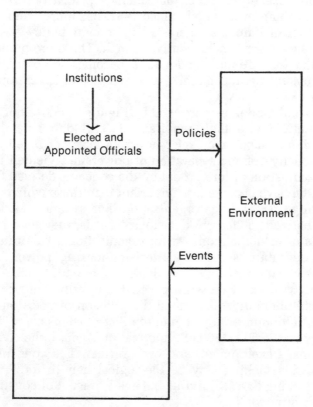

FIGURE 1.3
THE ORGANIZATIONAL INSTITUTIONAL MODEL

graphic and power position vis-à-vis the outside world. It is more than coincidence that the discipline of political science grew out of history and that it has moved away from the historic and institutional perspective since it has emerged in its own right.

This very brief description of the institutional model, like those in this chapter of other models, cannot do justice to the scholars who have worked within the framework of the model. Many, for instance, have combined elements of the classical democratic model with the institutional model, thereby suggesting that the public and the institutional structure act to shape the decisions made.

The growth of strength in the U.S. federal institutions vis-à-vis states and of the executive branch vis-à-vis other federal branches, have increasingly discouraged the study of the U.S. Constitution as a principal source of understanding for foreign policy. The growth of a massive executive branch bureaucracy, primarily in the twentieth century, and even largely since 1932, has increasingly shifted the attention of students interested in foreign policy away from Congress and toward the executive branch. The more modern version of the institutional model thus becomes an organizational model focusing on the massive bureaucratic organization of the executive.

The general model, as portrayed by Figure 1.3, does not change: The institutions and their requirements still dominate the individuals. Some major concepts, however, have changed. As the constitutionally defined separation of powers has yielded to presidential domination of foreign policy, the concepts derived from the Constitution have become less important than those which describe the workings of any large organization. For instance, all large organizations tend to "factor" decisions. That is, they tend to designate areas of principal concern for organizational subunits and to allow those subunits principal decision-making power in those areas, even though overall coordination may suffer and subunits may actually work at cross-purposes. Many critics of our foreign policy institutions have lamented the division of decision-making authority in foreign policy among the State, Defense, and Treasury Departments, the CIA, the U.S. Information Agency, the Agency for International Development, and even further. The concept of factored decision making may be the logical heir in foreign policy decision making to a still living, but aged concept of constitutional separation of powers.

Another organizational concept is incrementalism—step by step change in policy. Decisions taken by organizations seldom, if ever, follow the rational model prescription, whereby, regardless of past policy, all the alternatives are evaluated and a decision is made. For organizations, past policy is extremely important. First, the actual structure of the organization and the positions of personnel within it reflect past policy, and any change in policy can greatly threaten the organization. Second, organizational members and units generally cannot agree on criteria for evaluation of policy or on the probable consequences of policy. Thus small or incremental changes in past policy serve the dual functions of providing information about policy consequences and of preserving the organization.

The Bureaucratic Politics Model

The organizational model has increasingly gained acceptance within the discipline of political science as an important representation of foreign policy making. Even the steady increase in the Vietnam involvement from the early 1950s through 1968 has been explained in terms of incremental policy making. The rise within the discipline of specialists in the study of management and public administration (reflecting the rise of bureaucracies at all levels of government) has paralleled the increasing acceptance of organizational models.

Yet Figure 1.3 shows no linkage at all to the domestic sector. The bureaucratic politics model, which is something of a variation on the organizational model theme, does posit such a linkage. Whereas the organizational model focuses on the entire organization, the bureaucratic politics model draws our attention to the subunits. It stresses the factored nature of decision making less than the competition of decision-making units involved in the same decision area. More than by any other phrase, the essence of the bureaucratic politics model is captured by the saying "Where you stand depends on where you sit." Again, this implies the domination of institutional role over individual or idiosyncratic factors.

Decisions that involve allocation of budget among organizational units can probably best illustrate the model. Every unit portrays itself capable of performing intelligence, planning, and field functions better than any other unit. The conflict within the organization leads eventually to broadening of the arena of conflict. For example, when the Air Force feels that it is not receiving its share of the budget, it will let its supporters in Congress and its organizations within the general public know. The intention is clearly to

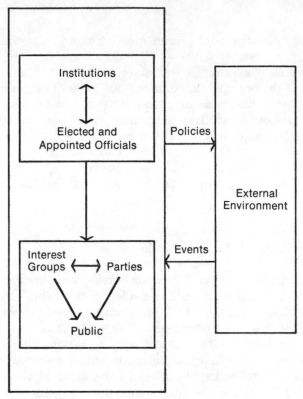

FIGURE 1.4
THE BUREAUCRATIC POLITICS MODEL

strengthen the Air Force's internal bureaucratic position by bringing outside pressure to bear. Of the same nature, although certainly more spectacular, were General MacArthur's criticisms of American policy, made when he was U.N. commander of the forces in Korea. Other organizational units, to the extent that they have larger constituencies, will also broaden the area of conflict. Even the State Department, which has a much smaller and weaker public constituency than the armed forces, uses the same tactic:[9]

> Since 1943, liaison with private groups, particularly the public-interest organizations, has become a permanent major aspect of the public affairs operations of the Department. About 3000 organizations are represented in the files of the Organization Liaison Branch of the Office of Public Services. Active contact is maintained with about 300 of this list and upwards of 100 of these receive the attention accorded "important customers."

Hence Figure 1.4 shows the entrance into the bureaucratic politics model of some societal elements—the organizational model placed no emphasis on such elements.

The Power Elite Model

Of the models discussed thus far for the explanation of foreign policy making, only the rational actor model and classical democratic model stress the clear dominance of those making decisions over the institutional framework within which they work. There are, however, two competing foreign policy models that begin with the assumption that the decision makers are dominant and proceed to ask another set of questions: Who are the decision makers? What is the process by which they determine foreign policy? These two models, the power elite and pluralist models, arrive at very different answers to those questions.

According to the power elite model, given its most famous expression by C. Wright Mills, a relatively small number of individuals, a subgroup of the total set of elected and appointed officials, is dominant in the decision process.[10] More importantly, these people are a cohesive group of like-minded individuals who really do constitute an elite. The elite springs from common upper-class socioeconomic orgins, shares a common private eastern school educational experience, and goes on to the upper positions in three areas: civilian government, the military, and the corporate world. The family and social interrelationship among the three elites is very close, and the ease by which the individuals move from one to another suggests to Mills the existence of really only one elite.

Figure 1.2 (the rational actor model) portrays this version of our more general foreign policy model quite adequately—the primary determinant of foreign policy is the small group of elected and appointed officials (in consultation with nongovernmental elements of the elite, of course). Different versions of the power elite model vary in their portrayal of the relationship between the public and the elite. In its purest form, the model portrays an elite largely unconcerned about the public. Leftist scholars normally argue that the elite policy contradicts that desired by the public. More frequently it is suggested that the public acquiesces in the elite policy, accepting it uncritically most of the time. For instance, a variant called the *establishment orchestration model* sees the elite as very successfully manipulating opinion throughout the rest of government and the public.[11] Other, less pure versions of the model have become widely accepted and are associated with the catchwords *establishment* and *military-industrial complex*. These words suggest a somewhat larger and less cohesive policy-making elite than the power elite model of the left.

The issue areas most frequently used to draw attention to the power of the elite are the size of the military budget and the duration of the cold war. The argument, at least implicitly, is nearly always that the elite stands to profit economically from both. A hot war, such as Vietnam, it is further pointed out, provides an even better opportunity for profit to both the corporate and military elements in the elite and, given the traditional public support of wars, also to the civilian government elite.

The Pluralist Model

Many observers of politics and probably most political scientists reject the pure thesis of the power elite model. Their observations lead them to a more complex model, probably most clearly stated by Robert Dahl.[12] The proponents of the pluralist model argue that in every issue area there are specialists and to that extent elites but that in the policy-making process there are many different sets of such elites and the elites are in nearly constant conflict. While there may be a military elite with allies in the corporate world and civilian government and while that elite may push for higher defense expenditures, there also are, say the pluralists, other elites who oppose higher defense budgets, if only because they realize that there is a budget pie to be split and that increased military expenditures may decrease their own share or force an unwanted increase in the pie. Thus, for instance, we shall see in later chapters that those who want a wide variety of social expenditures increasingly find themselves in conflict with the military. The pluralists do not assume that the military will win every battle. In fact, as governmental social expenditures have outstripped military budgets and as the military budget has declined in terms of the percentage of the GNP it constitutes, many political scientists and many on the right wing of the political spectrum have suggested the existence of very different power elites than those discussed above—elites not at all compatible with C. Wright Mills' vision.

The pluralist version of our model requires all of the linkages in Figure 1.1, the general model. It clearly is the most complex variation we have examined. At the decision-making process level, institutions and officials are seen as interacting. Although the pluralists recognize the importance of institutional roles in shaping policy advocacy, they are more inclined to identify those filling roles as the key variable. Whereas those developing institutional models are likely to point to the highly role-shaped foreign policy positions of functionaries in the State or Defense Departments, the pluralists are more likely to point to the debates that rage among key foreign policy advisors to the president, especially in the White House office. These advisors fill less clearly defined roles, which more frequently allow individual preferences to surface.[13]

The pluralist relationship between the decision makers and the public looks much like that in the bureaucratic politics model. Because of the conflicts internal to the governmental process, the arena of conflict will be extended outward to encompass prospective allies in the parties, interest groups, and general public. The relationship between decision makers and others differs in the two models, however. Whereas in the bureaucratic politics model the officials reach out to find allies for their institutionally defined role, pluralists are more likely to perceive the officials as extensions or representatives of groups within the public. Thus the pluralists suggest the possibility of a two-way relationship in which officials do try to manipulate constituencies but in which the public also has some ability to place those it desires in the governmental fray.

Relationships are also complex within the larger society. Interest groups and parties are derivative from the public, yet, once established, they are entities in themselves capable of proselytizing and shaping the public. Interest groups and parties interact to the point that even definitions are not always clear—the American Independence party of George Wallace, for example, fits most definitions of *interest group* as well as it fits those of *party*.

Domestic Setting Role Submodels

This book examines especially the domestic setting elements of the foreign policy process. Interestingly, few of the models discussed above outline any real role for those elements in the direction of foreign policy. Specifically, only the classical democratic model, the pluralist approach, and to a lesser degree the bureaucratic politics model see a significant role for the general public or subgroups of the public. The nature of that domestic setting role remains unclear. There exist at least five applicable submodels to describe it, most clearly listed by Norman Luttbeg.[14] The first three are coercive models, requiring punishment of unresponsive legislators or other representatives. The last two models do not require coercion to obtain representation.

The rational activist submodel stands first in Luttbeg's list. This model posits an informed, involved, and politically active general public capable of selecting candidates rationally and watching their performance once elected. If representatives perform unsatisfactorily, the public removes them. The rational activist submodel frequently comes with the classical democratic model in civics textbooks. A second coercive approach is the political parties submodel, and a third is the interest groups submodel. In both cases, an intermediate institution assists the public in its candidate selection and evaluation duties. The pluralist and bureaucratic politics models are highly compatible with these two submodels' descriptions of the domestic setting role. Actually, of course, some combination of these three mechanisms to ensure representation could operate in any given political system.

Representation of the domestic setting in the foreign policy decision process can theoretically also occur without reliance on strictly coercive mechanisms. Luttbeg's fourth approach is the attitude-sharing submodel, in which those elected actually share the opinions of their electors (or the elected assemblage shares the distribution of opinion in the public), so that when representatives act on their own opinions they also act on behalf of the public. Finally, and perhaps the only alternative remaining, the role-playing model suggests that even if the elected representatives do not share public attitudes they may, without coercion, play the role of representatives and act on the basis of public sentiment rather than their own.

There are thus a multitude, although not a confusion, of general frameworks or models for the explanation of the foreign policy process. We have discussed six models of the overall process and, for those in which the domestic setting plays a part, five submodels of the public role.

This book will not present an argument for one or another of the above foreign policy decision-making models, not even the most complex, the pluralist. There already exists more than adequate advocacy of that type. The reader may have noticed that the discussions of the models generally noted an example or two that proponents use to illustrate the working of their model. Frequently, however, it becomes apparent that the example appropriate for one model may be inappropriate for another. At other times, more than one model appears to offer insights into the decision-making process.[15] This book will argue that the various models differ in their appropriateness as descriptions of the foreign policy decision-making process, depending on the type of decisions being made. No one model adequately explains all decisions or even all "important" decisions.

The Procedure

A number of very specific questions need to be answered during our analysis of the relationship between the domestic setting and American foreign policy.

1. What do the American people think about various foreign policy issues? Remember that this study has two purposes—to describe the foreign policy opinions of the general public and subgroups of that public and to analyze the importance of these opinions. This question is basic to both of the purposes.
2. What do those making foreign policy decisions think about various issues? This question assumes that we know the answer to another question: Who makes foreign policy decisions? Although we cannot here, nor can anyone, draw up a list of names and seek out their opinions, we can focus in on a small subset of Americans with the greatest input and find out what they think.
3. To the extent that foreign policy opinions of the general public and decision makers differ, are the opinions of the public in some way represented by the decision makers in the policy process? Such representation of opinions not held by decision makers presumes that those other opinions are known by decision makers and that some incentives exist for making decisions on behalf of them.
4. Of what importance are political parties in differentiating among opinions within the public, and to what extent do parties introduce opinions thus differentiated into the decision-making process? Many have lamented that the parties are too much alike to serve such a function, particularly in foreign policy, and this issue merits investigation.
5. Of what importance are interest groups in differentiating among opinions within the public, and to what extent do they introduce diverse opinions into the

decision-making process? Few have argued that interest groups fail to express different opinions (although
little comparative analysis of groups exists).

6. Under what circumstances (if any) are the opinions of
the general public, or those of parties and interest
groups, especially important in the decision process,
and under what circumstances are such opinions of
little or no importance? An attempt to answer this
question must build on answers to the five preceding
ones. It is this question that specifically attacks the
issue of the relative importance of decision-making
models in a variety of decision settings.

Frequently, a political scientist will rely on the detailed analysis
of a particular case in his or her attempts to answer questions like
these six. Unfortunately, the selection of cases can bias the answers
a great deal. For instance, if we wanted to prove the importance of
the power elite model, we would direct our attention toward decisions such as were involved in building and dropping the atomic
bomb in World War II. If we wanted to show that foreign policy was
dominated by bureaucratic politics decisions, we would look only
at budget decisions. Pluralists might look at the details of the
foreign aid program. This study will draw on a large number of
case studies already performed. It will supplement those cases with
analyses of public opinion data, voting behavior of congressmen,
policy actually made by the government, and various government
and private (e.g., interest group) documents. The next six chapters
will consider in turn the six questions just listed.

Notes

1. The division made here was dictated by ease in presentation of the
models to follow. It roughly follows the divisions made by Richard
Snyder, H. W. Bruck, and Burton Spain, eds., *Foreign Policy
Decision-Making: An Approach to the Study of Foreign Policy
Decision-Making* (New York: Free Press, 1962), and by J. David Singer,
"The Level-of-Analysis Problem in International Relations," in Klaus
Knorr and Sidney Verba, eds., *The International System: Theoretical
Essays* (Princeton, NJ: Princeton University Press, 1961), pp. 77–92.

2. Quoted by Lester B. Pearson, "Democracy and the Power of Decision,"
in Harold Karan Jacobson, ed., *America's Foreign Policy* (New York:
Random House, 1965), p. 27.

3. Walter Lippmann, *The Public Philosophy* (Boston: Little, Brown, 1955).

4. Thomas A. Bailey, *The Man in the Street: The Impact of American Public Opinion on Foreign Policy* (New York: Macmillan, 1948), pp. 7–8.

5. A similarly positive evaluation has been made by Kenneth Waltz, who was happy to report that "One need not fear that pusillanimity is especially encouraged by the pressures of public opinion as it operates in the American democracy"—*Foreign Policy and Democratic Politics* (Boston: Little, Brown, 1967), p. 291.

6. Lippmann, *op. cit.*, p. 267.

7. See discussions by William Yandell Elliott, *United States Foreign Policy* (New York: Columbia University Press, 1952); Max Beloff, *Foreign Policy and the Democratic Process* (Baltimore: Johns Hopkins University Press, 1955).

8. Graham T. Allison, "Conceptual Models and the Cuban Missile Crisis," *American Political Science Review*, 63, No. 3 (September 1959): 589–718; or Graham T. Allison, *Essense of Decision: Explaining the Missile Crisis,* (Boston: Little, Brown, 1971).

9 John S. Dickey, "The Secretary of State and the American Public," in Don K. Price, ed., *The Secretary of State* (Englewood Cliffs, NJ: Prentice-Hall, 1960), p. 156.

10. C. Wright Mills, *The Power Elite* (New York: Oxford University Press, 1956).

11. John C. Donovan, *The Cold Warriors: A Policy-Making Elite* (Lexington, MA: D. C. Heath, 1974), p. 23. Another variant of the small and generally homogeneous group theories for describing foreign policy making has been proposed by Irving L. Janis, *Victims of Group Think: A Psychological Study of Foreign Policy Decisions and Fiascoes* (Boston: Houghton Mifflin, 1973). He stresses personality and group dynamics factors that conspire to considerably lessen rationality in decision making.

12. Robert A. Dahl, *Preface to Democratic Theory* (Chicago: University of Chicago Press, 1956).

13. Even congressmen, however, are strongly influenced by the roles of party and committee membership. See James Rosenau, "Private Preferences and Political Responsibilities: The Relative Potency of Individual and Role Variables in the Behavior of the U.S. Senators," in J. David Singer, ed., *Quantitative International Politics* (New York: Free Press, 1968), pp. 17–50.

14. Norman R. Luttbeg, ed., *Public Opinion and Public Policy* (Homewood, Ill.: Dorsey Press, 1974, revised edition), introduction.

15. This was the point of Graham Allison, *op. cit.*, in laying out his three alternative models.

2

Public Opinion on Foreign Policy Issues

The preceding chapter listed two primary goals for this book: to describe the domestic setting of American foreign policy and to analyze the importance of various domestic factors in the formation of that policy. The description of public opinion must precede the analysis of its role in foreign policy making. Hence this chapter will provide the description and create the base for subsequent analysis of the relationship between public opinion and U.S. foreign policy.

The History of Public Opinion Characterization

Prior to the widespread use of survey research, descriptions of public opinion were of necessity painted in broad strokes and with little detail. Concepts like "isolationism" and "internationalism" were well suited to such general pictures; many have noted the jingoism of the Spanish-American War period, the swing from isolationism to interventionism in the periods of both world wars, and the movement back to isolationism after World War I. It is difficult not to wonder, however, about the finer details of such attitudinal sketches of American history. We have more recently become accustomed to thinking in terms of X percent of the public supporting, Y percent dissenting from, and Z percent not knowing about a particular policy.

It is also quite natural to wonder about the accuracy of some of the earlier characterizations. For instance, the bellicosity of Americans in the late nineteenth century has been judged largely by the example set in the press of the period. Under normal circumstances, a relationship between press position and public opinion exists; but should the public be judged by the press? One also cannot help but wonder how the supposedly isolationist eighteenth- and early nineteenth-century United States so quickly became interventionist. William Appleman Williams argues that there actually was no rapid change—that rural America was expansionist throughout the eighteenth and nineteenth centuries, and that the supposed change was a result of the perceived absence of continental new frontiers and open land.[1] And it is certainly doubtful that American Indians have ever characterized the United States as isolationist. Similarly, the supposed swings in the twentieth century from isolationist sentiment to internationalist (during World War I) and back to isolationist (after World War I) gave rise to some questions about the accuracy of each characterization. It is difficult to conceive of such massive changes of public opinion in view of recent findings that widespread apathy toward and ignorance of foreign policy exists and in view of increasing evidence of the stability of basic attitudes over time. Is it possible that only the tip of the public opinion iceberg, namely the press and some of those especially attentive to foreign policy, was rapidly changing? And for that matter, even at the tip of the iceberg in 1914, was there ever a serious internationalism, or was there just a flurry of support for a presumed quick and easy intervention in Europe? Dozens of largely unanswerable questions can be raised about historic characterizations of public opinion.

The rapid growth of survey research in the post-World War II period has allowed replacement of the earlier general sketches by more finely detailed pictures of public opinion. Although this has been a blessing for students of politics, it has not been an unmixed one. Public opinion surveys have provided more information and more detail than anyone might have guessed. As a result, however, our mental picture of post-World War II public opinion is never really finished. One problem is that it becomes difficult to provide easy labels. If polling techniques had not been developed, the 1945–1975 period would almost certainly have been characterized as one of considerable internationalism and even imperialism. The polls, however, show that much of the public remained uninterested in foreign policy and frequently opposed to the use of domestic resources abroad. Moreover, polls have allowed us to trace the peaks and valleys of support for international involvement, and this, too, makes simple labels impossible. Still another complication arises from the complexity of individual attitudes. Polls have not only made it more difficult to characterize eras but also have led us to try to categorize individuals and groups, thus further complicating once simple matters.

Can We Really Talk about Public Opinion?

Is it possible to talk about public opinion when 30 percent of the U.S. population seems completely to lack foreign policy knowledge on which to base opinions? And how can we describe a public opinion that can change dramatically in response to seemingly minor changes in question wording? The answers only become possible when we recognize that there is not one "public," but several. We can describe three publics.[2]

The first segment of the public consists of people who are unaware of all but the most major events in foreign affairs—say, the launching of Sputnik[3]—and have either no opinions or have vague and generally weakly held ones. This segment is sometimes referred to as the "mass public." Studies consistently show this group to be about 30 percent of the total adult population. Another 45 percent can be said to be aware of many major events, but not deeply informed. This group constitutes the "attentive public." The attitudes held by individuals within this group frequently lack intensity and internal consistency, and they often fluctuate markedly in response to reports of international events or public officials' positions. The remaining 25 percent of the electorate is generally knowledgeable about foreign affairs and has fairly stable and consistent attitudes. These people communicate their opinions to others and are sometimes characterized as "opinion leaders."[4] A still smaller segment of this last category can be identified. Those who give money or time to political activities and communicate their opinions beyond their own acquaintances can be called "mobilizables" and constitute only 1 or 2 percent of the public.[5]

Divisions such as this one are inevitably rough and vary considerably over time and across issues. Yet the consistency with which this breakdown occurs can be illustrated by a study done in Cincinnati in September 1947.[6] A survey showed that 30 percent of the Cincinnati adult population could not identify the basic purposes of the United Nations. Fifty-five percent of the remaining adults (39 percent of the total population) were confused about the purposes and scope of the world body. The remaining 30 percent of the population was quite knowledgeable. Civic leaders supported a large-scale information campaign by the mass media in Cincinnati. The survey was repeated after the information campaign but found no appreciable change in the distribution of public knowledge. Clearly, the survey data must indicate the level of public interest as well as of public knowledge. Those in the least knowledgeable grouping prove least likely to pay attention to the type of information that could provide them with the basic knowledge they lack.[7]

In short, "public opinion" is an uneasy aggregate of individual opinions based on widely varying levels of concern and information. It can be uncertain and unstable. An early but good example of the instability of public opinion can be found in retrospective American attitudes toward entry into World War I. The four years preceding the 1941 attack on Pearl Harbor were marked by a dramatic change in American perceptions of the earlier war. Table 2.1 shows the reversal by 50 percent of the public, from a belief that U.S. entry into World War I was a mistake to a belief that it was not a mistake.

We must exercise exceptional care in describing public opinion.

TABLE 2.1

PERCENTAGE OF THE AMERICAN PUBLIC BELIEVING ENTRY INTO WORLD WAR I WAS A MISTAKE

Date of poll	Percent believing it a mistake
January 1937	70
February 1939	48
October 1939	59
January 1941	40
December 1941	21

Source: Constructed from Frederick H. Hartmann, *The New Age of American Foreign Policy* (New York: Macmillan, 1970), p. 115.

In particular, we should realize that any data purporting to capture public opinion represent both the stable opinions of highly informed individuals and the responses of some who say yes because it is easier to say than no, of some who sense a position of the interviewer and adopt it, of some who answer randomly, and of some who "feel strongly" about a position today but who tomorrow will feel equally strongly about its opposite.

The discussion of foreign policy attitudes throughout the rest of this chapter will proceed in three steps. The next section searches, with limited success, for general structures or patterns of attitudes within the general public. The succeeding section narrows our vision to particular issues and allows us to probe more deeply into postwar opinions of the general public on each of the issues. The last major section of the chapter directs our attention still deeper to differences within the general public on various foreign policy issues.

Patterns of Belief:
Isolationism and Internationalism

Journalists, scholars, and politicians use the terms *isolationist* and *internationalist* to describe both foreign policies and attitudes. This chapter has already used these terms frequently. Yet, like the words *liberal* and *conservative* in discussions of domestic policy, the terms *internationalist* and *isolationist* remain loosely defined.

All of these concepts are often used as if most individuals fell quite clearly into one category or the other: either liberal or conservative, either isolationist or internationalist. Even more presumptuous is the frequent assumption that liberals tend to be internationalist and that conservatives tend to be isolationist. Studies generally show a very slight tendency for liberals (either self-identified or those favoring government economic action) to be more internationalist than conservatives. But the relationship holds primarily during Democratic administrations (led by liberal, internationalist presidents such as Truman, Kennedy, and Johnson). During the Eisenhower administration and again under Nixon, the presence of a president taking both conservative and internationalist positions practically eliminated the relationship between liberalism and internationalism within the general public.[8] As we shall see shortly, the concept of internationalism itself has become much less useful as the split between military and nonmilitary internationalist attitudes has developed and deepened.

An Early Study of Belief System Structure

There exist, of course, many dimensions of public opinion within the American public—a fact recognized by critics of the two-party system and ignored by advocates of two-party realignment along some supposedly universal or overwhelmingly important ideological dimension. Philip Converse showed that most people do not structure either their domestic or foreign attitudes into the commonly applied categories.[9] Converse looked at beliefs of Americans on several domestic issues: federal public works programs to prevent unemployment, federal aid to education, federal funds for public housing, and federal prevention of racial discrimination in employment. He also looked at attitudes on three international issues: economic aid, military aid, and general U.S. commitments around the world. He measured the relationship between the responses of the public to each question with the responses to each other question, using a tau-gamma correlation coefficient as his measure of relation.[10]

On the whole, Converse found that a position on any one issue was not tied closely to a position on any other issue. The average coefficients can be seen in Table 2.2. The fact that most of the coefficients in Table 2.2 are quite low means that respondents to the questions did not have a common perception of interrelationship among the questions. That is, they saw and took no consistently "liberal" or "conservative" stances on the domestic issues and no consistently "isolationist" or "internationalist" positions on the foreign issues.

TABLE 2.2

AVERAGE CORRELATIONS AMONG DOMESTIC AND INTERNATIONAL ISSUES (1958)

	Among domestic issues	*Between domestic and international*	*Among international issues*
Congressional candidates	.53	.25	.37
General public	.23	.11	.23

Source: Adapted from Philip E. Converse, "The Nature of Belief Systems in Mass Publics," in David Apter, ed., *Ideology and Discontent* (New York: Free Press, 1964). Reprinted with permission of Macmillan Publishing Co., Inc. Copyright © 1964 by The Free Press of Glencoe, a Division of The Macmillan Company.

Note also (Table 2.2) that Converse computed his correlation coefficients for both the general public and for a sample of candidates for the U.S. Congress. Higher correlations for the candidates indicate that they did have more pattern, structure, or ideology in their belief systems—that is, they could somewhat more accurately be characterized as either liberals or conservatives on domestic policy and as internationalists or isolationists on international policy. It has been frequently noted that the more educated and more knowledgeable in politics evidence more internal attitudinal consistency and ideological orientation.[11] Yet even for the congressional candidates, the average correlation among foreign policy issues was only .37.

More Recent Data on Belief System Structure

Converse used data from 1956. The Survey Research Center at the University of Michigan, which collected the data Converse used, has also collected data more recently, including data for the years 1968 and 1972. This is an especially interesting period, because the Vietnam War provides a chance to discover whether the supporters of that war were more or less likely to be "liberal" domestically and to support other "internationalist" measures. Table 2.3 presents correlations summarizing the relationship between public support of several different foreign measures (such as trade with the communists, foreign aid, and the Vietnam War) and various domestic measures (federal aid to education, federal health care programs, and civil rights policy).[12] The questions in 1968 and 1972 were not identical, so that comparison over time can only be fragmentary. As in 1968, neither in 1968 nor in 1972 was there any strong relationship between the attitudes.[13] In general, those who held "internationalist" positions on foreign aid and trade with communist countries were slightly more likely than others to take "liberal" positions on aid to education or civil rights and somewhat more likely to want to get out of the Vietnam War and to decrease defense spending.

The correlation between opposition to continuation of the Vietnam War and positions of liberalism or internationalism on trade and aid issues reverses the situation in the earlier stages of the war—in fact, initially the internationalists and liberals supported the war most strongly. Note that in 1972 the question asked about the war was whether our initial involvement was correct. There were still positive correlations between belief in the initial in-

TABLE 2.3
CORRELATIONS AMONG VARIOUS ISSUES, 1968 AND 1972

	1968				
	1	2	3	4	5
1. Support foreign aid	—	—	—	—	—
2. Support Vietnam War	−.03	—	—	—	—
3. Support trade with communists	.24	−.25	—	—	—
4. Support federal aid to education	.19	NA	.25	—	—
5. Support civil rights movement speed	.28	−.24	.39	NA	—

	1972							
	1	2	3	4	5	6	7	8
1. Support foreign aid	—	—	—	—	—	—	—	—
2. Support Vietnam War	.20	—	—	—	—	—	—	—
3. Support trade with communists	.44	.07	—	—	—	—	—	—
4. United States should stay home	−.43	−.56	−.39	—	—	—	—	—
5. Cut military spending	.02	−.39	NA	.13	—	—	—	—
6. Feel big war unlikely	.13	.18	NA	−.35	−.09	—	—	—
7. Support government health plan	.01	−.27	NA	.21	.22	−.08	—	—
8. Feel men and women are equal	.13	.01	.31	−.21	.14	.18	.12	—

Note: The 1968 and 1972 questions on support for the Vietnam War differed. In 1968 the question concerned what to do at that time (escalate or pull out), while in 1972 it asked whether or not the initial involvement was desirable. The foreign aid question also differed in the two surveys. For items marked NA, data was not available.

Source: Computed from 1968 to 1972 Survey Research Center National Election Studies, data from which was obtained on tape from the Inter-University Consortium for Political Research, Ann Arbor, MI.

volvement and support for foreign aid and trade with the communists. Already by 1968 and again in 1972 there were negative correlations between support for continuation of the war (or defense spending in general) and support for foreign aid or trade with the communists.

Table 2.3 suggests in general the difficulty of categorizing the public. Even among those who in 1972 felt that the United States should leave Vietnam, there was no consistent attitude toward the questions of whether we were initially right in our Vietnam involvement and whether the defense budget should be raised or lowered. Those who wanted to leave Vietnam were about equally divided on the issues of foreign aid and trade with the communists. To see more clearly how weak these relationships among attitudes are, refer to Table 2.4. It can be seen that the 1968 correlation of .24 (in Table 2.3) between support for foreign aid and support for increased trade with the communists actually indicates a weak relationship. Of those who supported increased trading, 55 percent also supported aid and 25 percent opposed it; of those who opposed additional trade, the plurality again supported foreign aid—41 percent compared to 39 percent opposed.

Two Kinds of Internationalism

Some members of the public exhibit generalized internationalism or isolationism. As we shall see below, these terms can be somewhat appropriate for certain subgroups of the population, such as the most educated. Yet the concepts should not have the descriptive importance frequently accorded them. They may, in fact, mislead. This book will of necessity use the terms. Rather than avoid their use, we shall try to use them carefully. Internationalism will indicate a position of support for action on any issue in the international arena: giving foreign aid, talking, meeting, or trading with the communists, signing treaties, keeping forces abroad, and even fighting wars. Isolationism will signify the position opposing action on the issue. It makes sense to talk about internationalist and

TABLE 2.4
DISTRIBUTION OF PUBLIC ATTITUDES ON TWO INTERNATIONAL ISSUES

	TRADING WITH THE COMMUNISTS		
FOREIGN AID	*Support* (N = 462)	*It depends* (N = 57)	*Oppose* (N = 543)
Support	55.2%	36.8%	40.7%
It depends	19.5	50.9	20.8
Oppose	25.3	12.3	38.5

Source: Computed from 1968 Survey Research Center National Election Study, data from which was obtained on tape from the Inter-University Consortium for Political Research, Ann Arbor, MI.

isolationist positions on individual or groups of issues, even if very few people consistently espouse all internationalist or all isolationist opinions. Whenever possible, we will focus our attention on specific issues or groups of issues, not on the general concepts of internationalism and isolationism.

The relatively large difference between support for international policies not involving military forces or action (such as foreign aid and support for the United Nations) and support for international policies involving the military (like alliances and military action) merits explicit recognition. This book will call the former *nonmilitary* internationalism and the latter *military* internationalism. Although not particularly colorful terms, they more accurately and less prejudicially portray the distinction among the two kinds of internationalists than do words like *dovish, pacifistic, hawkish, jingoistic,* or *militaristic.* It should be noted that this military/nonmilitary distinction became important in the 1960s. For instance, Converse found correlations (albeit low ones) in 1958 between foreign aid support and support for keeping soldiers abroad, military aid, and other military measures.[14] Some of the first evidence of a split between military and nonmilitary internationalism came early in the Vietnam War. A great many "doves" remained quite internationalist in their support for foreign aid and an active detente policy, but they questioned the war, the level of defense spending and alliance commitments. Instead of correlations (albeit low) between domestic liberalism and generalized internationalism, studies began to find correlations (again low) between "dovishness" and liberalism.[15] This realignment of attitudinal structures has persisted into the mid-1970s, and we shall return to it.

Certainly, other important dimensions besides the military/nonmilitary distinction divide internationalists among themselves. For instance, internationalists on nonmilitary issues might fall into categories either in support of or in opposition to the strengthening of international organizations. Similarly, internationalists on military issues such as the stationing of troops in Europe might not support an American military presence in Asia. Although other dimensions exist in international affairs attitudes, the military/nonmilitary distinction has normally been the strongest and most useful. In sum, however, the reader must remember that a statement characterizing an individual or a group as internationalist or isolationist on one issue provides limited information as to positions on other issues.

Trends in Internationalism

Before moving to a discussion of American public opinion on specific issues, we should comment on how scholars have viewed the internationalism or isolationism of the American post-World War II public. Theoretically, one can ask questions about international attention and involvement in general, without reference to any specific issues, and obtain some notion of generalized support for an active foreign policy—a type of support that can be crucial to a government. There has, however, been some debate over how exactly to measure such support. Some have tried to gauge the internationalism of the public through the emphasis that the public places on international as opposed to domestic issues in response to questions about the major concerns of those being interviewed. Researchers doing such studies have found that the emphasis has varied considerably. For instance, it shifted dramatically to domestic issues in 1945–1946; it shifted back to international issues in 1947–1948.[16] These shifts have provided the basis for discussions of the instability of American "mood" on foreign policy and have supported the accusations of Lippmann and others that the American public cannot guide foreign policy satisfactorily.

William Caspary and John Mueller both present another, contradictory type of data. They report responses to questions such as "Do you think it will be best for the future of the country if we take an active part in world affairs, or if we stay out of world affairs?"[17] Surprisingly, there has consistently been 60 to 80 percent support for an active world role, from 1949 through 1969. Some slight decreases can be noted during both the Korean and Vietnam War periods, but the stability is remarkable even during war periods. In 1974, even after Vietnam, 66 percent of Americans surveyed still responded that it is best for the United States to take an active role.[18] This type of question more reasonably measures very generalized internationalism and isolationism. After all, it does not indicate a lesser commitment to an active international position to suggest during a given period (such as a recession) that domestic problems deserve increased attention. For instance, in December 1974, during a deepening recession, 80 percent of Americans identified the economy as the major concern, and only 13 percent listed any foreign policy issue.[19] Thus it should be safe to conclude that "internationalism," in the sense of a generalized mood and divorced from any specific issue positions, was quite widespread throughout the postwar period.

Specific Issue Positions

The previous section found relatively little general attitudinal structure on foreign policy in the public. As noted at the beginning of this chapter, the widespread use of terms like *isolationist, internationalist,* and *jingoist* to characterize time periods prior to widespread survey analysis leaves many questions unanswered. How, then, can we use survey analysis to present a more accurate picture? One way is by narrowing our attention to specific issues and looking at opinion on those issues over time. Although the wording of questions frequently changes, thus frustrating the effort to describe patterns and trends in foreign policy opinion, some trend analysis remains possible. In this section, we will look at American attitudes on a few foreign policy issues, including foreign aid, trading and talking with the communists, the admission of China to the United Nations, and the Vietnam War.

Foreign Aid

Figure 2.1 summarizes responses over time to questions designed to elicit support or opposition to foreign economic aid. It is clear that for many years a majority of respondents consistently supported foreign aid and thus supported the broad outlines of actual U.S. policy. It appears, however, that support peaked in the late 1950s and 1960s and that by 1968 it had waned considerably. In 1968, only a plurality of 46 percent supported foreign aid. Finally, in 1972 a majority of 52 percent opposed foreign aid. Specifically, they disagreed with the statement that "the United States should give help to foreign countries even if they don't stand for the same things we do."

This decline in support, of course, parallels a decline in actual U.S. aid. Although exact figures on foreign aid are confused—because of the irregular inclusion, exclusion, and valuation of multilateral aid, military aid, loans, and grants in surplus equipment and produce and because of increasingly tight stipulations on where and how the money can be spent (returning most to the United States)—economic grant aid decreased in the 1960s, and total aid has decreased as a percentage of both the national budget and the GNP. Thus the public shift away from support for foreign aid in 1968 and 1972 parallels (or follows with some time lag) a shift or attitudes and action in both the executive and congressional branches of government. Only time will tell if these shifts represent

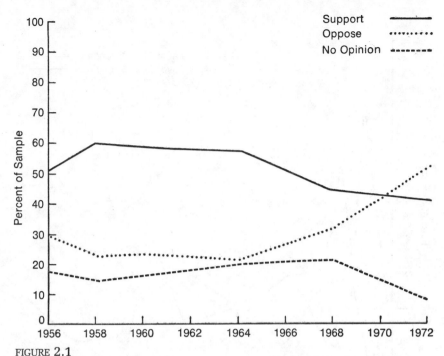

FIGURE 2.1

PUBLIC ATTITUDES ON FOREIGN AID (*Note:* The question used from 1956 through 1960 differed somewhat from that used in 1964, 1968, and 1972. *Source:* Compiled from codebooks of the Survey Research Center National Election Studies, as distributed by the Inter-University Consortium for Political Research, Ann Arbor, MI.)

temporary disillusionment, largely as a result of the Vietnam War, or signify longer-term developments. However, a survey of 1974, using a similar question about foreign aid, found that 52 percent of the public supported it and only 38 percent opposed, suggesting that the Vietnam War may have been an important factor and that support may be increasing.[20]

Military Spending

Figure 2.2 shows the opinions of Americans since 1946 about military spending. Specifically, it traces the percentages favoring greater and lesser amounts of defense spending in response to very similar questions asked over time.

Interestingly, the late 1940s and early 1950s provide a period of flux and relatively unstable attitudes, presumably in part because of

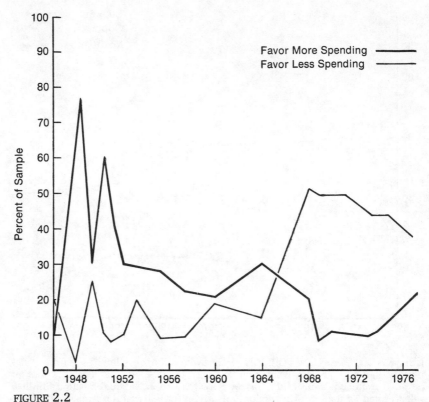

FIGURE 2.2

PUBLIC ATTITUDES ON DEFENSE SPENDING (*Source:* Adapted from Bruce M. Russett, "The Revolt of the Masses: Public Opinion on Military Expenditures." Published by permission of Transaction, Inc. from *New Civil-Military Relations*, Eds. John P. Lovell and Philip Kronenberg, copyright © 1974 by Transaction, Inc. 1973–1974 data from Gallup Polls. 1976 data from Bruce M. Russett and Miroslav Nincic, "American Opinion on the Use of Military Force Abroad," *Political Science Quarterly*, *91*, No. 3 (Fall 1976), fn. 18.)

uncertainty about the Soviet Union's intentions and the appropriate U.S. response. In general, however, a plurality of the public favored greater defense spending. The greatest level of support for increased spending came in March 1948, at the time of the coup in Czechoslovakia, and the next greatest levels came in February and March of 1950 (interestingly, *before* the outbreak of the Korean War). As the cold war stabilized in the 1950s, so did attitudes—specifically, a small plurality supported greater defense spending throughout the period of Eisenhower's term as president, during which cold war tensions remained high but during which the United States began to spend less of the GNP on defense. Support for higher spending continued into the 1960s, and 1964 was a year of fairly widespread support for the Vietnam War and the greater spending it required.

A major shift occurred between 1964 and December 1968, and evidence that we will present later suggests that it was probably continuous, but with an acceleration in late 1968. This shift led for the first time since World War II to a strong plurality support (in fact, in December 1968, to actual majority support) for decreased military expenditures. By 1974 the incremental military costs of the Vietnam War had largely been paid, and the intensity of desires for less spending may have decreased. Nevertheless, nearly four times as many Americans wanted to decrease spending further as wanted to increase it.

Two polls in 1976 have shown still further erosion of the Vietnam War impact. By early in the year, only 36 percent of Americans still felt we were spending too much on defense, and those believing that we spend too little had increased to 22 percent.[21]

Relations with the Communists

The decreased public support for both foreign aid and military spending can be explained by an unwillingness to accept foreign burdens engendered by the Vietnam War. An alternative or additional explanation for the decreased support is the growing detente with the communists. The fear of communist expansion always stood as a major rationale for both foreign aid and military spending. The fear has decreased generally, although by no means steadily, through the postwar period.[22] By 1959, a relatively peaceful year preceding the aborted Paris summit meeting between Eisenhower and Khrushchev, only 15 percent of the American population named communism when asked about their national fears or worries. This increased to 29 percent during 1964, probably in large part because of the issues raised in that presidential election. In 1972, only 8 percent mentioned communism as a fear. Perhaps as indicative of the decreasing fears of communism is the decrease in fears of war. In 1959, even during a period of relative quiet, 64 percent of the population mentioned their fear of war when asked to name their major national fears—far more than those who mentioned any other single issue. By 1964, this had dropped to 50 percent, and by 1972 it had fallen to 35 percent.[23]

One of the most interesting aspects of the changing picture of communism in the eyes of the public is the fact that change has continued throughout the period of the war in Indochina—a war heralded as a war against communist expansion. For instance, in the 1964 election, prior to the massive U.S. involvement, only 37 percent of the population thought farmers and businessmen should be allowed to engage in nonmilitary related trade with the communists.[24] By 1968, at the peak of the effort, 43 percent supported such trade. By 1970, a sizeable majority of the public supported a wide range of cooperative efforts with the Soviet Union, as shown in Table 2.5.

Perhaps the best measure of the changing image of communism over time lies in American public support of U.N. membership for China, prior to its admission to actual membership in October 1971. Support for U.N. membership fluctuated in the postwar period. The communists captured China in 1949. Figure 2.3 shows that support for their U.N. membership was already low by June 1950, prior to the invasion of South Korea. It dropped further by 1954. Membership support rose in 1955 and 1956, the period of the Camp David summit meeting and an era of improving relations with the communists. It dropped again in late 1956 (after the Hungarian invasion by the Soviets) and in 1958. Public support for admission rose to a new high (20 percent) in August 1958 and was still relatively high in 1961. But in early 1964 support dropped again to the levels

TABLE 2.5

PUBLIC ATTITUDES ON AGREEMENTS BETWEEN THE UNITED STATES AND SOVIET UNION IN 1970 (PERCENTAGES)

	Percent in favor	Percent opposing	Percent not sure
Limiting antimissile (ABM) systems	68	16	16
Exploring outer space	62	27	11
Expanding trade	74	14	12
Exchanging scholars and culture groups	79	11	10
Taking joint action if another nation threatens to use nuclear weapons	74	12	14
Joint action to keep communist China from starting wars	77	10	13
Getting European countries to pledge not to war against each other	79	8	13
Joint exploration of the oceans	70	15	15

Source: *Harris Survey Yearbook of Public Opinion, 1970,* (New York: Louis Harris and Associates, 1971), p. 104.

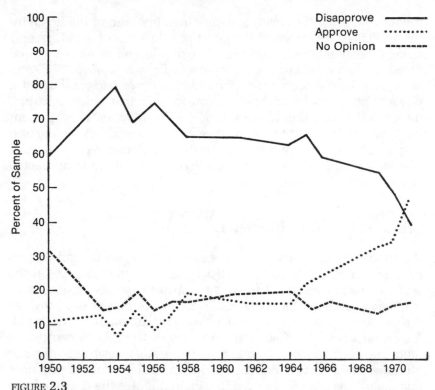

FIGURE 2.3

PUBLIC ATTITUDES ON ADMISSION OF CHINA TO THE UNITED NATIONS
(Note: The 1960 and 1953 surveys used somewhat different question wording. The
standard question was "Do you think Communist China should or should not be
admitted as a member of the United Nations?" *Source:* AIPO poll, compiled by John
Mueller, *War, Presidents and Public Opinion* p. 15. Copyright © 1973. Reprinted by
permission of John Wiley and Sons.)

of the early 1950s—paralleling the increasing fear of communism
noted earlier for that year. But, surprisingly, by late 1964 support
for admission again increased, and it did so steadily thereafter. The
Vietnam War clearly did not prevent an improvement of relations,
even with the nation most feared by many Americans supporting
the war in Indochina.

The Vietnam War

It has been suggested above that attitudes toward the Vietnam War
affected other foreign policy attitudes, particularly those on foreign
aid and military spending. We should thus look at those war at-

titudes directly. After 1965, the American Institute of Public Opinion (AIPO) regularly asked the question, "In view of developments since we entered the fighting in Vietnam, do you think the United States made a mistake sending troops to fight in Vietnam?" Figure 2.4 shows the responses. In August 1965, only 24 percent thought it was a mistake (many of those, of course, said that, mistake or not, the United States should stick it out).[25] By May 1971, 61 percent were willing to admit that a mistake had been made. A similar and nearly as striking erosion of war support characterized the Korean War, suggesting a more general public reaction pattern to protracted and unsuccessful wars.

Crises and Military Intervention

We showed earlier that the vast majority (between 60 and 80 percent) of the public have supported an active American role in the world. This general or "diffuse" support, not specific to any issue, is of considerable importance to the U.S. government and provides the government with considerable flexibility in making foreign policy. Other evidence of such support comes from American public attitudes during crises. It appears that, almost regardless of prior attitudes of the public, regardless of the popularity of the president and regardless of how well the president handles the crises, a large proportion of the population will support him.

For instance, Kennedy's popularity rose in the polls from 61 percent to 74 percent at the time of the Cuban missile crisis.[26] Eisenhower's popularity rose from 49 percent to 58 percent when he introduced troops in Lebanon. It is apparently not necessary that the action be successful. For instance, President Kennedy was surprised to discover that his popularity actually rose after the highly unsuccessful Bay of Pigs invasion—to 85 percent, the highest point during his period of office. Nor is it necessary that the president be popular. At the outbreak of the Korean War, only 37 percent of the American population felt that Truman was performing well as president. His support then rose to 46 percent. Moreover, a rather impressive 81 percent of the public supported his commitment of U.S. troops in the "police action." Nor is it necessary that the policy be consistent with previous desires of the public. Consider the answers that Detroit residents gave to this question in 1960:[27]

> Now suppose that fighting is breaking out somewhere abroad, and the president thinks it *important* to send American troops there. He knows, however, that most Americans are opposed to

> sending our troops there. Now, what do you think: should he
> send those troops, which he may *legally* do as president, or
> *should* he follow public opinion and keep them home?

Of those interviewed, 75 percent said the president should send the
troops. The skeptical reader might argue that this was before Vietnam. Yet consider the 1972 decisions of President Nixon to escalate
the Vietnam War by greatly intensified bombing and by mining the
ports of North Vietnam. This came at a time when public and congressional opposition to the war was well established. Yet a poll
after his actions confirmed the finding of the Detroit study: 59 percent of the public supported the actions and only 24 percent opposed.[28] This level of support is especially striking given that there
was no major external development to justify the declaration of a
"crisis." In spite of the manner in which the public rallies behind a

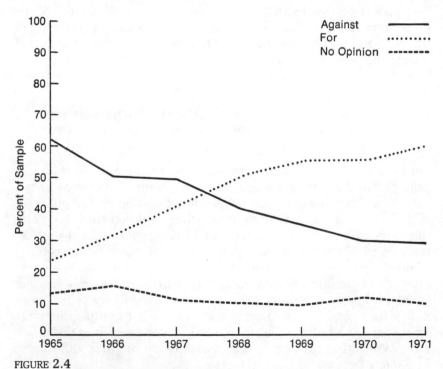

FIGURE 2.4

PUBLIC OPINION ON THE VIETNAM WAR (Note: The question was: "In view of
the developments since we entered the fighting in Vietnam, do you think the United
States made a mistake in sending troops to fight in Vietnam?" *Source:* AIPO poll,
compiled by John Mueller, *War, Presidents and Public Opinion* pp. 54–55. Copyright
© 1973. Reprinted by permission of John Wiley and Sons.)

president and military intervention during a perceived crisis, surveys show that in the abstract there is a great deal of the world in which the public does not want to intervene. Questions asked in 1969, 1971, and 1975 indicate that fewer than half of all Americans would want to send troops to Yugoslavia, Thailand, India, Brazil, Japan, or, most surprising, West Germany, even if those countries were "threatened by communist-supported invasion and takeover."[29] Although the Vietnam War has undoubtedly made many Americans literally gun-shy, other studies show generally comparable willingness (or unwillingness) to defend Europe against attack in the 1950s and 1970s.[30]

Although support for the president in crises is overwhelming, it should be pointed out that public support can be fickle and depends on the longer-run success of policies, or, as in the case of the Bay of Pigs invasion, on the absence of long-term negative consequences. For instance, whereas 81 percent reported support for Truman's decisions in 1950, two years later only 35 percent of the public reported that they favored Truman's original commitment of troops in Korea. This parallels the change of attitudes that occurred during the Vietnam War.

Sociological Characteristics and Foreign Policy Attitudes

Up to this point, we have presented a picture of American foreign policy attitudes without much detail. Such an overview is necessary. It has been made at the cost, however, of treating the public as if it were one group—an assumption that, as noted earlier, ignores the gross differences in the amount of information about and activeness of interest in foreign policy. It also ignores the possibility of major differences in opinion by region, sex, education level, and other demographic characteristics. In politics, all people are not equal, and some groups clearly are much more likely to influence policy than others. It is important to know what group differences exist in foreign policy opinion and to know the extent of the differences. We turn now, therefore, to a discussion of group differences in foreign policy.

Table 2.6 shows the relationships in 1964 between a large variety of social characteristics and position on a scale of nonmilitary internationalism.[31] Many of the patterns remain nearly unchanged. In examining the relationship between groups and foreign policy, we

TABLE 2.6

RELATIONSHIPS IN 1964 BETWEEN SOCIOLOGICAL CHARACTERISTICS AND NONMILITARY INTERNATIONALISM.

	Percent completely internationalist	Percent predominantly internationalist	Percent mixed	Percent predominantly or completely isolationist
Nation as a whole	30	35	27	8
Sex				
Male	30	36	27	7
Female	30	35	27	8
Age				
21–29	35	36	24	5
30–49	34	36	24	6
50 & over	24	35	31	11
Education				
Grade school	19	34	34	13
High school	30	38	26	6
College	47	30	19	4
Income				
Under $5000	23	36	29	12
$5000–$9999	32	35	27	6
$10,000 & over	45	32	18	5
Occupation				
Professional, business	43	31	23	4
White-collar workers	35	35	24	6
Farmers	25	39	28	8
Blue-collar workers	27	37	27	9
Nonlabor	20	35	32	13
Religion				
Protestant	28	36	27	9
Catholic	38	32	26	4
Jewish	43	37	17	3
City Size				
500,000 & over	33	34	25	8
50,000–499,999	36	33	25	6
2500–49,999	27	39	27	7
Under 2500 & rural	24	36	30	10
Region				
East	35	34	25	6
South–Goldwater	19	33	33	16
South–Johnson	25	39	28	8
Midwest	32	37	25	6
West	30	32	29	9
Ethnic Groups				
English	33	35	26	6
German	31	38	24	7
Scandinavian	32	36	26	6
Irish (Catholic)	35	32	29	4
Italian	35	35	23	7
Eastern or Central European	43	21	22	5

Source: Lloyd A. Free and Hadley Cantril, *The Political Beliefs of Americans: A Study of Public Opinion*, pp. 227–228. Copyright © 1967 by Rutgers, The State University. Reprinted by permission of the Rutgers University Press.

will look first at the two characteristics that appear to be associated with the greatest differences in foreign policy attitudes: education and social class.

Education

Attitudes differ quite sharply between those with a college education and those without. Educational attainment has in fact generally proven the single best predictor of foreign policy attitudes.[32] Table 2.6 shows that the more educated respond with substantially more internationalist positions (at least on the largely nonmilitary issues included in the scale) than the less educated. Of those with college degrees (Table 2.6), 47 percent were classified as completely internationalist, while only 19 percent of those with no more than grade school education fall into that category. No other characteristic has as large an impact on attitudes. Data from studies between 1956 and 1972 support the same conclusion, suggesting continuity of the pattern over time.[33]

The internationalism of the educated remained true into the early 1970s on nonmilitary issues, such as support of foreign aid and of the United Nations, and on most military issues, such as support of NATO membership and of the initial Vietnam commitment. It is perhaps surprising, in view of the college campus protests, that the college educated prove to have been the greatest supporters of the Vietnam War through 1968. By 1968 the college educated were no more supportive of the war than those with high school educations, but both of these groups remained considerably more supportive than those with only a grade school education.[34] Even in 1972 the educated more often believed that the initial Vietnam involvement was correct, although they were by then as likely as the less educated to want to get out. By 1975 the college educated had marginally shifted toward greater opposition to military measures in Vietnam, while strongly retaining greater support for humanitarian efforts. In April 1975, 84 percent of the college educated who had an opinion opposed military aid to South Vietnam, while 80 percent of those with a grade school education opposed such aid. Of the college educated, 68 percent supported humanitarian aid, compared with 49 percent support from the grade school educated.[35] Throughout the war period, however, there was less intense belligerence among the more educated, who were less likely than the rest of the public to support the use of nuclear weapons in Vietnam.

By 1972 the growing disenchantment of the educated with the Vietnam War was spilling over into related areas. For instance, a definite tendency to more heavily support cuts in military spending had emerged. In 1974, 55 percent of the university educated felt that the United States was spending too much on military aid, compared to only 41 percent of the high school educated and 40 percent of those with grade school education. Moreover, 63 percent of the college educated felt U.S. NATO troops in Europe should be reduced, compared to 48 percent of the grade school educated, thus reversing the pattern of traditionally greater support among university graduates.[36] This should *not* be interpreted as meaning that the more educated have become more pacifistic. In response to questions about the appropriate U.S. response to military attacks by communist-backed forces on various allies or other noncommunist countries, the more educated consistently are more likely to suggest either troop use or supplies and less likely to suggest noninvolvement. For instance, 73 percent of the college educated, 56 percent of the high school educated, and only 37 percent of the grade school educated would send troops in defense of Canada.[37]

While support by the most highly educated portion of the public for military internationalism has slipped somewhat, the same group continues its greater support for nonmilitary internationalist policies, such as economic foreign aid and the strengthening of the United Nations, in spite of considerable skepticism about their effectiveness. For example, the college educated more frequently say that the United Nations has done a poor job, that it cannot be made an effective organization for peace, and that it has lost their respect. At the same time, they conclude more often than the less educated that the United Nations is worthwhile.[38]

Other differences characterize the attitudes of the educated and the uneducated. Not surprisingly, the educated are substantially better informed. One study in the early post-World War II period found that there were between two and three times as many "don't know" and "no opinion" among those limited to grade school education as there were among the college educated.[39] That has not changed. Education has been shown to relate not just to a greater ability to respond (perhaps also partly to a greater willingness) but also to a very substantially higher level of factual knowledge.

The educated differ in still another way from the less educated: They are more optimistic about the United States' ability to handle the international situation and are less afraid of that situation. A study of attitudes toward nuclear testing found that the educated feared fallout considerably less than the uneducated.[40] They are even less likely to believe that nuclear weapons would be used in another world war.[41] A 1970 Harris survey found that 37 percent of those with a college education felt that U.S.-Russian relations were improving, as compared to 25 percent of those with a high school education and 22 percent of those with an eighth-grade education or less.[42] Similarly, the educated have been found to be less wary of confrontation with the Soviet Union, even when a threat of war exists.[43] In 1972 the more educated were more likely to feel that the danger of a big war had diminished. Perhaps among the benefits of education are lessened fear of the unknown in the environment and a commensurate increase in confidence to deal with whatever dangers the environment does hold.

Socioeconomic Status (SES)

Scholars have a variety of measures for social class: Social class can be looked at either as an objective function of occupational status or income or as based on the subjective belief of the individual. Higher social status, however measured, relates to foreign policy attitudes in essentially the same way that higher education does, obviously because of the strong relationship between education and social class. As in the case of higher education, both increased occupational status and larger income have normally been closely related to greater military and nonmilitary internationalism, with a recent slippage of military internationalism. This can be seen in the 1964 data shown in Table 2.6 and has been shown as clearly in 1956, 1960, 1968, and 1972 data.[44] Those with lower incomes generally prove more nationalistic and isolationist.[45] As with more education, those with more income or higher social status possess more information and profess greater optimism about world affairs. Lower income is occasionally associated with a kind of fatalism in international affairs.

Not all statements about education and foreign policy attitudes also extend to socioeconomic status. For instance, the recently greater desire of the college educated to cut military expenditures has not been paralleled by attitudes of the most wealthy. In fact, those in the highest income categories have proven more prone to believe that the United States spends too little.[46]

Although both the more educated and those with higher social status more frequently than other people indicate support for general involvement in foreign affairs (an internationalist orientation), we should not exaggerate the differences in issue positions from

TABLE 2.7

THE RELATIONSHIP OF INCOME TO ATTITUDES ON FOREIGN AID IN 1968 AND 1972

| | INCOME | | |
| | 1968 | | |
Foreign aid	Up to $5999 (N = 499)	$6000– $9999 (N = 422)	$10,000 and up (N = 447)
Support	37.9%	44.3%	55.5%
It depends	18.3	25.4	23.3
Oppose	43.9	30.3	21.3

| | 1972 | | | |
	Up to $3999 (N = 492)	$4000– $7999 (N = 606)	$8000– $11,999 (N = 666)	$12,000 and up (N = 826)
Support	39.6%	37.1%	40.8%	47.3%
It depends	6.1	6.8	5.4	6.9
Oppose	54.3	56.1	53.8	45.8

Note: 1968, gamma = −.25; 1972, gamma = −.10.

Source: Computed from 1968 and 1972 Survey Research Center National Election Studies, data from which was obtained on tape from the Inter-University Consortium for Political Research, Ann Arbor, MI.

the rest of the public. Table 2.7 shows, for instance, the greater support of those with higher income for foreign aid in 1968 and 1972. Yet 38 percent of those with an income (in 1968) of less than $6000 felt we should give foreign aid. Data from 1956, 1960, and 1972 show even weaker relationships between income and willingness to give aid.[47]

Religion

At this point, it should not surprise anyone to find that higher-status Protestant denominations are more internationalist than are Protestants in general. Moreover, since such denominations contain a high proportion of Americans with higher educations and incomes, it comes as no surprise to find that they are more internationalist than the generally less-educated and poorer Catholics.[48] Yet, as can be seen in Table 2.6, Catholics are more internationalist than Protestants in general, and Jews are by far the most internationalist of the major religions. Given the popular conception that Catholics generally fall lower on education and social status scales than Protestants, this result is surprising. In reality, that relative socioeconomic image of Catholics and Protestants is a *misconception*. An extensive 1975 study discovered that a wide range of Catholics (from Irish, Italian, German, and Polish backgrounds) have higher average incomes than even the highest-income Protestant group, the Episcopalians.[49]

Another reason for the greater internationalism of Catholics may lie in the relatively recent immigration and stronger ethnic identity of many of the Catholic ethnic groups: Irish Catholics, for example, and especially Italians and East Europeans.[50] These ethnic ties would also explain why Catholics (generally Irish, German, and Italian) often opposed internationalist foreign policy moving the country toward involvement in World War II on the British side. In part because U.S. post-World War II policy has involved cooperation with Catholics' countries of origin, Catholics shifted from a pre-World War II position of isolationism, relative to Protestants, to a postwar position of relative internationalism. Yet Catholics have not been internationalist only in attitudes relating to their countries of origin. Other parts of the total explanation for Catholic internationalism include the attachment of Catholics to the historically more internationalist Democratic party and the tendency of urban dwellers (which Catholics largely are) to be more internationalist than rural citizens.[51] As for the college educated, the late 1960s and 1970s appear to have caused the Catholics to reevaluate their commitment to both greater military and nonmilitary internationalism. Recent polls show continued greater Catholic than Protestant commitment to the United Nations and foreign aid but less support for military spending. The evidence remains ambiguous, however, because more Protestants favor reduction in U.S. NATO troop strength in Europe.[52]

One special and perhaps religion-based attitude difference between Catholics and Protestants *was* the slightly greater opposition of the former to communism. Catholics have been not only more supportive of the Vietnam (anticommunist) War but have also been more opposed to trading with the communists.[53] Catholic-Protestant differences on all of these issues, however, are slight. In fact, the 1972 Survey Research Center study indicates that in that year Catholics more frequently than Protestants favored foreign aid, the initial Vietnam involvement, *and* trading with the communists. At the same time, Catholics in 1972 indicated, by more often urging a withdrawal, greater current dissatisfaction with the Vietnam War than did Protestants. Protestant-Catholic differences overall are *negligible*. The more major religious differences separate Jews and the rest of the population.

Jews are highly internationalist, but in a nonmilitaristic way. They intensely opposed the Vietnam War, even though most of the internationalist groups discussed so far supported that war. This opposition, incidentally, reversed the pattern of Jewish support for the Korean War. Historically, Jews have very strongly supported foreign aid and international organizations, although recent surveys show them to be the religious group least inclined to view the United Nations as effective.[54] The hostility of the United Nations toward Israel, especially recognition of the Palestine Liberation Organization and the 1975 U.N. General Assembly vote equating Zionism with racism, will obviously greatly further erode or destroy the historic Jewish support for that body. The 1972 study also indicates that Jewish support for foreign aid slipped below that of Protestants and Catholics. They remained in large numbers opposed to the Vietnam War and overwhelmingly in favor of cuts in the defense budget. An exception, a not surprising one, to the Jewish nonmilitaristic internationalism arises on attitudes toward the Mid-East. Their greater domestic liberalism, tendency to live in urban areas, and higher education cannot entirely explain the differences between the attitudes of Jews and other religious groups. The historical and cultural basis for these differences, deriving from two millenia of persecution and international migration, has high salience for Jews.

Race and Ethnicity

White ethnic differences hardly merit comment. To the extent that they exist, Anglo-Saxon groupings are slightly more isolationist. The somewhat greater internationalism of more recently immigrated non-Anglo-Saxon groups may reflect primarily attitudes toward the country of origin or, as in the Irish attitudes toward Britain, attitudes toward a principal adversary of the country of origin. Nor surprisingly, immigrants from eastern Europe, many of whom fled the imposition of communist regimes, frequently hold bitterly anticommunist attitudes.

Earlier studies showed that a large percentage of blacks were isolationist.[55] Many remnants of that isolationism persist into the 1960s and 1970s. For instance, blacks were considerably more likely to oppose the Vietnam War than whites. Blacks were particularly opposed to any extension of the fighting to Cambodia or Laos. Blacks may also be less optimistic than whites about the international setting. In 1970, whereas 30 percent of whites felt relations with Russia were improving, only 17 percent of blacks did.[56]

Much of the earlier black isolationism, however, was reversed in the 1960s. Blacks became more likely than whites to support foreign aid, trading with communists, and the United Nations. Table 2.8 contrasts white and nonwhite (overwhelmingly, black) attitudes on foreign aid and trading with the communists in 1968. Quite considerable differences existed. In fact, in that year support for these measures was more dependent on race than on education or income. Blacks also increasingly showed a greater interest than whites in Africa, although not comparable to the identification that many Jews felt and feel with Israel.

Table 2.8 also shows the difference that four years can make. For 1972, positions of the two racial categories reversed completely. The attitudes of blacks (and a few other nonwhites in the sample) toward foreign aid shifted from one of strong support to one of considerable opposition. Although whites also became less sup-

TABLE 2.8

THE RELATIONSHIP OF RACE TO ATTITUDES ON FOREIGN AID AND
COMMUNIST TRADE IN 1968 AND 1972

	1968			
	FOREIGN AID		COMMUNIST TRADE	
	Whites (N = 1215)	Others (N = 136)	Whites (N = 1025)	Others (N = 96)
Support	43.6%	66.2%	40.9%	62.5%
It depends	23.0	11.8	5.2	4.2
Oppose	33.3	22.1	54.0	33.2
	1972			
	FOREIGN AID		COMMUNIST TRADE	
	Whites (N = 2374)	Others (N = 301)	Whites (N = 832)	Others (N = 80)
Support	42.0%	38.5%	63.7%	57.5%
It depends	7.2	4.7	3.2	1.3
Oppose	50.9	56.8	32.8	41.2

Source: Computed from 1968 and 1972 Survey Research Center National Election Studies, data from which was obtained on tape from the Inter-University Consortium for Political Research, Ann Arbor, MI.

portive of aid, their change cannot compare to the increase in the percentage of blacks opposing aid, from 22.1 percent to 56.8 percent. Blacks' attitudes toward trade with communist countries changed little, while whites shifted dramatically. Although the differences between attitudes in 1968 and 1972 may seem impossible to explain, a great deal of the explanation almost certainly lies with party preferences. Blacks vote overwhelmingly Democratic, while whites are fairly evenly split. Between 1968 and 1972, the Democrats, especially highly visible Democratic senators, changed from their traditional support for foreign aid to a position of criticism. Many of the whites, especially Democrats, followed this change in attitudes, while most blacks apparently did. Similarly, between 1968 and 1972, a Republican president reversed traditional Republican antipathy toward commercial ties with the communists and led the way to new trade agreements. Many whites, presumably the Republicans in particular, followed the lead, while blacks remained nearly unaffected. Table 2.8 thus allows us to remake one old point, namely that public attitudes are not very stable, and to make a new point, namely that a major source of the instability lies in governmental and political party behavior.

A renewed relative isolationism of blacks seems to be the pattern of the mid-1970s. More frequently than whites, they favor reduced defense spending and reduced NATO troop commitments. They are much less likely than whites to want to support other nations with troops in case of communist-backed attack. In 1975 they more often opposed both military and humanitarian aid to Vietnam.[57]

Region

Evidence suggests that ethnic differences underlay pre-World War II regional differences in foreign policy attitudes, especially the isolationism of the Midwest and internationalism of the South. For instance, in July of 1940, 42 percent of those in the Midwest opposed involvement in the European war and also opposed any aid to England.[58] Only 15 percent of those in New England or the Mid-Atlantic states felt the same way. The South and Southwest were most willing to go to war to prevent allied defeat. Ethnic identifications of the South with Britain and of many midwesterners with Germany partially explained these attitudes, especially in the Midwest. As further support for the importance of ethnicity, it is interesting to note that prior to the Spanish-American War the Midwest was particularly belligerent.[59]

Commercial ties, especially tobacco and cotton sales to England, not ethnicity, probably determined many of the seemingly internationalist attitudes in the South prior to World War II. Southern internationalism was particularly evident in the areas of international economic cooperation and lower tariffs. Now that the South has a broadened industrial base, increasing numbers of southern congressmen vote for protectionist measures, that is, for restrictions on international trade. It should be noted that much of the evidence for internationalism in the pre-World War II South came from the voting patterns of southern congressmen. That voting may not accurately indicate public attitudes in any region of the country, especially in the South, with its somewhat oligarchic structure and the relative freedom that southern congressmen enjoy in formulating policy.[60]

Survey data for the postwar period support these interpretations of the earlier ethnic and commercial bases of regional attitude differences. Table 2.6 shows that the regions now differ little. In general, the southern states, particularly those which supported Goldwater in 1964, are now more isolationist than the rest of the country on nonmilitary issues. They were, however, along with the West, slightly more willing to accept a military solution in Vietnam. The southern pattern thus illustrates the basic independence of attitudes on military and nonmilitary forms of internationalism. In fact, recent surveys indicate that the South and the Midwest now share a less positive attitude toward foreign aid than the rest of the country, and the South stands alone as slightly less positive toward the United Nations. In contrast, the South provides noticeably greater support than elsewhere for military spending.[61]

Midwesterners now appear no more isolationist than inhabitants of other regions on most issues. The area of the country that was most consistently internationalist over a long period of time (if the voting patterns of its congressmen accurately indicate attitudes before widespread polling) is the Northeast and Mid-Atlantic area.[62] That region obviously has always had commercial motivation for continuing international ties. The region also served as the port of entry for most immigrants, and, once again, recent immigrant groups generally retain some international bonds. Current surveys, however, show no greater internationalism of the general public in the Northeast than that of citizens in the Midwest or West.

On most issues, regions differ little. As an illustration, see Table 2.9, which shows regional differences in 1968 and 1972 on Vietnam. Regional differences on that issue exceeded those on issues such as foreign aid or trading with the communists but are small in absolute terms.

TABLE 2.9

THE RELATIONSHIP BETWEEN REGION OF RESIDENCE AND ATTITUDES ON
VIETNAM WAR IN 1968 AND 1972

What to do in Vietnam?	1968			
	Northeast (N = 339)	Midwest (N = 416)	South (N = 424)	West (N = 217)
Get out	26.0%	21.6%	20.0%	18.4%
It depends, mixed	43.7	41.1	38.9	40.1
Stay	30.5	37.3	41.0	41.5
	1972			
	Northeast (N = 281)	Midwest (N = 347)	South (N = 398)	West (N = 190)
Get out	53.0%	40.3%	38.2%	48.9%
It depends, mixed	21.4	32.0	24.1	20.0
Stay	25.6	27.7	37.7	31.1

Source: Computed from 1968 and 1972 Survey Research Center National Election
Studies, data from which was obtained on tape from the Inter-University Consortium
for Political Research, Ann Arbor, MI.

Urban-Rural

Moving from a discussion of geographical region to another ecological variable, we find that urban-rural differences once again parallel education and socioeconomic status difference. Urban dwellers are on average better informed, more optimistic, and, for most of the postwar period, somewhat more internationalist on military and nonmilitary issues.[63] This should hardly surprise anyone—urban areas also have concentrations of many groups that have been found to be internationalist: Jews, those with high SES, and recent immigrants. It should also not surprise anyone that urban dwellers in the 1970s remain more internationalist than small-town and rural residents on foreign aid and the United Nations but more often oppose defense spending and NATO troop strength in Europe.

Sex

Although characterizing sociological groupings as more or less internationalist often provides a useful description, many situations exist in which it misleads. Seldom, if ever, do two dimensions of belief invariably correlate, and what we have called *nonmilitary internationalism* and *military internationalism* frequently do not. The discussion above noted, for instance, that in the 1960s Jews, blacks, and people on the East Coast more frequently than others supported nonmilitary international measures but less often supported the Vietnam War. In contrast, the more educated and those with higher incomes or social status generally supported both military and nonmilitary internationalism. As the Vietnam War progressed, the greater war support of these latter groups declined, as did their general support for military internationalism.

Sex proves to be a characteristic for which the general internationalist/isolationist distinction has considerable utility in recent years. Women, often more than men, have tended throughout the 1960s and 1970s to support the United Nations. And Table 2.6 shows little sexual difference for general and largely nonmilitary internationalism in 1964. On the recent issues, however, women seem generally more isolationist. Women gave considerably less support in 1968 and 1972 to trade with communists. That fact is compatible with the frequent generalization that women are preservers of societal values, perhaps including anticommunism. But a more encompassing and thus convincing explanation is that women have been and remain generally less internationalist than men on military and nonmilitary issues. For instance, in 1972 men more frequently supported foreign aid than did women. Women also oppose defense spending and maintaining U.S. troops in Europe more often than men.

Although men give greater support to military and nonmilitary measures in international affairs, the differences are greatest for military measures. Men more frequently supported involvement in

TABLE 2.10

THE RELATIONSHIP BETWEEN SEX AND ATTITUDES ON VIETNAM WAR IN 1968 AND 1972

	1968		1972	
What to do in Vietnam?	*Male* (N = 617)	*Female* (N = 779)	*Male* (N = 553)	*Female* (N = 663)
Get out	17.7%	24.9%	41.6%	45.9%
It depends, mixed	37.0	44.0	22.4	27.3
Stay	45.4	31.1	36.0	26.8

Source: Computed from 1968 and 1972 Survey Research Center National Election Studies, data from which was obtained on tape from the Inter-University Consortium for Political Research, Ann Arbor, MI.

TABLE 2.11

THE RELATIONSHIP BETWEEN SEX AND ATTITUDES ON WHEN WAR WOULD BE JUSTIFIED

War would be justified if	WOMEN			MEN		
	Justified	Not justified	Not sure	Justified	Not justified	Not sure
The United States were invaded	99%	1%	0%	99%	1%	0%
Canada were invaded	78	13	9	84	11	5
Castro took over a country in South America	31	49	20	43	43	14
The Russians tried to take over West Berlin	37	42	21	50	38	12
The communists invaded Australia	37	41	21	54	34	12
Israel were losing a war with the Arabs	17	58	25	28	54	18
Western Europe were invaded by the communists	42	36	22	59	28	13
The communists were to take over South Vietnam	33	48	19	39	50	11

Source: *Harris Survey Yearbook of Public Opinion, 1970* (New York: Louis Harris and Associates, 1971), p. 86.

Vietnam and the extensions of the conflict to Cambodia and Laos. Table 2.10 shows sexual differences in support for the Vietnam War. In view of the seemingly greater anticommunism of women (if that is indicated by their opposition to trade), it is interesting that they did not support the Vietnam War as actively as men. This provides more evidence for the frequently touted relative pacifism of women. Further evidence comes from a Harris poll in 1970 on the circumstances in which the United States would be justified in going to war. In each hypothetical situation provided, women are less likely than men to think war is a proper policy. Table 2.11 presents the data. Again, in a 1975 study, the same result emerges. While 52 percent of women surveyed thought that war was an outmoded manner of settling international disputes, only 37 percent of men believed that.[64] Both studies also show that women less frequently have an opinion on the question—a fact found more generally on other international affairs issues.

Age

Age groupings also fit uneasily into categories of more or less internationalist. Many were surprised by the finding that it was the oldest Americans, not the young of draftable age, who most consistently opposed the Vietnam War (see Table 2.12). The youngest were in 1968 the most belligerent, although relatively little difference characterized those under fifty—the oldest group stands out. By 1972, the youngest age group had begun to recognize its interests as the group most burdened by the war. In fact, the four-year period witnessed a dramatic shift by the young from the most supportive group to the least supportive.

On foreign aid issues or support for the United Nations, however, the younger groups have historically stood out in their support for the more internationalist positions, perhaps thereby obtaining the label "idealistic" that is sometimes applied.[65] Recent polls have suggested that American young people are now nonmilitary internationalists, compared to those over thirty. For instance, they are more likely to feel that the United States is spend-

TABLE 2.12

THE RELATIONSHIP BETWEEN AGE AND ATTITUDES ON THE VIETNAM WAR
IN 1968 AND 1972

What to do in Vietnam?	1968				
	20–29 (N = 262)	30–39 (N = 269)	40–49 (N = 306)	50–59 (N = 239)	60 plus (N = 314)
Get out	16.4%	20.8%	18.6%	20.5%	30.6%
It depends, mixed	38.2	45.7	43.1	38.1	39.2
Stay	45.4	33.5	38.2	41.4	30.3
	1972				
	18–30 (N = 393)	31–40 (N = 212)	41–50 (N = 193)	51–60 (N = 175)	61 plus (N = 239)
Get out	50.9%	42.0%	37.3%	41.7%	41.0%
It depends, mixed	20.6	18.4	34.2	32.6	25.5
Stay	28.5	39.6	28.5	25.7	33.5

Source: Computed from 1968 and 1972 Survey Research Center National Election Studies, data from which was obtained on tape from the Inter-University Consortium for Political Research, Ann Arbor, MI.

ing too much on defense, less likely to suggest that the United States should give up U.N. membership, and considerably more likely to argue "that war is an outmoded way of settling differences between nations."[66]

In discussing the impact of age on attitudes, it should be remembered that there are at least two distinct factors involved. One is the process of aging itself, which takes us all through various "life stages." The other is the fact that different experiences have shaped the beliefs of different age groupings (or "cohort groups") whose members progress through life simultaneously. For example, a man of sixty in 1970 may express foreign policy beliefs similar to those reported by a different man of sixty in 1950, because they shared life stages at the time of the surveys. In general, progressive life stages tend to be less interested in foreign affairs, less aware of international crises, and less supportive of nonmilitary commitments abroad.[67] Yet the two men may also have differed significantly in foreign policy beliefs because of different life experiences (belonging to different cohort groups). The man who was sixty in 1960 came into his early twenties about the time of World War I, while the man of sixty in 1970 belongs to the cohort group reaching maturity in the Great Depression. These experiences of the early adult years have been shown to be very important in shaping beliefs throughout a lifetime. A study by Bobrow and Cutler reports that[68]

> The World War I cohort is isolationist in that it is least attentive to the external world and least in favor of American commitments to the external world. The Great Depression cohort is pessimistic about peace (i.e., most expects war and local nuclear attack) and is skeptical about unilateral military solutions (e.g., it most perceives the Soviets as strategically superior and least supports American initiation of war and preparation for war). The Nuclear Era cohort is internationalist in that it is most attentive to the external world and most in favor of all American efforts to affect that world.

One study suggested that the Vietnam War, over a period of about ten years, may have created a new and pacifistic cohort group. Whereas 72 percent of college students surveyed in 1962 thought that the "United States must be willing to run any risk of war which may be necessary to prevent the spread of communism," only 25 percent believed that to be true in 1972. More significantly, in 1962 only 17 percent answered that it was "contrary to my moral principles to participate in war and the killing of other people," whereas 49 percent of the college students in the survey answered thus in 1972.[69] The author's argument that Vietnam may become for this age group what "Munich" and appeasement became for the World War II generation, however, needs more study—for instance, people of all ages were affected by Vietnam, and it has not been proven that the Vietnam cohort was especially affected.

In conclusion, however, it bears repeating that neither age nor sex differences in attitudes should be exaggerated. They generally prove considerably less important than educational, social status, or racial differences.

Conclusions

As noted at the beginning of this chapter, the marvels of survey research have not made it easy to get an overview of foreign policy attitudes. It certainly is easier to talk about moods or swings of isolationism and interventionism or internationalism throughout American history than to portray the complex patterns that actually exist. People do not fall neatly into categories. Moreover, the attitudes of demographic groups, to the extent that they can be labeled and differentiated, have changed frequently over time.

Clearly, however, the amount of information we now have available has expanded our ability to describe public opinion. We have learned that attitudinal structures of Americans do not fall easily into categories such as internationalism, domestic liberalism, or (and especially) a general liberalism transcending domestic and international issues. More common structure exists for the more educated and those with higher socioeconomic standing.

In fact, we have caught a glimmer in this chapter, among the educated, of a new attitudinal structure development, for which we will see more evidence in a discussion of other elites in the next chapter. Specifically, while continuing to support most nonmilitary international measures, the educated have become more selective of military measures. They stand willing to support nations under attack, but they perceive the permanent defense structure (defense spending and U.S. troop levels in Europe) as unnecessarily well developed. There appear to be large segments of the more educated public that have reevaluated their internationalism in light of their liberalism and begun to question our ability to provide both guns and butter—this was not true before or in the early years of the Vietnam War. It does not appear appropriate to call these people *doves*—they are liberals and internationalists with an increased emphasis on domestic spending priorities. We shall learn more about this restructuring in the next chapters.

We have also seen in this chapter how support for foreign aid and defense spending has slipped generally, how antipathy toward communism has lessened, and how Vietnam War support evolved into opposition. Demographic differences have been clarified. In addition to providing some understanding of post-World War II foreign policy opinion, this discussion has set the stage for an analysis of the relationship between public opinion and American foreign policy. That relationship is the subject of the next chapters.

Notes

1. William Appleman Williams, *The Tragedy of American Diplomacy* (New York: Delta, 1962).

2. There are many different divisions of the public, although the public is often divided into three classes, frequently with the same names as used here. One of the earlier divisions was made by Martin Kreisberg, "Dark Areas of Ignorance," in Lester Markel, ed., *Public Opinion and Foreign Policy* (New York: Harper and Bros., 1949), pp. 49–64. For a listing of many of the terms and their sources, see James N. Rosenau, *Citizenship Between Elections* (New York: Free Press, 1974), pp. 91–92.

3. This event apparently attracted the maximum amount of attention. Awareness reached 74 percent in England and up to 97 percent in Norway. See Gabriel Almond, "Public Opinion and Space Technology," *Public Opinion Quarterly*, 24 (Winter 1960): 553–572.

4. See the more conservative categories of James Rosenau, *Public Opinion and Foreign Policy* (New York: Random House, 1961). Rosenau puts only 1 to 2 percent in his "opinion maker" category, and 70 to 90 percent in the "mass public" category.

5. James N. Rosenau, *op. cit.*, p. 20.

6. S. A. Star and H. M. Hughes, "Report on an Educational Campaign: The Cincinnati Plan for the United Nation," *American Journal of Sociology*, 55 (1950): 389–440.

7. To illustrate the frequency with which these percentages arise, we can point out that, in a survey in the late spring of 1964, approximately 25 percent of the U.S. population were unaware that China was ruled by a communist government. Twenty-five percent also were unaware that the United States was fighting in Vietnam. These figures were reported by Lloyd A. Free and Hadley Cantril, *The Political Beliefs of Americans* (New York: Simon & Schuster, 1968), p. 59. Another study dis-

covered that 25 to 50 percent of the public were unable to accurately define the word *tariff*—see Raymond A. Bauer, Ithiel de Sola Pool, and Lewis A. Dexter, *American Business and Public Policy* (Chicago: Atherton Press, 1963), p. 82. A *New York Times* survey published on March 23, 1959, at the height of a Berlin crisis, found that nearly 40 percent of those interviewed were not aware that Berlin was surrounded by communist territory—reported in Harold Karan Jacobson, ed., *America's Foreign Policy* (New York: Random House, 1965), p. 18.

8. Alfred O. Hero, Jr., *American Religious Groups View Foreign Policy* (Durham, NC: Duke University Press, 1973), pp. 141–142.

9. Philip E. Converse, "The Nature of Belief Systems in Mass Publics," in Norman R. Luttbeg, ed., *Public Opinion and Public Policy* (Homewood, IL: Dorsey, 1968), pp. 246–274. Also see Robert Axelrod, "The Structure of Public Opinion on Policy Issues," *Public Opinion Quarterly*, *31*, No. 1 (Spring 1967): 51–60; Alfred O. Hero, "Liberalism-Conservatism Revisited: Foreign vs. Domestic Federal Policies, 1937–1967," *Public Opinion Quarterly*, *33*, No. 3 (Fall 1969): 399–408; Free and Cantril, *op. cit.*; Norman Nie, "Mass Belief Systems Revisited: Political Change and Attitude Structure," *Journal of Politics*, *36*, No. 3 (August 1974): 540–591. There is considerable inconsistency among these studies. Free and Cantril actually find a moderate relationship between domestic liberalism and internationalism in the general public (p. 288), while Axelrod finds no relationship between domestic liberalism and internationalism for "participants." Some of the discrepancies among the studies can be accounted for by the inclusion of different items in the scales. In particular, there is evidence to suggest that "militaristic" and "pacifistic" international attitudes no longer scale well, and the inclusions of differing numbers of these by the various scholars could well determine results. Still another problem is the use of data from different time periods. Attitudinal interrelationships have changed. Hero, using data over a substantial time period (1937–1967) finds a fairly recent relationship between attitudes favorable to federal aid and support for the United Nations, even in the general public. Free and Cantril also use more recent data (1964), and with an internationalism scale that included no specifically military items they found a general public relationship between liberalism and internationalism. Nie found that there was no relationship between liberalism and dovish international attitudes in the 1950s, but a definite if small one in the mid- and late 1960s.

10. A coefficient of 0 (zero) would indicate no relation; that is, it would mean that those responding yes to one question were equally likely to respond yes or no to the other. Similarly, a "no" response to the first question would provide no indication of response to the second question. A correlation of 1 would mean that a perfect relationship existed; that is, a "yes" response on one question would always be associated with a "yes" response on the other, and "no" responses would be simi-

larly related. A correlation of −1 indicates a perfect inverse or negative relationship. Clearly this means that those individuals responding yes to one question respond no to the other, and vice versa.

11. William C. Rogers, Barbara Stuhler, and Donald Koenig, "A Comparison of Informed and General Public Opinion on U.S. Foreign Policy," *Public Opinion Quarterly*, 31, No. 2 (Summer 1967): 242–252. We will return to this issue in the next chapter.

12. Converse used a tau-gamma correlation; those reported in Table 2.3 are gammas.

13. A study of the relationship in 1964 found an even smaller correlation. See J. S. Robinson *et al.*, *Measures of Policy Attitudes* (Ann Arbor, MI: Survey Research Center, Institute for Social Research, University of Michigan, 1969).

14. Converse, *op cit.*, p. 268.

15. For an excellent review of changing attitudinal structures, see Bruce M. Russett and Elizabeth Hanson, *Interest and Ideology* (San Francisco: W. H. Freeman, 1975), pp. 130–144. See also Norman Nie, *op. cit.*

16. Gabriel Almond, *The American People and Foreign Policy* (New York: Praeger, 1960), p. 73.

17. William R. Caspary, "The 'Mood Theory': A Study of Public Opinion and Foreign Policy," *American Political Science Review*, 64, No. 2 (June 1970): 536–547; John E. Mueller, *War, Presidents and Public Opinion* (New York: John Wiley, 1973).

18. John E. Reilly, ed., *American Public Opinion and U.S. Foreign Policy 1975* (Chicago: The Chicago Council on Foreign Relations, 1975), p. 12. Although generally agreeing with the conclusion presented here of consistent internationalism, William Watts presents some data that show a considerable decline in internationalism between 1972 and 1974, with some rebounding in 1975. See "New Yeast in the Old Internationalism," *New York Times*, September 19, 1975, p. 37.

19. Reilly, *op. cit.*, p. 10.

20. Reilly, *op. cit.*, p. 27.

21. See the report of the January 1976 AIPO poll in Footnote 18 of Bruce Russett and Miroslav Nincic, "American Opinion on the Use of Military Force Abroad," *Political Science Quarterly*, 91, No. 3 (Fall 1976): 411–431; see also the report of a March 1976 Gallup poll with identical results in Walter Slocombe *et al.*, *The Pursuit of National Security: Defense and the Military Balance* (Washington, DC: Potomac Associates, 1976), p. 39.

22. See the data presented in Sophia Peterson, "International Events, Foreign Policy-Making Elite Attitudes and Mass Opinion: A Correlational Analysis," paper delivered at the Twelfth Annual Convention of the International Studies Association, San Juan, Puerto Rico, March 1971, p. 10.

23. William Watts and Lloyd Free, ed., *State of the Nation* (New York: Universe Books, 1973), p. 258.

24. From the Codebook of the Survey Research Center, *1968 American National Election Study* (Ann Arbor, MI: Inter-University Consortium for Political Research, 1973).

25. Mueller, *op. cit.*, pp. 54–55.

26. Unless otherwise noted, these and the following data on crises are reported by Kenneth Waltz, "Opinion and Crisis in American Foreign Policy," in Douglas Fox, ed., *The Politics of U.S. Foreign Policy Making* (Pacific Palisades, CA: Goodyear, 1971), pp. 47–48.

27. Thomas Halper, *Foreign Policy Crises* (Columbus, OH: Charles E. Merrill, 1971), p. 225.

28. Report of Harris Poll, *Cleveland Plain Dealer*, May 14, 1972, p. 14a.

29. Reported by Bruce Russett and Miroslav Nincic, "American Opinion on the Use of Military Force Abroad," *Political Science Quarterly*, 91, No. 3 (Fall 1976): 425, Table 8.

30. *Ibid.*, Table 2.

31. The Free and Cantril scale of internationalism is somewhat unique in that none of the items are explicitly "militaristic." It is also unique in that the types of international cooperation suggested do not include any that appear to have a clear price tag—such as economic aid. Instead, all items are relatively general statements, such as "The United States should mind its own business internationally and let other countries get along as best they can on their own" or "The United States should cooperate fully with the United Nations." This is unfortunate, because it results in a great shift of all sociological categories to internationalist responses. It may have some benefit, however, in that it avoids cues to specific issues that would elicit varied and probably nonscalable responses. See Lloyd A. Free and Hadley Cantril, *The Political Beliefs of Americans* (New York: Simon & Schuster, 1968).

32. Alfred O. Hero, *Americans in World Affairs* (Boston: World Peace Foundation, 1959).

33. See J. S. Robinson *et al.*, p. 561, for the 1956 and 1960 correlations; the 1968 and 1972 verification came from analysis of the SRC National Election Survey.

34. Mueller, *op. cit.*, p. 125.

35. *Gallup Opinion Index* (Princeton, NJ: American Institute of Public Opinion, April 18–21, 1975).

36. On military aid, *Gallup Opinion Index* (Princeton, NJ: American Institute of Public Opinion, September 6–9, 1974); on NATO, *Gallup Opinion Index* (September 21–24, 1973).

37. *Gallup Opinion Index*, April 18–21, 1975.

38. *Harris Survey Yearbook of Public Opinion, (1970)* (New York: Louis Harris and Associates, 1971); *Gallup Opinion Index* (Princeton: NJ: American Institute of Public Opinion, February 4–7, 1972, and February 7–10, 1975).

39. Almond, *The American People and Foreign Policy,* p. 127.

40. Eugene Rosi, "Mass and Attentive Public on Nuclear Weapons Tests and Fallout, 1954–1963," *Public Opinion Quarterly, 29,* No. 2 (Summer 1965): 280–297.

41. *Gallup Opinion Index* (September 21–24, 1973).

42. *Harris Survey Yearbook of Public Opinion, 1970,* p. 103.

43. Rogers *et al., op. cit.*

44. The 1968 and 1972 data examined were from the Survey Research Center. See J. S. Robinson *et al., op. cit.,* for the 1956 and 1960 data.

45. Almond, *The American People and Foreign Policy,* p. 125; Hero, *Americans in World Affairs;* Johan Galtung, "Social Position, Party Identification and Foreign Policy Orientation: A Norwegian Case Study," in James N. Rosenau, ed., *Domestic Sources of Foreign Policy* (New York: Free Press, 1967), pp. 161–194.

46. *Gallup Opinion Index* (September 21–24, 1973, and September 6–9, 1974).

47. Robinson *et al., op. cit.,* p. 561.

48. Hero, *op. cit.*

49. National Opinion Research Center (NORC) poll, reported in the *Cleveland Plain Dealer,* October 19, 1975, p. 6.

50. Most studies have found practically no differences between Catholics and Protestants on foreign policy issues. See, for example, Gerhard Lenski, *The Religious Factor* (Garden City, NY: Doubleday, 1961). Hero, *Americans in World Affairs, op. cit.,* found slightly greater isolationism among Catholics. More recently, Hero, *American Religious Groups View Foreign Policy,* p. 14, said that Catholics have become more internationalist than Protestants, and that the greater internationalism cannot be explained by ethnic differences.

51. Hero, *American Religious Groups View Foreign Policy,* argues that none of these are adequate explanations in themselves. However, perhaps, together they are.

52. On the United Nations, see the Gallup Polls, February 7–10, 1975; on foreign aid, see the SRC 1972 Election Study; on military spending, see *Gallup Opinion Index* (September 21–24, 1973, and September 6–9, 1974); on NATO, see *Gallup Opinion Index* (September 21–24, 1973).

53. SRC 1968 National Election Study data.

54. *Harris Survey Yearbook of Public Opinion, 1970.*

55. Hero, *Americans in World Affairs,* p. 99.

56. Harris Survey Yearbook of Public Opinion, 1970, p. 103.

57. On defense spending, see Gallup Opinion Index (September 21–24, 1973, and September 6–9, 1974); on NATO, see Gallup Opinion Index (September 21–24, 1973); on Vietnam aid and troop support, see Gallup Opinion Index (April 18–21, 1975).

58. Almond, The American People and Foreign Policy, p. 131.

59. Ray Allen Billington, "The Origins of Middle Western Isolationism," Political Science Quarterly, 60, No. 1 (March 1945): 44–64.

60. Hero, Americans in World Affairs, op. cit., p. 99.

61. SRC 1972 Election Study and Gallup Opinion Index, op. cit.

62. George Grassmuck, Sectional Biases in Congress on Foreign Policy (Baltimore: Johns Hopkins University Press, 1951), p. 160.

63. Hero, Americans in World Affairs, p. 97; Almond, The American People and Foreign Policy, p. 132.

64. Gallup Opinion Index (April 18–21, 1975).

65. Hero, op. cit., p. 82; Almond, op cit., p. 118.

66. On defense spending, see the Gallup Opinion Index (September 21–24, 1973, and September 6–9, 1974); on the United Nations, see the Gallup Opinion Index (February 7–10, 1975); on war, see the Gallup Opinion Index (April 18–21, 1975).

67. Davis B. Bobrow and Neal E. Cutler, "Time-Oriented Explanations of National Security Beliefs: Cohort, Life-State and Situation," Peace Research Society: Papers, 8 (1967): 48.

68. Ibid., p. 47.

69. Roger B. Handberg, Jr., "The 'Vietnam Analogy': Student Attitudes on War," Public Opinion Quarterly, 36, No. 4 (Winter 1972–1973): 612–615.

3

The Foreign Policy Attitudes of Decision Makers

The last chapter focused on the opinions of the public. This chapter looks at the similarity of, or differences between, general public foreign policy opinions and the foreign policy opinions of elected and appointed officials in the United States.

Leaders can represent followers in one of two ways. First, they can *literally* represent them. That is, public officials can hold the same attitudes, or at least attitudes in the same proportions, as held by the general public. Chapter 1 discussed this possibility and adopted Norman Luttbeg's label for it: the attitude sharing model. That model provides the framework for analysis in this chapter. It seems to be the model that John Adams had in mind when he said that a representative assembly "should be an exact portrait, in miniature, of the people at large, as it should think, feel, reason, and act like them."[1] An alternative or second category of models for representation posits that officials hold different attitudes but nevertheless act in accordance with public sentiment, as a result of public pressure or because of a perceived obligation to do so. These alternative representation models constitute the subject matter of the succeeding chapters. The remaining possibility is nonrepresentation: Officials hold attitudes other than those in the public and act on the basis of their own attitudes. If we do not uncover mechanisms of representation in this review of possibilities, we will be forced to conclude that in foreign policy decision makers *do* fail to represent the public.

Some evidence suggests considerable similarity between attitudes of the general public and attitudes within our foreign policy leadership. There appeared, for instance, a change in the attitudes of our high elected and appointed officials toward the Vietnam War that roughly paralleled the disillusionment of the general public. Public opinion polls reported that not until early 1968 did the size of the group opposing the war exceed that supporting it (review Figure 2.4). At about the same time, President Johnson withdrew from the race for reelection and began to deescalate the war. One could also point to the high level of support throughout the cold war period for the general foreign policies of the United States, as shown in Chapter 2.

On the other hand, many of those who have at one time or another opposed governmental policy in foreign affairs have questioned the representativeness of the governmental foreign policy machinery. Many opponents of the Vietnam War argued that public officials not only failed to share public attitudes but also failed to respond to public pressure. Critics cite in particular the period between 1968 and the 1973 Vietnam ceasefire, when the opposition of the public to the war did not result in U.S. withdrawal.

Comparing General Public and Decision Makers' Attitudes

Comparing the general public and decision makers presents methodological difficulties. Chapter 2 discussed the problems in even describing the opinions of the general public: the high level of ignorance, the instability of opinion, and the great variation within the public. Equally great problems arise in any attempt to characterize the attitudes of foreign policy decision makers. The most basic problem lies in identification of those who make foreign policy. Congress generally wields less power in foreign affairs than in other issue areas, such as social welfare, and the Supreme Court has little influence in making foreign policy. Yet even if we were to focus only on the executive branch, the problem of identifying those making policy, not to speak of the problem of measuring their attitudes, would remain. Another alternative would be to ignore attitudes and to look directly at governmental behavior in foreign policy—this would avoid the need to specify those involved in the process of decision making. Chapter 4 will use this approach. Yet since external forces and domestic pressures constrain leaders, their actions reflect more than their own beliefs. Thus full understanding of policy maker's attitudes requires a direct look at those attitudes.

This chapter will proceed in two stages and will use two different methodologies. The first stage will be an inductive examination of decision makers' attitudes through a process of identifying characteristics of decision makers and looking for the attitudinal correlates of these characteristics in the general public. This procedure builds on the description of general public characteristic/ attitude relationships presented in the last chapter. Fortunately, foreign policy decision makers are a segment of the population. Decision makers differ from the general public in that they somewhat misrepresent various behavioral, sociological, and perhaps psychological characteristics of the general population. To the extent that those characteristics shape the foreign policy attitudes of decision makers, they should also shape the attitudes of those individuals in the general population with the same characteristics.

Thus we will first identify characteristics of decision makers, look next at the attitudes held by people in the general public with those same characteristics, and finally extrapolate to decision makers. This first and "inductive" procedure has the advantage of involving direct comparison and contrast of the general public's attitudes and decision makers' attitudes. It can provide a basic understanding of the magnitude of the attitudinal differences. The procedure is, however, a rather blunt tool. The "decision maker" identified in the inductive approach will be in reality a sizeable segment of the population, perhaps better identified as the societal elite from which political, business, and other decision makers are drawn.

Some studies have been done that used interviews and questionnaires to focus directly on attitudes of those in various decision roles. Thus the second stage and methodology in our examination of decision-maker and general public attitude differences involves a review of studies on decision makers. Because these studies infrequently look simultaneously at decision makers and the general public, comparison and contrast will not be as direct as in the first portion of the chapter. However, our understanding of decision makers, especially of the differences among business, society, and political elites, will benefit considerably from the survey.

There is still another concern for the following analysis. The attitudes of decision makers presumably change over time. The studies on which this analysis draws were completed at various times during the post-World War II period. It would be inappropriate to assume that the decision makers held the same attitudes before World War II or will continue to hold current ones in the future. The last section of this chapter discusses the possibilities of generalizing to other time periods and countries.

Decision Makers' Attitudes: An Inductive Look

The most obvious and most important behavioral characteristic of decision makers is political activism. We will look first at the relationship between political involvement and opinions on foreign affairs. Thereafter the focus will shift to the sociological characteristics of decision makers and the relationship between those characteristics and foreign policy attitudes. Although some scholars have attempted to identify psychological characteristics of decision makers and to tie those characteristics to attitudes, their studies have generally not been convincing and will not be reviewed here.[2]

Political Involvement and Opinions on Foreign Policy

Those actively involved in politics do hold somewhat different attitudes on foreign policy issues than the less involved. Substantial evidence supports the proposition that political involvement is related positively to internationalism—that is, those politically more involved more often have internationalist attitudes. This holds for both nonmilitary internationalism (e.g., support of U.S. participation in alliances or support of U.S. forces abroad) and for military internationalism. Table 3.1 reports 1956 data relating political involvement and degree of internationalism. Two aspects of the table merit comment. First, those who do not participate, especially those who do not vote, much less frequently hold opinions and

TABLE 3.1

THE RELATIONSHIP OF POLITICAL PARTICIPATION TO POSITION ON FOREIGN ISSUE SCALE (1956)

	PARTICIPATION LEVEL[a]		
Internationalism[b]	Low (N = 394)	Medium (N = 770)	High (N = 515)
High	35%	45%	55%
Medium	14	21	23
Low	16	16	12
Not scaled[c]	35	18	10

[a]Levels of participation: High (voted and talked about politics or engaged in some other political activity), medium (voted only), low (no participation and did not vote).

[b]Internationalism scale included items on foreign aid and on maintaining troops overseas.

[c]Respondents with too few opinions to permit placement scale.

Source: V. O. Key, Jr., Public Opinion and American Democracy, p. 187. Copyright © 1964 by Alfred Knopf, Inc.

TABLE 3.2

THE RELATIONSHIP BETWEEN FOREIGN POLICY ATTITUDES AND EFFORTS (TRY) TO CONVINCE OTHERS IN 1968 AND 1972

	1968		1972	
	Try	Don't try	Try	Don't try
Foreign Aid	(N = 413)	(N = 760)	(N = 686)	(N = 1486)
Support	49.4%	44.3%	46.2%	41.3%
It depends, mixed	26.9	20.1	6.0	6.6
Oppose	23.7	35.5	47.8	52.2
Trade with communists	(N = 361)	(N = 614)	(N = 315)	(N = 448)
Support	44.6%	42.5%	72.4%	56.5%
It depends, mixed	7.5	3.7	4.4	2.7
Oppose	47.9	53.7	23.2	40.8
What to do in Vietnam?	(N = 410)	(N = 797)	(N = 370)	(N = 612)
Stay	41.7%	34.8%	34.9%	29.9%
It depends, mixed	40.7	41.4	22.7	26.8
Get Out	17.6	23.8	42.4	43.3

Source: Computed from 1968 and 1972 Survey Research Center National Election Studies, data from which was obtained on tape from the Inter-University Consortium for Political Research, Ann Arbor, MI.

TABLE 3.3

THE RELATIONSHIP BETWEEN KNOWLEDGE AND ATTITUDES ON FOREIGN
POLICY IN 1968

| | KNOWLEDGE | | |
	High	Medium	Low
Foreign aid	*(N = 882)*	*(N = 231)*	*(N = 236)*
Support	48.8%	48.5%	32.6%
It depends, mixed	24.5	17.7	16.9
Oppose	26.8	33.8	50.4
Trade with communists	*(N = 786)*	*(N = 181)*	*(N = 156)*
Support	45.5%	37.0%	35.3%
It depends, mixed	5.9	5.0	1.9
Oppose	48.6	58.0	62.8
What to do in Vietnam?	*(N = 872)*	*(N = 251)*	*(N = 268)*
Stay	42.2%	32.7%	26.5%
It depends, mixed	39.9	42.6	42.5
Get out	17.9	24.7	31.0

Note: High knowledge classification meant knowing both that there was a
communist government on mainland China and that it did not hold membership in
the United Nations; medium knowledge classification required knowledge of one or
the other; low knowledge reflects ignorance of both facts.

Source: Computed from 1968 Survey Research Center National Election Study, data
from which was obtained on tape from the Inter-University Consortium for Political
Research, Ann Arbor, MI.

thus cannot be placed on the internationalism scale. Second (and
more interesting), higher levels of participation associate clearly
with higher levels of internationalism.

The effort to convince another person of the validity of your own
political view also constitutes a form of political activity. Only
about one-third of the population, almost certainly including actual
and potential decision makers, engages in such efforts. Table 3.2
shows the positions in 1968 and 1972 on three foreign policy issues
(foreign aid, trading with the communists, and the Vietnam War) of
those who tried and those who did not try to convince others of
their opinions. Again, those who can be characterized as most
politically active are consistently the more internationalist—military and nonmilitary. They support foreign aid, they supported
trade with the communists, and they supported continued Vietnam
involvement.

Political knowledge is also related to political activism. Knowledge is partially a prerequisite for and partially a result of political
activism. Table 3.3 shows that in 1968 those with a higher level of

knowledge on one international relations issue, the political status of Communist China, more often take internationalist positions. The more knowledgeable generally support both foreign aid and trade with the communists and more frequently call for a strong stand on Vietnam.

To summarize, those members of the general public who prove most knowledgeable about foreign affairs and who are most politically active very definitely espouse more internationalist attitudes than does the average American, on both military and nonmilitary issues. The evidence reported here and a wider body of research both support that conclusion.[3] This implies that foreign policy decision makers, who are themselves more politically active and/or knowledgeable than the general public, probably hold more internationalist attitudes. We can continue this inductive look at decision-maker attitudes by turning to sociological characteristics.

Sociological Characteristics of American Foreign Policy Makers

Much of the American public believes that those elected and appointed to high public office share characteristics that differentiate them from the general public. Many people further believe that this demographic misrepresentation results in attitudinal and behavioral misrepresentation. This argument has not received careful analysis. Here, as in the case of political activity, we shall not explore the question by direct analysis of highly elected officials, but instead by abstracting sociological characteristics of decision makers and seeking the attitudinal correlates of those characteristics within the general public.

We can list a large number of characteristics overrepresented among the public leadership of the United States without any difficulty: male, Anglo-Saxon (and, of course, white), Protestant, college educated, high income, urban residence, middle age (30–59), and white-collar (especially professional) occupations. Clearly, not all decision makers possess all of these characteristics, but each is present more often among leaders than within the public.

Donald Matthews undertook two extensive studies of American government officials (primarily elected);[4] Dean Mann conducted a detailed study of political executives (cabinet members and other high-level appointees).[5] Their findings bear out the dominance of the characteristics listed above. Sex and race hardly need any comment—few women and non-Caucasians hold governmental positions, and, although an increasing number do, it is hard to imagine a future in which black women might constitute 5 percent of all congressmen and high executive officials. The facts also bear out the truth of the WASP image of government officials. Few congressmen are foreign-born. A number are second-generation, however, and those that are heavily overrepresent northwestern Europe (the British Isles, Scandinavia, the Low Countries, France, and Switzerland). Seventy-five percent of all second-generation American senators and 53 percent of all representatives in 1950 had origins in northwestern Europe, compared to 29 percent of the 1940 population.[6] All other areas of the world are underrepresented relative to their share in the U.S. population.

In religion, too, the WASP image is appropriate, although perhaps exaggerated. In 1960, 87 percent of all senators and 83 percent of all representatives were Protestant, compared to 59 percent of the general population.[7] Whereas Catholics and Jews made up 34 percent and 6 percent of the population, respectively, less than 16 percent of all congressmen were Catholics, and only 1 percent were Jews. Political executives somewhat better represent Catholics.[8]

Perhaps more interesting than the overrepresentation of Protestants is the misrepresentation of Protestant denominations. Four high-status denominations—Congregational, Episcopalian, Presbyterian, and Unitarian—are substantially overrepresented. These denominations claimed only 13 percent of the general population in membership, but claimed 39 percent of all congressmen as members. Methodists are also substantially overrepresented. At the other end of the scale, Baptists make up 20 percent of the public, but fewer than 13 percent of all congressmen are Baptists. The executive branch strikingly overrepresents Episcopalians. From the Roosevelt through the Kennedy administrations, 25 percent of all appointees have been Episcopalians, whereas only 4 percent of the public are Episcopalians. Moreover, Episcopalians were especially prominent in the high-status (and foreign policy making) departments: Treasury, Defense, and State.[9]

In educational level, differences between elected and appointed federal officials and the mass public are overwhelming. In 1940 only 10 percent of the population over twenty-five had a college education, yet over 80 percent of all congressmen, high-level executive officials, and Supreme Court justices had a college education.[10] In fact, a very substantial number of political officials have graduate degrees—57 percent of the political executives.[11] Much of their advanced work was done in law.

The occupations for which political officials are trained not only misrepresent the general public, but they also reflect the misrepresentation of their fathers' occupations.[12] According to Matthews, "The children of low-salaried workers, wage earners, and farm laborers, which together comprised 66 percent of the gainfully employed in 1900, contributed only 7 percent of the postwar senators."[13] Sons of professionals and proprietors or officials are heavily overrepresented in the U.S. Senate, and sons of farmers (as opposed to farm laborers) are somewhat overrepresented.

The public officials themselves come overwhelmingly from two occupations: law and business. In the 1950 Congress, 56 percent of the congressmen were lawyers (13 percent were other professionals, such as teachers), and 22 percent were proprietors or officials. Lawyers have dominated not only Congress but also the presidency. Fully two-thirds of all presidents have been lawyers.[14] In contrast, only .1 percent of the U.S. labor force hold law degrees.[15] Appointed executive officials exhibit a somewhat different occupational background, as shown in Table 3.4.[16] As do congressmen, political executives heavily represent law, but less than one-third of political executives claim law as their principal occupation. Businessmen have been more heavily represented in appointive positions, especially in the Eisenhower administration. The largest single occupation, however, is previous nonelective government work. This is especially true in the State Department, which is responsible for foreign affairs, and for the lower echelon of political appointees. Businessmen more frequently held cabinet-level and other positions in the Defense Department establishment.[17]

The machinery of the political system and the pressures of the society clearly shape the patterns of recruitment within the United States. Table 3.5 presents data on cabinet member occupations for four countries. Some substantial differences exist. None of the other three countries, for instance, has relied as heavily as the United States on businessmen, and only France exhibits a similar reliance on lawyers. If American dependence on businessmen and lawyers indicates our commercialism, the somewhat greater British dependence on the military and landowners reflects the impact of nobility; the strong presence of journalists in France relates to the ideological character of French politics; and the much greater use of civil servants in Germany before 1933 most likely results from a tradition of a paternalistic and well-liked executive establishment.

TABLE 3.4

PRINCIPAL OCCUPATION OF POLITICAL EXECUTIVES, BY ADMINISTRATION AND MAJOR OCCUPATIONAL GROUPS

| | Business (%) | Law (%) | Other professions[b] (%) | GOVERNMENT[a] | | | |
				Elective (%)	Nonelective (%)	Total (%)	Other[c] (%)
Persons (N = 789)	29	25	11	3	29	32	5
Roosevelt (N = 210)	23	26	16	3	30	33	2
Truman (N = 265)	23	24	5	2	43	45	4
Eisenhower (N = 293)	39	24	9	3	22	25	3
Kennedy (N = 124)	20	24	18	4	25	29	10

[a] All levels of government, including international agencies.
[b] Chiefly education, journalism, engineering, and science.
[c] Trade union officials, party officials, farmers, and foundation officials.

Source: Dean E. Mann, "The Selection of Federal Political Executives," *American Political Science Review*, 68 (March 1964): 81–99.

We can make some note of the ecological origins of officials. Not surprisingly, congressmen represent considerably better the various regions of the nation than do appointed officials. They also better represent urban/rural differences. Political executives frequently come from the Mid-Atlantic states, especially the New York and Washington metropolitan belt, or from regions of political party

TABLE 3.5

PERCENTAGE OF CABINET MEMBERS REPORTING SELECTED OCCUPATIONS

	United States 1889–1949	United Kingdom 1888–1950	France 1890–1940	Germany 1890–1933
Business and finance	61.1	29.3	13.5	12.5
Law	55.2	32.4	49.5	35.9
Journalism	22.6	28.6	43.7	10.5
Education	14.9	16.5	18.3	8.8
Civil service	3.2	3.2	15.4	56.4
Military	.5	8.7	6.5	12.2
Landowner	0.0	14.6	1.1	4.6
Other	28.2	26.1	16.3	10.1

Source: Harold D. Lasswell, Daniel Lerner, and C. Easton Rothwell, *The Comparative Study of Elites* (Stanford, CA: Stanford University Press, 1952), p. 30. Reprinted by permission of M.I.T. Press.

advantage—i.e., from the South in Democratic administrations and from the Midwest in Republican ones.[18] Political appointees even misrepresent population density more than they do geography. Ninety percent of all political executives were employed in urban areas at the time of government appointment, while only 59 percent of the 1950 population was. In contrast, the birthplaces of senators slightly overrepresent rural areas and small towns of 2500 to 5000 inhabitants.[19]

Sociological Characteristics and Foreign Policy Attitudes

Only with caution can we suggest the foreign policy attitudes of decision makers on the basis of attitudes held by those in the general public with the same demographic characteristics as the decision makers. Our task would be especially difficult if sociological analysis of decision-maker attitudes led to conclusions about those attitudes that differed from the earlier analysis of political activity and foreign policy attitudes. Fortunately, the two analyses suggest the same conclusions. Specifically, those individuals with the sociological characteristics of decision makers have more detailed and complex belief systems, higher levels of political knowledge, and more internationalist outlooks.

The last chapter outlined the relationship between demographic characteristics and foreign policy positions. We shall build on that discussion here. Table 3.6 summarizes the degree to which the sociological characteristics of leaders are associated with internationalist positions (broken into military and nonmilitary). We have already seen that behavioral characteristics of leaders are associated with internationalist positions on both dimensions of internationalism. Table 3.6 suggests the same conclusion for most of the sociological characteristics of foreign policy decision makers.

Decision Makers' Attitudes: A Direct Look

The indirect and inductive look at decision makers in the last few pages points to considerable differences between the attitudes of the general public and the "elite" from which political and other decision makers arise. As noted earlier, this information has value but needs the refinement of a direct look at decision makers. In

TABLE 3.6
SUMMARY OF MILITARY AND NONMILITARY INTERNATIONALISM OF MAJOR
SOCIOLOGICAL GROUPINGS (POST-WORLD WAR II)

	ARE GROUP MEMBERS MORE INTERNATIONALIST THAN NONGROUP MEMBERS?	
Leadership characteristic	Military	Nonmilitary
Educated	Yes (weak)	Yes
High socioeconomic status	Yes (weak)	Yes
High-status Protestant	Yes (weak)	Yes (weak)
White	Yes	Yes
Anglo-Saxon	No (weak)	No (weak)
Northeast and Mid-Atlantic region	Yes (weak)	Yes (weak)
Urban	Not clear	Yes (weak)
Male	Yes	Yes
Middle aged	Yes (weak)	Not clear
Total impact	Yes	Yes

particular, we want to know something about the way in which attitudes about foreign policy differ from one segment of the "elite" to another—from Republicans to Democrats, from politicians to businessmen, from civil servants to military leaders.

Some Earlier Studies

One relatively early attitudinal study was not done of foreign policy decision makers but of individuals clearly in touch with foreign policy decision making. A questionnaire study by James Rosenau tapped the attitudes of about 600 invited participants in a 1958 "Conference on Foreign Aspects of U.S. National Security," at which President Eisenhower, Vice-President Nixon, Secretary of State Dulles, and Adlai Stevenson were featured speakers. Not surprisingly, this select group had a high level of knowledge about and involvement in foreign affairs and were internationalist in attitude. For instance, conference participants were very supportive of foreign aid, with one-third of the respondents actually favoring an increase in the amount requested by the president and fewer than 10 percent supporting a decrease.[20]

Unfortunately, we have no real way of contrasting this group with the general public, because the same questions were not asked in general surveys at the same time. It would be desirable to review a study of both leaders and followers, preferably one also in which different kinds of leaders were examined and compared. In particular, it would be interesting to compare Republican and Democratic politicians, because of their alternation at the head of the foreign policy machinery.

In just such a study, Herbert McCloskey and colleagues sent questionnaires to convention delegates in the 1956 Republican and Democratic national party conventions; at the same time, national surveys were made, allowing us to differentiate between Democrats and Republicans in the general public, as well as between those who are politically active.[21] Table 3.7 summarizes the attitudes of the four groups on foreign policy issues.

The data in the table unfortunately cannot be relied on to compare the activists with the general public (or, as they were called in the study, the "leaders" with the "followers"), to see if, once again, leaders prove more internationalist than followers. The reason for this is that the launching of Sputnik occurred in the middle of the study and affected some attitudes of about one-half of the leaders, those who had not yet been surveyed, as well as all of the followers (who were not surveyed until after November 1957).

The important thing to note from the McCloskey data (see Table 3.7) is that very substantial differences existed between activists of the parties—much more substantial than the differences between Democrats and Republicans in the general public. Democratic leaders consistently provided more support for internationalist positions than did Republican leaders. Similar leadership differences exist for social welfare issues, civil rights issues, and also issues concerning government regulation of the economy. These issues, like the foreign policy issues, largely failed to differentiate followers of the two parties. Generally, public attitudes fell between the polls established by the party activists. Although commentators frequently characterize the parties as Tweedledum and Tweedledee, in 1956, this appeared true only for party followers and not for party leaders.

Analysis of Party Differences in Leaders: The Belief System

The relatively more rigorous belief systems of political activists in large part explain the existence of party differences among leaders, not followers. Democratic leaders consistently take more "inter-

TABLE 3.7

COMPARISON OF PARTY LEADERS AND FOLLOWERS ON FOREIGN POLICY ISSUES, BY PERCENTAGES AND RATIOS OF SUPPORT

ISSUES	LEADERS		FOLLOWERS	
	Democratic (N = 1788)	Republican (N = 1232)	Democratic (N = 821)	Republican (N = 623)
Reliance on the United Nations				
Percent favoring Increase	48.9	24.4	34.4	33.4
Decrease	17.6	34.8	17.3	19.3
No change	33.5	40.7	48.0	47.3
Support ratio	.66	.45	.54	.57
U.S. participation in military alliances				
Percent favoring Increase	41.5	22.7	39.1	32.3
Decrease	17.6	25.7	14.0	15.4
No change	40.9	51.6	46.9	52.3
Support ratio	.62	.48	.62	.58
Foreign aid				
Percent favoring Increase	17.8	7.6	10.1	10.1
Decrease	51.0	61.7	58.6	57.3
No change	31.1	30.7	31.3	32.6
Support ratio	.33	.23	.26	.26
Defense spending				
Percent favoring Increase	20.7	13.6	50.5	45.7
Decrease	34.4	33.6	16.4	15.4
No change	44.8	52.8	33.0	38.8
Support ratio	.43	.40	.67	.65
Level of tariffs[a]				
Percent favoring Increase	13.0	19.2	16.6	15.2
Decrease	43.0	26.3	25.3	21.3
No change	43.9	54.5	58.1	63.4
Support ratio	.35	.46	.46	.47
Immigration into United States[b]				
Percent favoring Increase	36.1	18.4	10.4	8.0
Decrease	27.0	29.9	52.0	44.6
No change	36.9	51.7	37.6	47.4
Support ratio	.54	.44	.29	.32

Note: The support ratio is an index of responses in which a weight of one is assigned each "increase" response, a weight of zero to each "decrease" response, and a weight of one half to each "same" or "no change" response.

[a]The internationalist and isolationist positions are reversed on this issue.

[b]This issue is not clearly one of foreign policy.

Source: Herbert McCloskey, Paul J. Hoffman, and Rosemary O'Hara, "Issue Conflict and Consensus Among Party Leaders," American Political Science Review, 54 (June 1960): 406–427.

nationalist" positions and more "liberal" domestic postures, while the Republicans are equally consistent in relatively "isolationist" and "conservative" stances (see Table 3.7). The magnitude of the differences between party leaders suggests something approaching party ideologies. The reader should realize, however, that the size of the interparty differences shown in McCloskey's study of convention delegates may not completely typify foreign policy decision makers. Not only popularly elected national and state officials but also an even larger number of *local party* activists attend national party conventions. These local activists, such as precinct committeemen, ward leaders, and county chairmen, do not need to compete for voters in an electorate clustered in the center ground, as do officials elected by the general public.

In general, these earlier studies (in the 1950s) found that the attitudes of political activists and of the more educated segment of the population exhibited two types of structure to a greater degree than did the rest of the public. First, such individuals showed greater coherence or interrelationship among various domestic attitudes and again among various foreign policy attitudes. That is, a political activist taking the "internationalist" view on foreign aid was more often "internationalist" in support for the United Nations than was a member of the general public who supported foreign aid. Second, a small positive relationship between domestic liberalism and military and nonmilitary internationalism existed in the attitudes of political activists and the educated. The Converse study reported in Chapter 2 discusses this relationship for congressional candidates.[22]

Several interrelated variables underlie such internal consistency of political belief systems: political knowledge, political interest, and political involvement. These are all in turn related to the level of education. Apparently political knowledge is especially crucial in determining the degree to which a belief system will be fully developed and have a rigorous structure. One study of the general public found, as did McCloskey, that opinions of Democrats and Republicans differed little.[23] When party adherents were rated by level of information, however, the better-informed partisans differed very substantially. Still another study of political knowledge contrasted a set of "knowledgeables" (in this case, participants in a World Affairs Center) with a general public sample and a general college-educated sample. The college sample differed in attitudes from the general public, and the "knowledgeables" stood out as dramatically different in attitudes.[24]

Some More Recent Studies

More recent studies generally confirm the conclusion of earlier studies about greater attitudinal structure among political decision makers than in the general public but indicate that the content within the structure has changed somewhat. In particular, we should review two recent studies of a variety of elite groups. In 1971–1972, Allen Barton and associates at Columbia sent questionnaires to Democratic and Republican politicians, labor and business leaders, high-ranking civil servants, representatives of the media, and heads of voluntary associations.[25] Nearly a year and a half later, Bruce Russett of Yale sent a questionnaire incorporating many of the same questions to another sample of business leaders, as well as to a group of high military officials.[26] Table 3.8 reports the percentage within each elite grouping who offered liberal or dovish responses to the questions.

First note the considerable variation of response to the questions. Our examination in Chapter 2 of the general public in the 1950s, 1960s, and 1970s, showed relatively little opinion variation across religious, occupational, education, income, and other categories of the public. In Table 3.8, we see a great deal of variation. At the extremes, only 12 percent of the military leaders wanted to reduce defense spending, while 79 percent of media leaders did. Only 37 percent of Republican politicians felt that the United States had contributed to the cold war, while 77 percent of Democratic politicians did.

Next note the party positions of Republicans and Democrats on international issues. In McCloskey's 1956 study, Democratic leaders were slightly more likely to want an increase in defense spending. By the time of Barton's 1971–1972 study, positions had reversed: Of the Democratic leaders, 71 percent wanted to decrease spending, and only 43 percent of Republican leaders did. Similarly, in 1956 41.5 percent of Democratic leaders wanted to increase participation in military alliances, in contrast to only 22.7 percent of Republicans. By 1971–1972, 52 percent of Democratic politicians wanted to dismantle alliances, compared with 32 percent of the Republicans. In general, Democrats were more internationalist on this type of military foreign policy issue in 1956, while Republicans were in 1971–1972. Remember, of course, that different kinds of politicians were interviewed in the two studies; specifically, Barton interviewed senators, ranking House committee members or chairmen, and administration and party officials, in contrast to McCloskey's convention delegates.

TABLE 3.8
FOREIGN POLICY ATTITUDES OF ELITE GROUPS (IN PERCENTAGES)

	YALE SAMPLE		COLUMBIA SAMPLE							
	Military	Business	Business	Republican politicians	Democratic politicians	Labor	Civil servants	Voluntary organizations	Media	Total Columbia sample
1. United States should reduce defense spending	12	51	63	43	71	76	74	78	79	66
2. United States should dismantle alliances	22	34	47	32	52	55	53	51	62	48
3. United States should keep ahead in nuclear (disagree)	26	22	30	28	38	31	40	57	63	39
4. United States contributed to cold war	58	52	65	37	77	81	70	74	82	67
5. Third World is nationalist	84	74	70	77	72	60	84	83	91	77
6. United States should accept socialist governments	78	78	81	78	83	83	88	87	93	84

Source: Bruce M. Russett and Elizabeth C. Hanson, Interest and Ideology (San Francisco: W. H. Freeman and Company, Copyright © 1975), p. 71.

Chapter 5 will provide additional information about the changing attitudes of Democratic and Republican politicians (specifically,
senators and members of the House). We will see that Republicans
have replaced Democrats as the primary supporters of military aid
and defense spending since the mid-1960s and that in the Senate
they have also taken over the role of primary economic foreign aid
supporters.

A number of studies of foreign policy elites, especially of congressmen, have discovered a reorganization of attitudinal structures
that is directly related to the changing party positions. Remember
again that Converse found in 1958 a correlation for congressional
candidates between domestic liberalism and both military and
nonmilitary internationalism. The McCloskey data (1956) suggest
the same conclusion, since Democrats were more liberal and more
internationalist than Republicans on all issues.

A study of the 87th Congress (1961–1962) by Russett found no
significant relationship between voting on domestic and foreign
policy issues. But his study of the Senate in the 90th Congress
(1967–1968) found a sizeable correlation between voting on defense and foreign policy issues on one hand and civil rights and
urban affairs issues on the other—a correlation of domestic
liberalism with more dovish positions.[27] The realignment took
place, however, primarily in the last few years of the 1960s. Moyer
found a very strong correlation (.82) between dovish positions on
foreign policy issues and liberal civil liberties votes in the House
during the 90th Congress.[28] This was not yet true, however, for
defense voting—few liberal senators or representatives dared to
oppose defense appropriations. In the 91st Congress (1969–1970),
Moyer found, however, that the realignment of voting patterns extended to defense spending.

In other words, by 1970, many liberals in Congress began to
perceive a trade-off between spending on defense and spending on
domestic programs. This had not been true in the 1950s and early
1960s when the feeling of a great many of those liberals and internationalists was that the federal budget pie was expandable and
both types of programs could be and should be funded at higher
levels.[29] Moyer notes that while liberals in the 91st Congress continued to support foreign economic assistance (although not military) they began to oppose defense expenditures and no longer
indiscriminantly favored expanded federal expenditures. Chapter 2
found that this same kind of restructuring of attitudes seems to
have taken place within the general public, particularly among the
most highly educated, but to a less significant degree.[30]

This discussion of a restructuring of attitudes on international issues by political elites raises a related question: Has there been an absolute change over time in the level of internationalist sentiment among politicians? Chapter 2 reported on studies showing a high and relatively constant level of generalized internationalist feeling in the general public since World War II. Although some specific instruments of an active foreign policy, in particular economic aid and counterinsurgency, lost support during the 1960s, other instruments, such as trade and general cooperation with the communists, gained support.

There has not been the same kind of sampling over time done of foreign policy elite attitudes. In general, we must rely on their behavior as a key to their actions, but this allows us to make the same statement for politicians as for the general public. Specifically, economic aid and military instruments of foreign policy have become less popular. Figure 3.1 shows the percentage of the GNP that

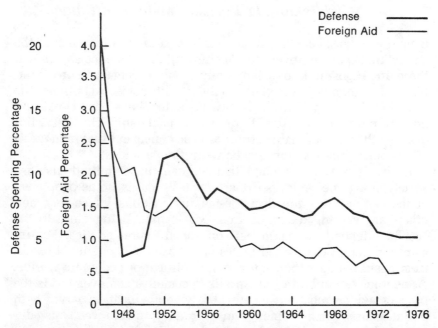

FIGURE 3.1

NET FOREIGN AID AND DEFENSE SPENDING AS PERCENTAGE OF GNP (*Source:* Computed from data in U.S. Department of Commerce, *Historical Statistics of the United States: Colonial Times to 1970* (Washington, DC: U.S. Government Printing Office, 1975); U.S. Department of Commerce, *Statistical Abstract of the United States, 1975* (Washington, DC: U.S. Government Printing Office, 1976); *Survey of Current Business, 56,* No. 11 (November 1976): 519.)

politicians have spent on aid and the defense budget. Were we to examine aid and defense as percentages of the total governmental budget, we would see even more rapid declines. At the same time, trade barriers have come down regularly, and diplomatic cooperation, especially detente with the communists, has been a major foreign policy preoccupation.

It appears that among both the general public and those making foreign policy, a fairly high level of interest in and commitment to foreign policy has been manifested, but an increasing reluctance to spend money has emerged. The Vietnam War can account for some of the change, but a sharpened focus on domestic priorities has been another factor. Assuming that we put our money where both our minds and mouths are, internationalism appears less strong now than it was in the 1950s and early 1960s.

A Framework for Understanding Decision Makers' Attitudes

Even if there has been a general decrease in internationalism in the United States (a yet uncertain conclusion), the evidence shows that those in a position to make foreign policy remain more internationalist than the rest of the public. With some exceptions, the results of the analysis in the last two chapters have been consistent on this point. In fact, the finding that leadership characteristics occur with internationalist attitudes is so consistent that it suggests some underlying relationship between the variables.

Johan Galtung has argued that we can place individuals in a society along one center-periphery scale.[31] That is, some people are at the center (near the decision-making nucleus) of society, and others are varying distances from that center. Being close to the "center" depends in large part on social characteristics. For instance, much of the United States has consciously excluded blacks from positions near the center of the political or economic worlds. As another example, in industrialized societies achievement is the basis on which most advancement is made; education serves both as a measure of achievement and as training to achieve. Thus education places an individual nearer the center of society.

Central position is also in part a function of societal communication. Urban dwellers are more exposed to formal communications media and to informal and interpersonal communications processes. Similarly, those near the capital of a country may be exposed to greater levels of political communication. Thus a middle-aged white male with an advanced education and a well-paying white-collar occupation and living in a major urban area near the capital of a country is very high in social position and close to the center. That is, he is close, in a social and a geographic sense, to the decision-making centers of business and politics. He can be dramatically contrasted with an elderly black woman married to a poor farm laborer and living in an area far from the country's major metropolitan centers.

Each of the characteristics listed earlier for decision makers is related in that the possession of it places the individual closer to the center of his or her society. Thus the characteristics are related in two ways. First, they tend to be associated with each other in the society. That is, the urban dweller is more likely to be educated than the rural dweller; the holder of a high-status job is more likely to be male than female; the middle-aged individual is more likely to have a higher income than younger or older people. Second and even more important, there appears to be an underlying social dimension that makes the impact of the characteristics on attitudes additive—each additional "center" characteristic possessed by the individual makes him more likely to share the dominant attitudinal and behavioral characteristics of the decision makers in the United States. Each characteristic will make him more informed, a more likely participant in politics, and more internationalist.[32]

A question that still remains is why the center is more internationalist than the social periphery. It is at least theoretically possible that the center would be more isolationist and that the accumulation of center characteristics would make an individual more likely to be isolationist. One explanation is that the periphery does not have the time or other resources to expend in thinking about foreign policy. The only policy positions possible without knowledge or thought may be isolationist (with perhaps an occasional outburst of jingoism). An exception to this may be a group like that portion of the blacks in this country who are not just part of a passive periphery but who are an actively alienated group and feel considerable empathy with the outside world, especially the less-developed countries.

Another explanation for the internationalism of the center lies in self-interest; members of the periphery may prefer to concentrate on domestic issues and expenditures because they see it to their advantage to do so. In fact, periphery members more often support social welfare issues than do members of the center.[33] The support for social welfare issues at the periphery tends to be a function of the recognition of short-term self-interest. For instance, those at the periphery more often favor federal aid to education and increased social security benefits than those in the center, but they often fail to support increased taxes. This may be short-sighted behavior, because in the long run such taxes could provide increased benefits at the expense of the center. In foreign affairs, the long-term economic benefits of an internationalist orientation are generally less obvious than the costs. One exception lies in a perception of an immediate threat to personal security; e.g., the launching of a Sputnik by an enemy. In this case, the periphery is in fact likely to support short-term measures such as increased armed forces and defense spending but is not likely to see value in increased foreign aid or reliance on the United Nations (see Table 3.7).

A third explanation for the concentration of internationalist attitudes at the center of society is psychological. Those who are near the bottom of social scales tend to be less well adjusted within society, to have greater anxiety about the outside world, to have less ego strength, and to be more likely to withdraw on contact, especially from the unfamiliar. These traits would rather naturally lead to isolationist attitudes toward the world and in fact are related within the general public to isolationism.[34]

All three of these explanations for the greater internationalism of the center are unrestricted by time or nation. Thus they would lead us to expect that in other nations and in other historical periods those who make foreign policy would be more internationalist than those who are far from the political "center" of the society.

There is a fourth explanation, however, one that would not lead to the same conclusion: It may be that those who make foreign policy in the United States have been influenced in the post-World War II period by a particular international environment and that this environment caused them to adopt internationalist positions not necessarily held by earlier decision makers. These attitudes may be communicated gradually from the political center to a political periphery still influenced by an isolationist history. This would mean that in the future the periphery may adopt internationalist attitudes, while the center again becomes more isolationist.

Such an explanation does not lack historic or contemporary support. W. A. Williams has argued, for instance, that in the late 1800s there was considerable expansionist attitude in the societal periphery (especially among farmers used to expanding land frontiers) and some reluctance to engage in such actions at the center.[35] Others might point to what has been called "neoisolationism" among many senators and congressmen, which grew in large part from opposition to Vietnam and has spilled over into disillusionment with foreign aid and other international programs, as evidence of a future in which the periphery could indeed be more internationalist than the center. A 1970 study found that whereas 27 percent of the general public wanted to speed up withdrawal from Vietnam, 30 percent of all congressmen and 45 percent of all senators did. Moreover, only 30 percent of the public wanted to "place less emphasis" on military weapons programs, a contrast to 37 percent of all congressmen and 45 percent of all senators.[36]

Conclusions

The reasons for the greater internationalism of the center clearly need more study. Yet whatever the reasons for the differences in attitudes of the general public and of decision makers, very noticeable differences exist. This has a number of implications for the foreign policy process. For instance, it means that the potential for conflicts over foreign policy exists as a result of the decision makers' inclination to act in accordance with their own, more internationalist, beliefs. It would also lead to shiftings in policies, depending on the degree to which either the decision makers or the public assert themselves. It was noted in Chapter 2, however, that there exists widespread and diffuse support for American foreign policy. Thus public rejection of policy or attempts to impose public sentiment on decision makers are infrequent.

Finally, even major differences in attitudes of the general public and decision makers need not necessarily lead to differences between public opinion and actual policy. The relationship between the public and policy involves more than attitudes. It also involves behavior—that of the elected and appointed officials and that of the public. In other words, we must look further into the processes of representation and into the behavioral linkages between public and leadership. That is the objective of the following chapter.

Notes

1. Hanna Fenichel Pitkin, *The Concept of Representation* (Berkeley: University of California Press, 1967), p. 61.
2. One of the best studies that has been done is Herbert McCloskey, "Personality and Attitude Correlates of Foreign Policy Orientation," in James N. Rosenau, ed., *Domestic Sources of Foreign Policy* (New York: Free Press, 1967), pp. 51–110.

3. See especially William C. Rogers, Barbara Stuhler, and Donald Koenig, "A Comparison of Informed and General Public Opinion on U.S. Foreign Policy," *Public Opinion Quarterly, 31,* No. 2 (Summer 1967): 242–252.

4. Donald Matthews, *The Social Background of Political Decision-Makers* (Garden City, NY: Doubleday, 1954) and *U.S. Senators and Their World* (New York: Random House, 1960). James Rosenau looked at the characteristics of another important group: opinion leaders and attenders of the 1958 conference on foreign aspects of national security. He found social background and attitude characteristics similar to those leaders discussed here. See James Rosenau, *National Leadership and Foreign Policy: A Case Study in the Mobilization of Public Support* (Princeton, NJ: Princeton University Press, 1963).

5. Dean E. Mann, "The Selection of Federal Political Executives," in Stephen V. Monsma and Jack R. Van Der Slik, eds., *American Politics* (New York: Holt, Rinehart and Winston, 1970), pp. 304–330. Also see Lloyd Warner, Paul van Riper, Norman Martin, and Orvis Collins, *The American Federal Executive: A Study of the Social and Personal Characteristics of the Civilian and Military Leaders of the United States Federal Government* (New Haven, CT: Yale University Press, 1963).

6. Matthews, *The Social Background of Political Decision-Makers,* p. 26.

7. *Ibid.,* p. 27.

8. Mann, *op. cit.,* p. 32.

9. *Ibid.,* p. 323.

10. Matthews, *The Social Background of Political Decision-Makers,* p. 29.

11. Mann, *op. cit.,* p. 321.

12. Apparently, however, adult socialization experiences are more important in determining attitudes than prior experiences or earlier characteristics. See Lewis J. Edinger and Donald D. Searing, "Social Background in Elite Analysis: A Methodological Inquiry," *American Political Science Review, 61,* No. 2 (June 1967): 428–445. This article also points up substantial cross-national differences in the characteristics that best predict attitudes.

13. Matthews, *U.S. Senators and Their World,* p. 19.

14. Matthews, *The Social Background of Political Decision-Makers,* p. 30.

15. Matthews, *U.S. Senators and Their World,* p. 33.

16. Mann, *op. cit.,* p. 324.

17. *Ibid.,* p. 325.

18. *Ibid.,* p. 321.

19. Matthews, *U.S. Senators and Their World,* p. 16.

20. James N. Rosenau, *National Leadership and Foreign Policy: A Case*

Study in the Mobilization of Public Support (Princeton, NJ: Princeton University Press, 1963).

21. Herbert McCloskey, Paul J. Hoffman, and Rosemary O'Hara, "Issue Conflict and Consensus among Party Leaders and Followers," *American Political Science Review, 54* (June 1960): 406–427.

22. See also Robert Axelrod, "Structure of Public Opinion on Policy Issues," *Public Opinion Quarterly, 31,* No. 1 (Spring 1967): 51–60; Philip E. Converse, "The Nature of Belief Systems in Mass Publics," in Norman R. Luttbeg, ed., *Public Opinion and Public Policy* (Homewood, IL: Dorsey, 1968), pp. 246–274.

23. George Belknap and Angus Campbell, "Political Party Identification and Attitudes Toward Foreign Policy," *Public Opinion Quarterly, 55* (Winter 1951–1952): 601–23.

24. William C. Rogers, Barbara Stuhler, and Donald Koenig, *op. cit.* See also Kurt Back and Kenneth Gergen, "Public Opinion and International Relations," *Social Problems, 2* (Summer 1963): 77–87.

25. Allen H. Barton, "Conflict and Consensus Among American Leaders," *Public Opinion Quarterly, 38,* No. 4 (Winter 1974–1975): 507–530.

26. Bruce M. Russett and Elizabeth C. Hanson, *Interest and Ideology* (San Francisco: W. H. Freeman, 1975).

27. Bruce M. Russett, *What Price Vigilance?* (New Haven, CT: Yale University Press, 1960), Chap. 3.

28. Wayne Moyer, "House Voting on Defense: An Ideological Explanation," in Bruce M. Russett and Alfred Stepan, eds., *Military Force and American Society (New York: Harper & Row, 1973).*

29. I am indebted to the discussion of voting studies in Bruce M. Russett and Elizabeth C. Hanson, *op. cit.,* pp. 130–138.

30. Another study lends some support for this restructuring of attitudes in the general public. Moreover, it suggests that the restructuring occurred between 1960 and 1964. Unfortunately, the question tapping military internationalism changed from a general cold war question in 1960 to a Vietnam War question in 1964, making definite conclusions impossible. See Norman H. Nie, Sidney Verba, and John R. Petrocik, *The Changing American Voter* (Cambridge, MA: Harvard University Press, 1976), pp. 124–138, 366.

31. Johan Galtung, "Social Position, Party Identification and Foreign Policy Orientation: A Norwegian Case Study," in James N. Rosenau, ed., *Domestic Sources of Foreign Policy* (New York: Free Press, 1967), pp. 161–194.

32. Interest in or the salience of foreign affairs also contributes to internationalism. See Bruce M. Russett, "Demography, Salience, and Isolationist Behavior," in *Public Opinion Quarterly, 24,* No. 4 (Winter 1960): 658–664.

33. Angus Campbell, Philip E. Converse, Warren E. Miller, and Donald E. Stokes, *The American Voter* (New York: John Wiley, 1964), pp. 115–120; Free and Cantril, *op. cit.*

34. Herbert McCloskey, "Personality and Attitude Correlates of Foreign Policy Orientation," pp. 51–110. On the relationship between psychological or personality characteristics and foreign policy attitudes, see Bjorn Christiansen, *Attitudes Toward Foreign Affairs As a Function of Personality* (Oslo: Oslo University Press, 1959). Many authors have stressed a relationship between authoritarianism and isolationist foreign policy attitudes. For example, see Hero, *Americans in World Affairs.* It is difficult to extrapolate to those making foreign policy, however, since we do not have information on how the personalities of the political elite differ from those of the general public, if they do.

35. William Appleman Williams, *The Tragedy of American Diplomacy* (New York: Delta, 1962).

36. Unfortunately, questions asked of public and representatives differed slightly, and other less military issues were not touched on. See Robert Erikson and Norman Luttbeg, *American Public Opinion* (New York: John Wiley, 1973), p. 257.

4

Policy Representation of Public Opinion

The last chapter discussed the attitudinal differences between the general public and decision makers. In spite of attitudinal differences, however, the behavior of public officials could still closely parallel the foreign policy preferences of the public. There are two major categories of reasons why elected and appointed officials might misrepresent their own attitudes and behaviorally represent those of the public. The first category contains coercive mechanisms. This chapter will examine one such mechanism: the public's electoral punishment of unrepresentative behavior. Luttbeg called this the *rational activist model*, because it requires rational behavior at the polls by an activist public. The second category contains noncoercive mechanisms. Again this chapter will examine one such mechanism: the possibility that foreign policy officials may feel a moral duty to seek out the opinions of their constituents and to act on them, even at the expense of their own beliefs. Luttbeg called this the *role playing model*.

The rational activist and role playing models help us understand the relationship between decision makers and the *general* public. The attitude sharing model examined in the last chapter did the same. Yet only segments of the public actually interact regularly with the decision makers. Hence the next two chapters turn to such segments within the public, specifically parties and interest groups.

Electoral Punishment:
The Rational Activist Model

There is a wide spectrum of opinion in the United States and other democracies on the question of whether or not the general public can influence foreign policy behavior. Some people obviously believe they can. Many write letters (27 percent of the public has at one time or another written to a public official[1]), or they faithfully return the questionnaires sent to them by their congressmen. Even war protesters during the Vietnam War obviously believed that they could mobilize public opinion to eventually force a change in governmental policy. Those who do believe in the force of public opinion make up a considerable percentage of the voting population.[2] Periodic statements from leaders reinforce that belief. Secretaries of state routinely stress the importance of public opinion.[3] At the height of the Cuban missile crisis, John F. Kennedy reportedly remarked to his brother that if he did not act he would be impeached.[4]

On the other hand, there remain many examples of situations in which the government has been accused of ignoring the public. Imagine the disillusionment of the recipient of the following letter from Congressman John McGroaty (California) in 1934:[5]

> One of the countless drawbacks of being in Congress is that I am compelled to receive impertinent letters from a jackass like you in which you say I promised to have the Sierra Madre mountains reforested and I have been in Congress two months and haven't done it. Will you please take two running jumps and go to hell.

While some of the public may believe they can influence their government's policy and others are undoubtedly disillusioned, still others believe that the government should sometimes act against majority opinion. Chapter 2 reported on a 1960 poll of Detroit residents that found that 75 percent of the respondents said the president should send troops into an overseas conflict *even if he knew most Americans opposed it.*[6] Our concern here is not, however, the level of influence the public may feel it has or should have over foreign policy so much as the actual degree of control.

For the public to control the foreign policy of its leaders through the mechanism of defeating those who act contrary to public beliefs and electing those who might better represent those beliefs, three basic conditions must be met within the public:[7]

1. Voters must know of foreign policy issues and have basic information about them.
2. Voters must have interest in the issues to the point that the interest will influence their voting behavior.
3. Voters must be able to distinguish between the party or candidate positions on the issues.

A fairly small segment of the population meets these three conditions for the vast majority of foreign policy issues. It is valuable to look at the data.

Information Level

Quite clearly a very large portion of the public was aware of the U.S. involvement in wars such as Korea and Vietnam and has been aware of the major cold war antagonisms. Substantial evidence, however, shows that a large portion of the population has little or no conception of the details of foreign policy. Approximately one-fourth to one-third of the American electorate is unaware of the most basic facts about foreign policy. In the late spring of 1964, a fourth of the American people were not aware of our activity in Vietnam or of the presence of a communist regime in China.[8] As late as March 1966, more than 80 percent of the public failed to identify the Viet Cong correctly.[9] Although events in the last few years have certainly improved this knowledge level, particularly concerning Vietnam, massive media coverage does not assure issue understanding.[10] On more technical matters, the knowledge of the public drops off rapidly. A Gallup poll in 1964 found that only 58 percent of the American people knew that the United States was a member of the North Atlantic Treaty Organization (NATO).[11] Furthermore, only 38 percent knew that the Soviet Union was *not* a member, and only 21 percent were aware that neutral Sweden did not belong.

Interest

One of the reasons that Americans are often not well informed about foreign policy is that they are less frequently concerned about it than about domestic issues. It has been a tenet of presidential campaigns that, barring exceptional foreign policy problems of the incumbent party (such as the Vietnam War posed for Democrats in 1968), the major issues will be the economic ones. This was proven again in the 1964 presidential campaign, when many pundits believed that the "hard-line" foreign policy positions of Barry Goldwater were influencing the vote of millions of Americans. A major study of political attitudes during the campaign found that "foreign affairs did intrude on the public's consciousness in the 1964 campaign more than in any election since 1952, but popular references to foreign issues in 1964 still had only about a fourth the frequency of references to domestic issues."[12]

Moreover, the personal image of Goldwater among the voters, more than either domestic or foreign policy issues, determined the shift away from the Republican party in the 1964 election. In general, the voters held a very negative image of Goldwater:[13]

> The detailed references to Goldwater are an impressive amalgam of doubts—a wild and erratic campaigner, muddled and unclear, unstable, poorly educated, and so on—with these themes very little offset by references to the advertised qualities of integrity, sincerity, and decisiveness.

Thus in 1964, even among those who understood the issue positions of the two major candidates, domestic issues more often shaped voting than did foreign issues.

Responses to general questions about presidential candidates and the two major parties provide an indication of the relative importance for an individual of domestic and foreign policy issues. Table 4.1 shows that in both 1952 and 1956, approximately three times more Americans spoke primarily of domestic issues than emphasized foreign policy issues. It is especially interesting that so few people concerned themselves principally with foreign policy issues in 1952, since the campaign issues of that year included the Korean War and cold war tensions.

Again in 1975 a study reported references to domestic and foreign policy issues (see Table 4.2) in response to a question asking what two or three problems the respondent would like the government to act on. Note that even if the energy crisis is classified as a foreign policy issue, there were four times as many

TABLE 4.1   93
PRIMARY ISSUE CONTENT OF POLITICAL CONCERNS EXPRESSED IN 1952
AND 1956

	1952	1956
Foreign policy	17%	16%
Domestic policy	54	47
Equal emphasis on foreign and domestic policy	10	8
No issue content	19	29

Source: V. O. Key, Jr., Public Opinion and American Democracy, p. 173. Copyright ©
1964 by Alfred Knopf, Inc.

domestic references as foreign ones by the general public. Leaders
were somewhat more concerned with foreign policy and much
more concerned with the energy crisis. The voting behavior of the
public obviously will reflect the lower level of concern with foreign
policy issues than with domestic economic issues. The low level of
public concern also underlies the relative ignorance on foreign policy issues.

Although the relative interest by the public in domestic and
foreign issues remains quite stable over time, it is, of course, feasi-
ble that the absolute interest in both is increasing. Some evidence
suggests that to be the case. Rosenau collected information from the
White House on letters received annually between 1949 and 1972.
Figure 4.1 shows these numbers expressed as letters per thousand
of U.S. population. The general trend is unmistakably upward, but
in steps representing the first year of new administrations. During
1953, the first year of Eisenhower's administration, the letter level
of 6.55 per thousand exceeded that of any year for which we have

TABLE 4.2
PERCENTAGE OF POPULATION MENTIONING PROBLEM BY CATEGORY
(DECEMBER 1974)

	Public	Leaders
Economy	80	85
Energy crisis, oil shortage (primarily domestic)	11	45
Foreign policy	13	23
Government corruption	15	17

Source: John E. Reilly, ed., American Public Opinion and U.S. Foreign Policy, 1975
(Chicago: Chicago Council on Foreign Relations, 1975), p. 10.

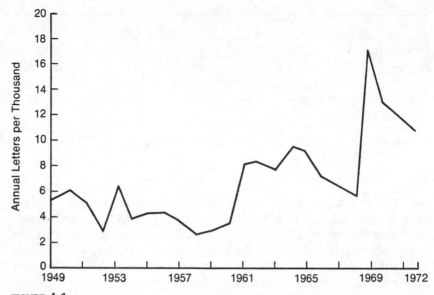

FIGURE 4.1

LETTERS RECEIVED BY THE WHITE HOUSE ANNUALLY PER THOUSAND OF U.S. POPULATION *(Source:* Calculated from James N. Rosenau, *Citizenship Between Elections* (New York: Free Press, 1974), p. 72; *The American Almanac* (New York: Grosset and Dunlap, 1974), p. 5.)

data of the Truman administration. Similarly, the letter rate during the first years in office of Kennedy, Johnson, and Nixon exceeded the peak years of their predecessors. The rate throughout Nixon's first term in office never fell below 10 per thousand and averaged more than three times the rate during Eisenhower's administration. Rosenau's conclusion is that a larger share of the public may be becoming attentive, presumably to both foreign policy and domestic issues.[14]

Party Differentiation and Voting

Given that only small segments of the population are informed about foreign policy issues and that foreign policy interest is low relative to domestic policy interest, it should not surprise us that voters do not perceive significant candidate and party differences on foreign policy issues. The McCloskey study of leaders and followers reported in Chapter 3 discovered that in 1956, even though party leaders did have ideological differences, party followers did not. More recent data and analysis indicate that attitudinal differentiation between partisans in the general public grew steadily from 1956 through 1968 (when the study ended) on a series of domestic issues but did not grow on foreign aid.[15] Data in the next chapter will show that again in 1972 Democrats and Republicans in the general public differed little in attitudes toward foreign aid or whether we should trade with the communists. Only on the issue of Vietnam was there evidence of significant party differences in the general public.

Obviously, only a relatively small segment of the population meet all three conditions underlying effective electoral control over foreign policy. Table 4.3 provides some information on the size of that group. It presents the percentages of the 1956 American public who knew in general terms what the present government policy was on six foreign policy issues (a basic piece of information), who held their own opinion about what should be done (indicating a minimum level of intensity), and who perceived some party differences on the issue.

The evidence suggests that about 30 percent of the public is capable of making voting decisions on the basis of foreign policy issues, although it is difficult to say how many actually do so. One should not assume that on every foreign policy issue it is always the same 30 percent of the public that has knowledge, is interested, and perceives party differences. Different issues attract the attention of different, although in large part overlapping, segments of the population. These segments are sometimes called "issue publics." In a study of those interested in military policy, Bernard Cohen found that one in four of those knowledgeable in military

TABLE **4.3**

PERCENTAGE OF 1956 POPULATION MEETING THREE CONDITIONS FOR ELECTORAL CONTROL

Issue	Percentage
Act tough toward Russia and China	36
U.S. international involvement ("stay home")	32
Friendliness toward other nations	32
Economic aid to foreign countries	23
Send soldiers abroad	22
Give aid to neutral countries	18

Note: The three conditions for electoral control are (1) awareness of and possession of basic information about issues; (2) sufficient interest in the issues to influence voting behavior; and (3) ability to distinguish candidate or party positions on the issues.

Source: Angus Campbell, Philip E. Converse, Warren E. Miller, and Donald E. Stokes, *The American Voter*, p. 106. Copyright © 1964. Reprinted by permission of John Wiley and Sons.

policy did not belong to the general foreign policy issue public. That is, they were not also knowledgeable on general foreign policy issues. He found that those in the military policy public are younger, more often male, better educated, and more frequently Democrats than those in the general foreign policy public.[16] Similarly, evidence suggests that different nonmilitary foreign policy issues attract different portions of the public.[17]

In general, we can conclude that the vote of a congressman or senator for or against foreign aid appropriation or even for or against a Gulf of Tonkin resolution will seldom have any impact on his reelection chances. Similarly, a president's decision to increase or decrease troop commitments to NATO or to build or not to build an ABM system should not affect his reelection. On the other hand, the public does set limits beyond which public officials cannot tread. President Johnson apparently went beyond them in the Vietnam War. In general, it is useful to make a distinction between (1) a few very salient foreign policy issues (such as Korea and Vietnam), about which the public does become concerned and (2) the vast majority of foreign policy activities, about which most of the public is either unaware or uninformed. Unfortunately, we cannot easily specify the issues that will arouse the public.[18]

A recent study of American voting behavior from 1956 through 1972 concluded that issue-based voting has risen significantly since 1956, although most of the increase occurred between 1960 and 1964.[19] It focused very heavily on domestic issues, however, providing no reason to change the conclusion here. The public as a whole cannot behave according to the rational activist model. At best, about two-thirds of it can; on most issues, only one-third can. This conclusion does not free the makers of foreign policy from electoral punishment. In a system where as little as 1 percent of the vote can determine an election outcome and quite frequently does, that one-third of the public wields great power. Again, however, only the most important foreign policy issues can galvanize the attitudes and direct the behavior of even this attentive segment of the public.

Representative Attitudes: The Role Playing Model

We have looked at two mechanisms for control by the general public over governmental foreign policy behavior. The first (see Chapter 3) was basic attitudinal similarity. If the attitudes of those making foreign policy reflect those in the public, then leaders literally represent followers. In Chapter 3, we noted that there are significant differences between the attitudes of the public and of those people the public places in high office. Now we are forced to reject electoral coercion as a mechanism by which the general public controls more than the broad outlines of most official foreign policy behavior.

Nevertheless, the behavior of leaders could closely represent the opinions of the public—at least that segment of the public that holds opinions. Behavioral representation could result from the attitudes concerning representation held by the makers of foreign policy. For instance, representatives might overestimate the awareness of their activities among the general public and act to avoid the apparently unlikely electoral censure. In a 1958 study of congressmen, more than four-fifths said that their records and personal standing were major factors in determining their reelection success or failure.[20] Also, representatives may value their role as delegates of the public in the process of making foreign policy and may desire to adequately represent public opinion. We now turn to these possibilities.

A number of theoretically possible roles exist for elected officials to play in their relationship with the public. Three of these are commonly labeled the *instructed delegate* role, the responsible party role, and the Burkean role.[21] The role of the instructed delegate is self-explanatory. He acts on the behalf of the majority view in his constituency, whether or not it corresponds to his own view.

The role of the responsible party member differs. He looks to the party for his cues to behavior. This role, quite logically, is best performed in a political system, such as the British, in which the parties generally vote cohesively or as a unit. It is not a role that can readily be filled in the American system, with its bipartisan foreign policy and split parties. Whereas a responsible party model might be appropriate for the United States in an issue area such as civil rights or domestic economics, the constitutional requirement that a treaty must be passed by a two-thirds vote acts as a basic structural barrier to its operations in foreign policy. Very seldom has an American party had a two-thirds majority within the Senate, thus permitting the luxury of party voting.[22] This constraint should not be exaggerated, however, since a great deal of U.S. foreign policy is made by the executive branch and thus does not necessarily require even the support of the president's own party, much less a two-thirds majority in the Senate. For instance, much of the escalation of the war in Vietnam was achieved by President Johnson in spite of the opposition of large portions of his own party. Moreover, with the change of administration in 1968, a rough responsible party model for attitudes toward the Vietnam War became a reality. Democratic legislators in large numbers favored more rapid deescalation and opposed resumption of the bombing and the blockade of North Vietnam. Republican congressmen and senators, on the other hand, largely supported the slower efforts of their Republican president.[23]

The Burkean role is one of trustee rather than delegate.[24] Edmund Burke, who was a member of the British Parliament in the late eighteenth century, argued that a representative must serve the constituency's *interest*, rather than its *will*. (He was quoted in Chapter 1.) Such a notion clearly attributes a greater knowledge concerning issues and a greater ability to formulate policy to the representative than to the constituency.[25]

There is little direct evidence concerning how representatives actually view their role in the United States. One study of congressmen by Charles Clapp reports that the congressmen are much freer of constituency domination than they are often portrayed and that they can in fact gain support by showing the "courage" to vote against the majority.[26] Much of our information about how legislators view their roles comes from studies of state legislators. A study of legislators in four states—California, New Jersey, Ohio, and Tennessee—found that the majority of legislators (63 percent) saw themselves as trustees, and only 14 percent perceived themselves as delegates. The remaining 23 percent adopted the perhaps more realistic position that a representative serves in both roles, depending presumably on the nature of the issues.[27] In general, then, it seems reasonable to conclude that a representative perceives himself to be relatively free of constituency opinion, especially in an issue area like foreign policy where constituency opinion can be ambiguous, if it exists.[28]

Information Sources as Keys to Representative Roles

Indirect evidence of the way a representative perceives his role can be found in the sources of information that the legislator relies on in his attempt to gauge constituency opinion. If he perceives his role to be that of a delegate, we would expect considerable effort to be spent in accurately ascertaining the opinions of the constituency. If, on the other hand, the representative views his role as that of a trustee, we would expect that his public opinion information gathering would focus first on those constituents most important to his reelection, whether or not they adequately represent majority opinion, and second on those reached with least cost to the legislator.

An early study of both congressmen and administrators in 1945 asked congressmen to rank order their sources of information from most important to least important. Table 4.4 provides a summary of the results. The most interesting aspect of the table is the rank given to public opinion polls. While administrators thought this to be the best source of information, legislators listed it last.

There are a number of reasons why we would expect administrators to rely heavily on polls, both in absolute terms and relative to legislators. First is the administrators' relative insulation from the information sources on which legislators rely heavily, such as public mail and visits to the public. A second, and perhaps important point, is that administrators represent in a sense the entire nation, and polls are generally national. These national polls undoubtedly can provide systematic and accurate information about the general national sentiment. This should be particularly useful to a government administrator trying to gain perspective under a barrage of pressure group demands.

Interestingly, however, studies since that of 1945 show consistent decreases in administrator (especially State Department) reliance on opinion polls. This is reflected both in the steady decrease in size of the State Department's own Public Opinion Studies Division, from seventy-nine to twenty-five men in the late 1940s and to three men in 1965 (with commissioned polls discontinued in

TABLE **4.4**
PERCEIVED USEFULNESS OF PUBLIC OPINION INDICATORS, AS RANKED BY LEGISLATORS AND ADMINISTRATORS IN 1945 (SCALE OF ONE TO FIVE)

| | RANK ORDER | |
	Legislators	*Administrators*
Polls	5	1
Visits to public	2	2
Newspapers	3	3
Mail	1	4
Visits from public	4	5

Source: Martin Kriesberg, "What Congressmen and Administrators Think of the Polls," *Public Opinion Quarterly, 60* (Fall 1945): 334.

1957),[29] and in the reports by State Department members that "intuition is the prevailing mode of opinion evaluation."[30] More important than the certain degrading of quality in public opinion assessment implied in this process is the indication that the State Department does not care to have high-quality information. Its treatment of mail says the same thing. The Public Opinion Studies Division does not handle mail; instead, mail goes to the Public Services Division, whose "function is liaison rather than opinion analysis."[31] Overall, the attitude of State Department officials has been summarized as "To hell with public opinion . . . we should lead, not follow."[32]

Although national polls at least hold the potential for offering those in the executive branch some knowledge of their national constituency, they almost certainly cannot be used by a legislator to gauge the opinion of a constituency potentially very different from the nation. Yet there is more behind the negative response to public opinion polls by legislators than their frequent inappropriateness for a particular constituency. Legislators have failed to use polls within their own districts for the purpose of tapping public sentiment. As of the mid-1960s, only around one-fourth of congressmen themselves used polling.[33] Of those who do use polls, there is much question as to whether they are used to gather information or to keep the legislator's name and a favorable image before the constituents. In a 1954 study of polls, Carl Hawver argued that the major purpose is the latter: "At the outset, it must be admitted that most Congressmen feel the poll is more valuable to them as an instrument of improving their public relations, than as a means of determining public opinion."[34]

A good many of the questions asked by congressmen are certainly not intended to provide an unbiased sampling of opinion. Consider an extreme example from a poll by Representative John Dowdy (D-Texas):[35]

> The Constitution established the Congress as the legislative branch of the government, the co-equal and independent of the executive and judicial branches. A drive has recently been announced to destroy the independence of the Congress by purging Congressmen who refuse to be rubber stamps for the executive arm of government. Would you want your representative in Congress to surrender to the purge threat and become a rubber-stamped congressman?

Similarly, the answers to the following question on a poll by another Texas Democrat (Ray Roberts), are hardly likely to aid him in the formation of a voting position on the United Nations: "In my opinion, the advantage of the United States remaining in the United Nations, working to solve problems without war, outweigh the disadvantages. Do you believe the United States should withdraw from the United Nations and abandon it to the communists?"[36] One study of polls found that approximately 19 percent of all poll questions were clearly biased.[37] In view of this, it seems reasonable to hypothesize that many of the more knowledgeable constituents are offended by the questions and fail to return the questionnaires.

Other evidence that polls are used at least as much for political as for information purposes lies in the widespread practice of saturation mailing. For a good estimate of opinion, a relatively small random sample of respondents is adequate. Follow-up letters should be sent to nonrespondents so that the response rate and accuracy will increase. Congressmen, however, generally mail to all households and do not send follow-up letters. When a sample is taken, it is of responses received. Some congressmen not only use polls but use them in a serious attempt to obtain information. These are, however, few.

A More Narrowly Defined Public

For congressmen, mail from their constituencies, although a biased indicator,[38] and visits to the constituencies are apparently more important sources of information than polls. For instance, the representative presumably wants to know the opinion of some special interests, since these play a more important part in his or her reelection than the less intense opinions of the general public. Yet even private representations to congressmen by mail or lobbyist approaches have been argued in some studies to be relatively unimportant in shaping congressional opinions. "We find that the net effect of communications was to heighten attention to an issue, rather than to convey specific content about it."[39]

There remain many political observers who would, however, disagree with this skeptical assessment of the influence of mail. James Reston, for example, has argued that letters have more impact on policy in both the White House and Congress than letter writers anticipate.[40] Moreover, it should be pointed out that the report of studies on mail treatment by the State Department may mislead us somewhat in our assessment of mail's impact on the executive. The State Department is supposed to be a collection of career officials analyzing foreign policy objectively and nonpolitically. In contrast, however, the White House has a considerable bureaucracy of its own, consisting in very large part of politically appointed officials. These officials may be more sensitive to mail than the State Department.

Perhaps even more important to the legislator than the opinions of what we might call "special interests" are the attitudes of those he or she would consider friends and supporters. These people, very frequently personal acquaintances, constitute those with whom the congressman checks on visits home, those who have access to his or her office in Washington, and those whose mail becomes more than a digit in the aide's report.

Although this public makes up only a subset of the opinion leaders in the constituency, it is nevertheless a widening of the representative's Washington circle and has an importance that should not be underestimated. The phenomenon has been quite well documented by Bernard Cohen for the State Department. He lists three categories of public opinion: that from "intimates" or friends and family; that from "specialists"; and that from "institutions" like interest groups and the press.[41] Cohen justifiably expresses surprise that political observers have largely ignored the first category. In particular, he presents a number of interview-based anecdotes that document the importance of "intimates" in shaking the bureaucracy's faith in Vietnam War policy. Moreover, both "intimates" and "specialists" provide information not only on their own views but also on patterns and changes in a wider public opinion. He also points out that congressional opinion serves for the State Department as a surrogate public opinion. We shall argue shortly that Congress is in fact a rather biased sample of the public but that it offers at least a broadening of view beyond that of the State Department.

The evidence to this point suggests that foreign policy decision makers do not actively assume the role of the delegate, either as a result of actual or perceived electoral control by the general public or as a result of a conception of the delegate as the proper role of representative. The trustee role is a much more appropriate description of the legislator-constituency relationship in foreign policy. This does not necessarily mean that all congressmen and members of the executive feel superior to others in their ability to make foreign policy decisions. Most look to *certain* constituents regularly. A great many congressmen, moreover, look to the executive (especially to the president) for foreign policy leadership, a point we shall elaborate, especially in Chapter 5.[42]

Public Opinion and Foreign Policy—
A Direct Look

Not only are there attitudinal differences between the general public and makers of foreign policy, then, but the general American public is also unlikely, except in unusual circumstances, to impose its attitudinal preferences on the decision makers. The evidence for this conclusion has been extensive but fragmentary. It is thus appropriate to look now at the few studies that focus directly on the relationship between public opinion and foreign policy.

Congress

One of the most interesting studies in this area was undertaken by Warren Miller and Donald Stokes. They interviewed 116 congressmen and examined their voting records. They also examined the opinion of constituents in each of the corresponding congressional districts.[43] They summarized the relationship between constituency opinion on foreign policy and the votes of congressmen with a correlation. The correlation is less than ".2."[44] In other words, there is very little relationship between representative votes and constituency attitudes for foreign policy. Miller and Stokes suggest that the congressman either votes as he or she feels best or looks to the administration, especially to the president, for advice. Here, then, is a case of basically Burkean representation in which the congressman feels free to act in the interest of his or her constituency as that interest is interpreted by someone other than the constituency.

Miller and Stokes present two other interesting correlations between constituency attitudes on the one hand, and both the representative's attitude and his or her perception of constituency attitudes on the other. It was argued in Chapter 3 that there can be considerable attitudinal differences between foreign policy makers and the general public. The correlation that Miller and Stokes found between constituency and representative attitudes is only .32, which bears this argument out. It has been argued in this chapter that representatives do not make an effective attempt to discover majority opinion in their constituencies. Miller and Stokes found that the correlation between constituency opinion and the representative's perception of that opinion is only .25, lower than the correlation with his own attitude.

This rather dismal picture for a democratic system should be tempered with the presentation of correlations between constituency attitudes and the representative's votes for issues other than foreign policy. On social and economic welfare issues, the correlation climbs to about ".4." This is still very unspectacular, and Miller and Stokes suggest that one reason is a relatively high degree of party voting on these issues. Thus the representative is looking to his or her party for voting cues, as well as, and perhaps more than to the constituency. It is on civil rights issues that we find congressmen voting much more consistently with their constituents—the correlation is .65. Civil rights issues were highly salient to the general public when this study was done in 1958 and continue to be among the issues that voters consider more important (witness "forced busing"). Thus constituencies tend to elect those who share their views on civil rights, and the elected congressmen closely follow the desires of the constituents.

There is some reason to believe that the Miller and Stokes study underestimates, at least slightly, the impact of constituency foreign policy opinions on the votes of congressmen. The data reported in a study of Leroy Rieselbach suggest a potentially stronger impact.[45] Rieselbach examined the relationship between demographic characteristics of the constituency and the internationalism of voting on foreign aid issues by members of the House of Representatives. On the basis of the previous chapter, we would posit that the more urban the district, the higher the education level of the district, and the higher the socioeconomic status (SES) level of the district, the greater the support we would find within the district for foreign aid. If congressmen are to represent these districts, then, we would expect more internationalist voting in such districts. In fact, Rieselbach found a fairly strong tendency for these suppositions to be borne out (see Table 4.5).

The data in Table 4.5 do not actually contradict the findings of the Miller and Stokes study, since it did find a correlation (even if a low one) between constituency attitudes and representative votes. The Rieselbach data do suggest, however, that the correlation might be somewhat higher.

Interestingly, Warren Miller himself, in another article, provides some data that raise questions about his and Stokes' conclusion.[46] He looked at congressmen in safe districts (those in which they have no trouble being reelected) and congressmen in marginal districts. Table 4.6 shows the results. In safe northern districts, Republicans and Democrats vote very differently. In marginal districts, they vote much alike on foreign policy issues. This implies that

TABLE 4.5

FOREIGN AID VOTING OF CONGRESSMEN, BY PARTY, REGION TYPE, EDUCATION, AND SOCIOECONOMIC STATUS (SES)

Party and Constituency Characteristic	83RD CONGRESS (1953–1954)			85TH CONGRESS (1957–1958)		
	Percent isolationist	Percent internationalist	N	Percent isolationist	Percent internationalist	N
Republicans						
Urban	14.7	78.7	75	26.4	70.8	72
Rural	70.2	23.4	47	65.7	25.7	35
Democrats						
Urban	2.4	92.9	85	3.3	80.2	91
Rural	23.3	59.3	86	52.5	24.2	97
Republicans						
Low education	52.5	37.5	40	54.3	34.3	35
High education	20.3	72.2	79	28.9	65.8	76
Democrats						
Low education	16.5	69.9	103	33.6	46.3	110
High education	8.1	75.7	37	17.5	50.0	40
Republicans						
Low SES	66.0	24.5	53	68.9	24.4	45
High SES	13.8	80.0	80	26.0	68.8	77
Democrats						
Low SES	19.1	64.8	105	40.5	37.7	116
High SES	2.2	86.7	45	8.3	66.7	48

Source: Leroy N. Rieselbach, "The Demography of the Congressional Vote on Foreign Aid, 1949–1958," American Political Science Review, 58 (September 1964): 584–87.

TABLE 4.6

DIFFERENCES BY PARTY OF NORTHERN CONGRESSMEN ON FOREIGN POLICY, 1958, ON A FIVE-POINT SCALE OF CONSERVATISM (1) AND LIBERALISM (5)

	Democratic congressmen	Republican congressmen	Difference
Safe districts	4.29	1.39	2.90
Marginal districts	3.83	3.38	.45

Source: Warren E. Miller, "Majority Rule and the Representative System of Government," in E. Allardt and Y. Littunen, eds., Cleaveages, Ideologies, and Party Systems (Helsinki: Transactions of the Westermarck Society, 1964), p. 358.

marginality forces congressmen toward the center, where the general public of both parties can be found (remember Table 3.7). In a safe district, however, representatives from the two parties can vote the more divergent positions of the politically involved. Our basic conclusion must be that there is a small (but not zero) relationship between constituency opinions and congressional voting.

The Executive

This discussion so far has focused on congressmen. Such a focus is somewhat inappropriate, since the making of foreign policy has come more and more to be an executive prerogative. Congressmen are left with what are in many cases relatively unimportant foreign policy decisions—decisions that very often do not attract the attention of the general public. The executive has even abridged the powers of Congress to make treaties and to declare war. Dissenters from the Vietnam War argued it to be an "illegal" war because of the absence of a congressional declaration. Many defenders of the executive have argued that modern technology no longer permits leisurely consideration in Congress of whether military force should be used, and Congress cannot act rapidly. Nor can it act secretly, and secrecy may well be crucial in situations such as the Cuban missile crisis. Whether or not these arguments for executive primacy in foreign policy are valid, the history of the post-World War II period is one of executive military actions in places such as Korea, Lebanon, Cuba, Vietnam, and the Dominican Republic.

The complexities and extensiveness of our involvement in the world have weakened the Senate treaty power. Senators have neither the time nor the resources to provide two-thirds approval of all the agreements into which the United States enters, and many are made without congressional approval. These "executive agreements" are generally of lesser importance than treaties but can be very significant. They include, for instance, the Korean armistice, the Agreement on Prisoners of War in Korea, and the agreement with Canada on the St. Lawrence Seaway project. There is often a fine line between an executive agreement and a treaty. President Theodore Roosevelt clearly recognized this. When he submitted a protocol to the Senate for U.S. administration of Santo Domingo customs and it was rejected, he acted on the basis of an executive agreement.[47] The number of executive agreements has mushroomed, as can be seen in Table 4.7.

TABLE 4.7   107
NUMBER OF UNITED STATES TREATIES AND EXECUTIVE AGREEMENTS,
1789–1964

Period	Executive agreements	Treaties	Ratio of agreements to treaties
1789–1839	27	60	.45
1839–1889	238	215	1.11
1889–1939	917	524	1.75
1940–1964	4358	244	17.86

Source: Elmer Plischke, *Conduct of American Diplomacy* (Princeton, NJ: D. Van Nostrand, 1967), pp. 423–424. Republished in 1974 by Greenwood Press, Westport, CN.

We should thus look carefully at the executive branch. It is conceivable, although hardly likely, that we might find a closer relationship between the foreign policy behavior of the administration and public opinion than we did with legislators. The State Department still does maintain a Public Opinion Studies Division to discover and circulate the character of public opinion in the United States, even if it is considerably reduced from its earlier size. The United States Information Agency even does considerable overseas polling (interrupted by Johnson when Vietnam War opinion soured). Although these information sources may be used to increase the sensitivity of the administration to the public, there are other uses as well. In 1957 it was discovered that the International Cooperation Administration (the forerunner of our present foreign aid machinery, the Agency for International Development) was leaking favorable reports of public opinion on foreign aid to the press.[48]

In spite of potential sensitivity to public opinion, the evidence we have seen suggests that the day-to-day conduct of foreign policy by the executive branch is almost completely unrelated to general public opinion. To that extent that there is a relationship, public opinion reacts to changes in foreign policy. For instance, in a study of U.S. tariff policy that included a look at public opinion toward the tariff issue, the authors concluded that[49]

> There is evidence of a general shift of opinion in the direction of a more liberal trade policy, a trend that parallels national policy on this issue. But the trend lagged behind policy. There is every evidence that opinions on this subject have not been well crystallized or firmly held and that a large proportion of the public has been neither informed nor interested in the topic.

This is only policy on a single issue—and a rather esoteric one, at that. More general evidence, however, corroborates the conclusion that public opinion reacts to foreign policy and generally supports it, but does not lead it.

This supportive reaction of the public appears not just in relatively unimportant foreign policy matters. On the contrary, it emerges most dramatically in major crises. Chapter 2 showed how the public will apparently support any president when he takes a dramatic step in foreign policy. Additional evidence from other democratic nations also indicates that public attitudes follow rather than precede foreign policy developments. Table 4.8 presents data showing the strength of the relationship between changes in foreign policy and *subsequent changes* in public attitudes for four European nations.[50] Note that the correlations in Table 4.8 differ substantially for the four nations. The longer democratic histories of France and Britain and the larger "attentive publics" in those countries, compared to Italy and Germany, may account for the closer government/public relationship in the former two countries. Studies of Italy frequently show that the general public is highly alienated from the government and is largely uninformed of government activities.[51] We would expect the United States to be more similar to France and Britain in this regard, and we might expect a similar correlation in the United States.[52]

Public Support of Foreign Policy

All of the data presented above indicate that those who react to governmental action in a democracy react *positively* or supportively. There almost certainly are individuals who react negatively to governmental foreign policy, presumably individuals who held negative attitudes toward the U.S. government. Few Americans, however, hold such negative attitudes.

Interestingly, studies show that there is in general a dramatically increasing willingness to support governmental policy among the more educated and those more knowledgeable about foreign policy.[53] These people stand close to the "center" of society and politics, so they understandably would feel a greater attachment to society and be more susceptible to its pressures. In support of this, we can contrast public opinion toward intervention in Cambodia in April 1970 with public opinion in May 1970. Between the times of the two surveys, the United States did in fact send troops into Cambodia. Table 4.9 presents Harris survey data for two center groups, the educated and whites, and for two periphery groups, the

TABLE **4.8**

RELATIONSHIP BETWEEN CHANGES IN FOREIGN POLICY AND SUBSEQUENT
CHANGES IN PUBLIC OPINION IN FOUR WESTERN EUROPEAN NATIONS
(1954–1965)

Nation	Average correlation
France	.47
Great Britain	.41
West Germany	.15
Italy	.05

Source: Martin Abravanel and Barry Hughes, "Public Opinion and Foreign Policy
Behavior: A Cross-National Study of Linkages," in the Yearbook of Foreign Policy
Studies, Volume 1, Patrick McGowan, ed., © 1974, p. 123, by permission of the
Publisher, Sage Publications, Inc.

TABLE **4.9**

PUBLIC SUPPORT FOR VARIOUS FORMS OF INTERVENTION IN CAMBODIA,
BEFORE AND AFTER ACTUAL INTERVENTION

	APRIL 1970 (BEFORE)			
	Send troops	Send advisors or conduct bombings	Stay out	Not sure
Race				
White	7%	25	58	10
Black	6%	10	64	20
Education				
Eighth grade or less	4%	13	62	21
High school	8%	22	59	11
College	8%	28	56	8

	MAY 1970 (AFTER)				
	Send troops	Send advisors	Conduct bombings	Stay out	Not sure
Race					
White	42%	14	8	29	7
Black	9%	21	3	56	11
Education					
Eighth grade or less	30%	5	7	44	14
High school	36%	19	8	31	7
College	50%	13	7	26	4

Source: Harris Survey Yearbook of Public Opinion, 1970 (New York: Louis Harris
and Associates, 1971), p. 120.

less educated and blacks. Note that before the invasion, none of the groups volunteered support for the sending of U.S. troops, although the educated and whites provided relatively more support for the use of advisors and bombings. Yet immediately after the sending of troops into Cambodia, support for the action jumped. Moreover, it increased primarily among the college educated and whites.[54] The contrast between whites and blacks is especially stark. It is also interesting that men were more likely to support the troops than were women, white Protestants more likely than white Catholics, and those over thirty more likely than those under thirty. Not surprisingly, Republicans were considerably more likely to support the action of their Republican president than were Democrats. In short, being close to the center makes support for the government considerably more likely.

There is, however, a factor that causes some individuals near the center not to change their beliefs—either in the direction of governmental policy or counter to it. As a person becomes more knowledgeable about foreign policy and a frequent observer of it, he or she tends to create a structured and thus less changeable belief system. This is not to say that he or she becomes an ideologue but that there is a pressure toward consistency. Thus some knowledgeable observers of governmental foreign policy action are pressured in two contradictory directions: toward consistency and toward governmental support.[55]

Some Examples of Attitude and Policy Change

The evidence we have seen thus far on the relationship between public attitudes and foreign policy can be supplemented with some graphs showing the relationship on specific issues. First let us examine two ongoing issues—the levels of spending on foreign aid and defense. Then we can turn to more discrete policy making—the decision to deescalate the Vietnam War and the admission of China to the United Nations.

Figure 4.2 shows the relationship between public opinion on foreign aid and foreign aid expenditures as a percentage of GNP. Support for foreign aid increased slightly between 1956 and 1968 and remained quite strong and stable until 1964. Thereafter it fell off markedly. Spending on foreign aid as a percentage of GNP declined quite sharply until 1959 and then roughly stabilized, with only slow erosion until 1972, and a fairly sharp decline again in 1973. The graph suggests that governmental behavior change led public opinion change in this case by a period of years. In fact, only

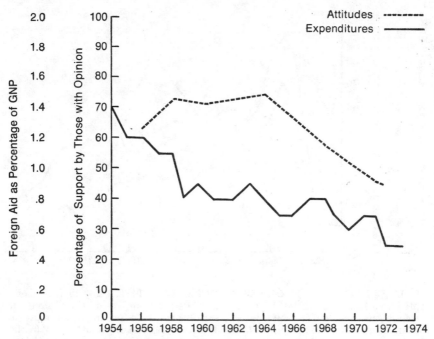

FIGURE 4.2
PUBLIC OPINION ON FOREIGN AID EXPENDITURES (*Source:* Codebooks of the Survey Research Center's American National Election Studies (Ann Arbor, MI: Inter-University Consortium for Political Research); U.S. Department of Commerce, *Historical Statistics of the United States: Colonial Times to 1970* (Washington, DC: U.S. Government Printing Office, 1975); U.S. Department of Commerce, *Statistical Abstract of the United States, 1975* (Washington, DC: U.S. Government Printing Office, 1976).)

in 1972 does a plurality of the public favor less spending. For foreign aid, the relationship between public opinion and public policy appears weak, and policy appears to affect attitude (with a time lag) rather than vice versa. It should be noted, however, that the relatively narrow range of the attitudinal variable (between 45 and 73 percent) implies satisfaction with policy, if not control.

Figure 4.3 traces the relationship between public opinion on defense spending and actual expenditures, again as a percentage of GNP. The two war spending peaks are evident in the expenditure data: 1952–1954 for Korea and 1967–1969 for Vietnam. The demobilization after World War II appears clearly, as does a general downward trend in expenditures (as a percentage of GNP) from the late 1950s to the mid-1970s.

The 1949 and 1950 attitudes reflect the cold war uncertainty and appear to question the demobilization. In 1951, support for Korea is

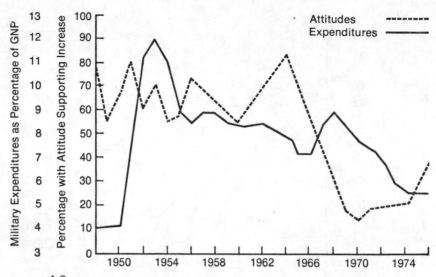

FIGURE 4.3

PUBLIC OPINION ON DEFENSE EXPENDITURES AND ATTITUDES (*Source:* Computed from Bruce M. Russett, "The Americans' Retreat from World Power," *Political Science Quarterly, 90,* No. 1 (Spring 1975): 3; 1973 and 1974 Gallup Polls as reported in various issues of *Gallup Opinion Index* (Princeton, NJ: American Institute of Public Opinion, monthly); U.S. Department of Commerce, *Historical Statistics of the United States: Colonial Times to 1970* (Washington, DC: U.S. Government Printing Office, 1975); U.S. Department of Commerce, *Statistical Abstract of the United States,* 1975 (Washington, DC: U.S. Government Printing Office, 1976).)

obvious, although it erodes by 1954. As expenditures moved downward (always as a percentage of GNP) under Eisenhower, the public appears to have resisted somewhat. Support for the Vietnam War is very evident in 1964, as is opposition by the time of the next survey in 1969. Only a few have come to question the quite significant downturn in expenditures since the Vietnam War, that downturn being the "peace bonus" so many have denied came at all.

Again, it is not obvious that any close relationship between attitudes and policy exists. In fact, the range of variability for attitudes (from 14 to 83 percent) is considerably greater than for foreign aid, suggesting less overall satisfaction with policy than in the foreign aid case. (Greater sensitivity of the public and interest in defense policy probably also account for some of that variability.) Clearly the public did favor spending to support the war efforts, although with erosion of support in Korea and collapse in Vietnam. In both cases, the beginning of the war led to attitudinal and policy changes, providing no indication of effect by either on the other. The major evidence of an impact of attitudes on policy is after 1969, when the great disillusionment of the public with spending leads and then coincides with a steady downward trend in the share of the national pie going to defense.

Turning to Figure 4.4, we see another and earlier instance in which public opinion clearly led policy, and we have every reason to believe that in this case it strongly influenced policy. The dashed lines show support for and opposition to the Vietnam War, with the emergence of a plurality in opposition during 1967–1968. In 1968 troop strength in Vietnam was at its highest. It declined thereafter, not just because of overall public opposition, of course, but in large part because of the intensity of opposition feelings, even when it was a minority. Interestingly, the graph shows that the dollar cost of the war climbed again in 1969. At that point, decision makers were still not committed to withdrawal, and spending was being substi-

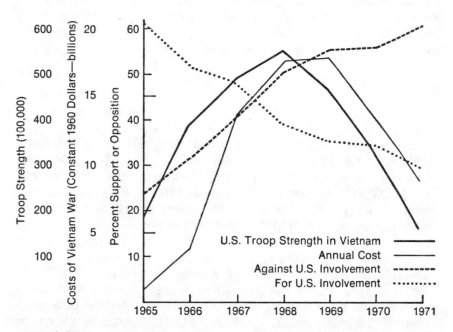

FIGURE **4.4**

PUBLIC OPINION ON THE VIETNAM WAR (*Source:* John Mueller, *War, Presidents and Public Opinion,* pp. 28, 54–55, for "Troop Strength and Attitudes." Copyright © 1973. Reprinted by permission of John Wiley & Sons; Stockholm International Peace Research Institute, *World Armaments and Disarmament: SIPRI Yearbook 1972* (New York: Humanities Press, 1972), p. 55 for "Annual Cost.")

tuted for soldiers to satisfy the opposition. As the public became even more clearly tired of the war, spending also declined.

As one last illustration of the relationship between public opinion and foreign policy, the reader might glance again at Figure 2.3. That figure showed the public's gradual acceptance of China's ultimate admission to the United Nations. Throughout the 1950s and 1960s, the public opposed admission of the People's Republic of China, but by a declining margin. Concurrently, in the United Nations growing numbers of nations made efforts to gain its admission. The United States resisted those efforts, but with decreasing enthusiasm once the final outcome became obvious. Although U.S. policy makers obviously did not have clear control over the date of admission, it is interesting that the substitution of Peking for Taiwan came in 1971, the same year that a plurality came to approve of the admission.

All in all, the four graphs indicate a definite, if not always strong relationship between opinion and policy.[56] The evidence corroborates our general conclusions that the public tends to be quite supportive of foreign policy, especially in a crisis, and that it frequently responds to policy rather than dictating it. Nonetheless, the evidence for some two-way relationship can also be found in Figures 4.3 and 4.4.

Conclusions

Some review and general discussion may help bring order and clarity to the picture of the relationship between public opinion and U.S. foreign policy. We should reconsider the evidence and what has been proved or not proved. First, "public opinion" on foreign policy, insofar as it can be ascertained, differs somewhat from the opinion of that segment of the population from which most foreign policy decision makers are drawn. The differences lie in the rigor of the belief system, the clarity of the beliefs, and the degree to which international involvement is accepted. The implication of this finding is that leaders, if they were to act without control from their constituencies, would act somewhat differently from the way they would act if they were to attempt to act on the basis of general public opinion. The significance of these differences is basically subjective. An isolationist might see them as more important than an internationalist; a convinced democrat might see them as more undesirable than an elitist.

Second, there appears to be little evidence of electoral control by the general public over the foreign policy made by decision makers. Decision makers appear, in general, to accept a role as a trustee of the public interest and to act in accordance with their own foreign policy beliefs or those of an especially important referent such as the president.

The data do not prove, however, that electoral control over foreign policy is a complete myth. There are groups in the population who are interested in foreign policy, who are aware of international relations, and who at least periodically cast their vote as a result of issue position differences between candidates. Some of these are the "swing voters," whose movement from one party to another often determines the outcome of elections.[57] It might be argued that these voters are often frustrated, in their efforts to control foreign policy, by the frequently insignificant differences between the two major parties and their candidates. In the 1968 presidential election, for instance, when the Vietnam War presented a salient issue to a widely attentive public, few voters and, for that matter, few foreign policy experts could see significant differences between the expressed positions of Humphrey and Nixon.[58] The 1976 election campaign also failed to give voters a clear image of candidate foreign policy differences.

There are two responses to this frequent lament. First, differences do exist between the foreign policy positions of the two parties; Chapter 3 indicated that, and the differences will be developed further in Chapter 5. It is often rational for candidates to deemphasize these differences during election campaigns. Second, to the extent that both parties and candidates act to reduce or eliminate these differences, both are moving their policies toward the center of the electorate attitude distribution. Thus in 1968, both Nixon and Humphrey presented images of themselves as favoring neither complete military victory (or hawkish positions) nor complete withdrawal (or dovish positions). At the same time the electorate was moving from generally hawkish to generally dovish beliefs, with the majority clustering of attitudes between the two poles. The election of either Nixon or Humphrey would have thus theoretically led to the representation of public opinion. In short, democratic control does not always mean (as perhaps in 1964 and 1972) the choice between clear alternatives, one representing public opinion and one not; it may mean that the alternatives presented to the public are all within a satisfactory range.

A moment's reflection on general U.S. policy toward various

nations in the world and on public opinion toward those same nations will lead to the conclusion that there is a high level of congruence between public attitude and policy. The U.S. government cooperates little and is often in conflict with the communist nations. Americans fear and distrust these same nations. The United States is generally on very good terms with the European and especially the Anglo-Saxon nations. Most Americans feel a cultural tie with Europe and hold favorable attitudes toward it. U.S. policies toward the underdeveloped world are much less developed and consistent. So are the attitudinal structures of Americans.

Although these arguments may salvage a role for democracy in foreign policy, they do not leave the role completely untarnished. The "swing voters" are, after all, generally going to be the white, educated, urban-dwelling males, and their votes still misrepresent much of the rest of the public. Moreover, they are the ones who belong at or near the "center" of society and who thus will often be supportive of a foreign policy, even when it conflicts with previous beliefs. Again, individual judgement of the seriousness of these deviations will be subjective. Those who currently favor the government's foreign policy would probably argue that the present weak control by the public of policy and the general public support of policy provides needed flexibility to an administration. Others who happen at the moment not to support the policies will complain of a lack of democracy. Many cheered a strong president leading a reluctant Congress and public to more liberal trade policies and more foreign aid. Some of those later decided that greater congressional control was necessary over a strong president who committed troops to South Vietnam. Those same newly convinced democrats (not necessarily Democrats) may yet cheer other strong presidents.

Notes

1. Computed from the 1972 Survey Research Center National Election Study (data received on tape from Inter-University Consortium for Political Research, Ann Arbor, MI).
2. In a British survey, 60 percent believed voters have a big influence on the way the country is governed, compared with only 35 percent who did not feel voters have much influence. See Richard Rose and Harve Mossawir, "Voting and Elections: A Functional Analysis," in Charles F. Cnudde and Deane E. Neubauer, eds., *Empirical Democratic Theory* (Chicago: Markham, 1960), pp. 69–93.

3. Bernard C. Cohen, *The Public's Impact on Foreign Policy* (Boston: Little, Brown, 1973), p. 21.

4. Robert F. Kennedy, *Thirteen Days* (New York: New American Library, 1969), p. 67.

5. Quoted in Frederick H. Hartmann, *The New Age of American Foreign Policy* (New York: Macmillan, 1970), p. 108.

6. Thomas Halper, *Foreign Policy Crises* (Columbus, OH: Charles E. Merrill, 1971).

7. Angus Campbell, Philip E. Converse, Warren E. Miller, and Donald E. Stokes, *The American Voter* (New York: John Wiley, 1964), p. 97.

8. Lloyd A. Free and Hadley Cantril, *The Political Beliefs of Americans* (New York: Simon & Schuster, 1968), p. 59.

9. Sheldon Appleton, *United States Foreign Policy* (Boston: Little, Brown, 1968), p. 280.

10. Shirley A. Star and Helen M. Hughes, "Report on an Educational Campaign: The Cincinnati Plan for the United Nations," *American Journal of Sociology,* 55 (January 1950): 389–440.

11. Free and Cantril, *op. cit.,* p. 59.

12. Donald E. Stokes, "Some Dynamic Elements of Contests for the Presidency," *The American Political Science Review,* 61 (1966): 19–28.

13. *Ibid.*

14. James N. Rosenau, *Citizenship Between Elections* (New York: Free Press, 1974), pp. 44–88.

15. Gerald R. Pomper, "From Confusion to Clarity: Issues and American Voters, 1956–1968," *American Political Science Review,* 66, No. 2 (June 1972): 415–428.

16. Bernard Cohen, "The Military Policy Public," *Public Opinion Quarterly,* 30, No. 2 (Summer 1966): 200–211.

17. David RePass, "Issue Salience and Party Choice," *American Political Science Review,* 65 (June 1971): 389–400; V. O. Key, *The Responsible Electorate* (New York: Random House, 1966).

18. Norman H. Nie, Sidney Verba, and John R. Petrocik, *The Changing American Votes* (Cambridge, MA: Harvard University Press, 1976).

19. For an interesting and logical discussion of this issue, see Cohen, *The Public's Impact on Foreign Policy,* pp. 17–19.

20. Warren E. Miller and Donald E. Stokes, "Constituency Influence in Congress," in Angus Campbell, Philip E. Converse, Warren E. Miller, and Donald E. Stokes, *Elections and the Political Order* (New York: John Wiley, 1966), p. 368.

21. *Ibid.,* p. 353.

22. Contrast this to party votes on Common Market entry in Britain and the Soviet Treaty in West Germany.

23. Quite remarkably, this alignment of legislators was followed by a shift in opinion by adherents of the two parties in the general public. Prior to 1969, a higher percentage of Democrats than of Republicans in the general public supported the military efforts in Vietnam. By mid-1969, this had reversed, and more Republicans supported the war. Note that the change in public opinion followed that in leadership alignment—a pattern that we will see repeated later in the chapter. For a fascinating presentation of this data, see John Mueller, *War, Presidents and Public Opinion* (New York: John Wiley, 1973), Chap. 5.

24. For a description of the trustee role, see Heinz Eulau, John C. Wahlke, William Buchanan, and LeRoy C. Ferguson, "The Role of the Representative: Some Empirical Observations on the Theory of Edmund Burke," *American Political Science Review*, 53 (September 1959): 742–756.

25. See Lester B. Pearson, "Democracy and the Power of Decision," in Harold Karan Jacobson, ed., *America's Foreign Policy* (New York: Random House, 1965), p. 27.

26. Charles L. Clapp, *The Congressman: His Work As He Sees It* (Washington, DC: Brookings Institution, 1963).

27. Eulau *et al., op. cit.*

28. Some scholars disagree with the view of the politician as a trustee on foreign policy decisions. A study of pre-World War I German governmental documents by Richard Fagen led him to the rather surprising conclusion that public opinion was very important to foreign policy decision makers. "In assessing public opinion as 'hard goods,' in attempting to influence public opinion through press control, and, finally in using public opinion symbolically, the decision makers seemed to conceive of public opinion as an active, initiating, coercive, reified, even personified force"—see Richard Fagen, "Some Assessments and Uses of Public Opinion in Diplomacy," *Public Opinion Quarterly*, 24 (1960): 457.

29. Cohen, *The Public's Impact on Foreign Policy*, p. 45. William Chittick reports that another reason for the decline in State Department polling is congressional wariness of such activities, which members perceive as related to administration propaganda efforts—see Chittick, *State Department, Press, and Pressure Groups* (New York: John Wiley, 1970), p. 43.

30. Cohen, *op. cit.*, p. 65.

31. *Ibid.*, p. 47.

32. *Ibid.*, p. 62.

33. Walter Wilcox, "The Congressional Poll—and Non-Poll," in Edward Dreyer and Walter Rosenbaum, eds., *Political Opinion and Behavior* (Belmont, CA: Wadsworth, 1970), p. 527.

34. Carl Hawver, "The Congressman and His Public Opinion Poll," *Public Opinion Quarterly*, 18 (Spring 1954): 128.

35. Wilcox, *op. cit.*, p. 527.

36. *Ibid.*, p. 533.

37. Leonard A. Marascuilo and Harriet Amster, "Survey of 1961–62 Congressional Polls," *Public Opinion Quarterly*, 28, No. 3 (1964): 497–506.

38. Converse *et al., op. cit.*

39. Raymond Bauer *et al., American Business and Public Policy: The Politics of Foreign Trade* (New York: Atherton Press, 1963), p. 413.

40. James Reston, "Washington: How Corrupt Is America?" *The New York Times*, February 26, 1976.

41. Cohen, *The Public's Impact on Foreign Policy*, p. 79.

42. Miller and Stokes, *op. cit.*, p. 362.

43. *Ibid.*

44. A correlation is a statistical measure of relationship. That is, when two variables (such as the attitudes held by a majority in the constituency and the votes of congressmen) are related, the correlation increases. In this case, the more often the positions of congressmen suggested by their votes are the same as the position of their constituents, the higher the correlation is. The arbitrary mathematical limit of a correlation is 1. In order to obtain a correlation of 1, the congressmen would need to always vote with their constituencies. If their votes were always against their constituency opinion, the correlation would be −1. If there were no relationship (the congressmen vote half the time with the constituency and half the time against), the correlation would be 0 (zero).

45. Leroy N. Riesselbach, "The Demography of the Congressional Vote on Foreign Aid, 1939–1958," *American Political Science Review*, 58 (September 1964): pp. 584–587.

46. Warren E. Miller, "Majority Rule and the Representative System of Government," in E. Allardt and Y. Littunen, eds., *Cleavages, Ideologies, and Party Systems* (Helsinki: Transactions of the Westermark Society, 1964), pp. 343–376. In a study of domestic policy, Robert Erickson also found evidence of constituency constraint. He found that conservative voting Republican congressmen were less likely to be reelected. The results for liberal Democrats were, however, inconsistent. See Erickson, "The Electoral Impact of Congressional Roll Call Voting," *American Political Science Review*, 65 No. 4 (December 1971): 1018–1032.

47. Elmer Plischke, *Conduct of American Diplomacy* (Princeton, NJ: D. Van Nostrand, 1967), p. 418 (Note 12). Needless to say, the Senate has not been happy with such actions; its resentment came out in the "Bricker Amendment" proposal.

48. For a fascinating discussion of this, see MacAlister Brown, "The Demise of State Department Public Opinion Polls: A Study in Legislative

Oversight," *Midwest Journal of Political Science*, No. 1 (February 1961): 1–17. For a more detailed examination of State Department public opinion activities, see William O. Chittick, *State Department, Press and Pressure Groups* (New York: Wiley Inter-Science, 1970).

49. Raymond Bauer et al., *op. cit.*

50. The changes in foreign policy are measured by events-interaction data. See Lincoln E. Moses, Richard A. Brody, Ole R. Holsti, Joseph B. Kadane, and Jeffrey S. Milstein, "Scaling Data on Inter-Nation Action," *Science*, 186 (May 26, 1967): 1056–1059. The correlations in Table 4.8 are averages of the no-lag and six-month-lag correlations presented in Martin Abravanel and Barry Hughes, "Public Opinion and Foreign Policy Behavior: A Cross-National Study of Linkages," in Patrick McGowan, ed., *Yearbook of Foreign Policy Studies* (Beverly Hills, CA: Sage, 1974).

51. Gabriel Almond and Sidney Verba, *The Civil Culture* (Boston: Little, Brown, 1965).

52. A somewhat similar study was done by Sophia Peterson for the United States and its relations with the Soviet Union. Although she found no correlation between conflictual foreign policy and attitudes, her data were too difficult to be comparable to those presented here. See Sophia Peterson, "International Events, Foreign Policy Making Elite Attitudes and Mass Opinion: A Correlational Analysis," a paper delivered at the 12th Annual Convention of the International Studies Association, San Juan, Puerto Rico, March 1971. See also a study of domestic opinion and the 1937 proposal to enlarge the Supreme Court, Frank V. Cantwell, "Public Opinion and the Legislative Process," in Bernard Berelson and Morris Janowitz, eds., *Reader in Public Opinion and Communication* (New York: Free Press, 1963), pp. 121–131. Also see Wilder Crane, Jr., "Do Representatives Represent?" *Journal of Politics*, 22 (1960): 295–299.

53. William Gamson and Andre Modigliani, "Knowledge and Foreign Policy Opinions: Some Models for Consideration," *Public Opinion Quarterly*, 30 (Summer 1966): 187–189.

54. It could be argued that this reflects a greater belligerence on the part of the educated, rather than a supportive reaction. A strong counterargument, however, lies in the greater desire of the educated to withdraw from Vietnam in 1970, even if the South Vietnamese government should collapse. See *Harris Survey Yearbook of Public Opinion, 1970* (New York: Louis Harris and Associates, 1971), p. 111.

55. Gamson and Modigliani, *op. cit.*

56. In a similar graphical comparison of policy and attitudes, primarily for domestic policy, Donald J. Devine also found "some relationship." See *The Attentive Public: Polygraphical Democracy* (Chicago: Rand McNally, 1970), Chap. 5.

57. V. O. Key has shown that policy-oriented swing voters outnumber considerably the generally apathetic and uninformed "independents"—see *The Responsible Electorate.*

58. Benjamin Page and Richard Brody, "Policy Voting and the Electoral Process: The Vietnam War Issue," *American Political Science Review,* 76, No. 3 (September 1972): 979–995.

5

The Parties and Foreign Policy

Up to this point, we have been talking about the general public and foreign policy. The last chapters suggest strongly that the public as a whole controls foreign policy only in the broadest outlines and on the most salient issues. It is time to narrow the focus. Some individuals within the public, particularly those who really understand foreign policy issues and who find those issues more than occasionally salient, can exercise more control over foreign policy. Electoral coercion is one of their tools. In the last chapter, we defined the portion of the public potentially able to exercise such control. Ongoing groups, which can wield power between as well as during elections, constitute another tool of such individuals. This chapter begins a look at these groups with an examination of political parties and foreign policy. The next chapter turns to interest groups.

In the study of political parties, as in the previous analysis of foreign policy decision makers, there exist two kinds of data we can examine: attitudinal and behavioral. Attitudinal data provide the best information about the type of and scope of party differences on foreign policy issues in the general public. Scholars have analyzed party differences within the public in behavioral terms as well, focusing on differences in voting patterns. Behavioral analysis could be especially valuable if the attitudinal studies showed significant differences between Democrats and Republicans in the public because we would then want to know the relative salience or importance to the voters of foreign policy and domestic policy issues. That is, given a conflict within a voter because he or she supports the foreign policy of one candidate and the domestic positions of another, which candidate draws his or her vote? We have seen (and will have additional evidence in this chapter) that the attitudinal studies show no significant differences in foreign policy positions of Democrats and Republicans in the public, and it should be no surprise that voters cast their ballots very largely from domestic concerns.

Attitudinal data to examine party differences on foreign policy among policy makers in Congress or the executive also exists, and previous chapters mentioned several studies, especially that of Barton. Yet surveys are infrequent, irregular, and generally not comparable. Thus we must turn primarily to behavioral data. Specifically, in this chapter we will look at congressional voting data since World War II for information about the impact of party membership on the behavior of policy makers.

Parties in the Public

Table 3.7 already introduced some data on the differences in foreign policy attitudes of Republicans and Democrats. The discussion of that table noted that the general public membership of the two party groups differed little in foreign policy attitudes—in contrast to the differences between the convention delegates of the two parties.[1] More recent data can update and supplement those 1956 data. Table 5.1 shows the differences in 1968 and 1972 between Democrats and Republicans on three issues: foreign aid, trading with communists, and the Vietnam War.

The data in Table 5.1 show few party differences on foreign policy. This may surprise some, since Democratic presidents such as Wilson, Roosevelt, and Truman have taken particularly strong

TABLE 5.1

FOREIGN POLICY ATTITUDES BY PARTY IDENTIFICATION OF GENERAL
MEMBERSHIP IN 1968 AND 1972

	PARTY IDENTIFICATION			
	1968		1972	
	Democrat	Republican	Democrat	Republican
Foreign Aid	(N = 835)	(N = 464)	(N = 1379)	(N = 903)
Support	42%	44%	43%	42%
It depends	18	25	6	7
Oppose	40	31	51	51
Trading with communists	(N = 613)	(N = 384)	(N = 460)	(N = 316)
Support	46%	40%	64%	65%
It depends	4	6	3	3
Oppose	50	54	33	32
What to do in Vietnam?	(N = 679)	(N = 458)	(N = 632)	(N = 405)
Get out	26%	20%	53%	30%
It depends	34	40	23	29
Stay	40	40	24	41

Source: Computed from 1968 and 1972 Survey Research Center National Election
Studies, data from which was obtained on tape from the Inter-University Consortium
for Political Research, Ann Arbor, MI.

internationalist positions during the twentieth century, often in the
face of Republican opposition in the Senate. Yet in light of our
earlier demographic analysis it should not be surprising. The
Democratic party includes more of the less educated, the poor,
southerners, and blacks, all of whom were shown to be relatively
isolationist. Of course, the Democratic party also has the majority
of urban dwellers and Jews—groups that are relatively internationalist, at least on nonmilitary issues. The net effect appears to
be little party difference. This finding is consistent as well with
previous studies of party identifiers in 1956, 1960, and 1964.[2]

In both 1968 and 1972, Democrats and Republicans responded
almost identically to questions about foreign aid and trading with
the communists. Similarly, in 1968 they both perceived the Vietnam
War in the same way. The only party differences appear on Vietnam
attitudes in 1972, when the Democrats announced themselves to be
much more eager to leave Vietnam than the Republicans. The reason almost certainly lies in the party leadership of the two parties.
On the issues of foreign aid and trading with the communists, the
two leaderships espouse much the same position. Similarly, in 1968

the two parties differed little on Vietnam. Most voters saw little or no difference in the Vietnam positions of Humphrey and Nixon, the presidential candidates of that year. Yet between 1968 and 1972 the Democratic leadership in the Senate and House moved toward intense opposition to the war. It culminated in the nomination of McGovern, an antiwar candidate, to oppose Nixon in 1972. Apparently, Democrats in the general public followed that lead.

Table 5.2 presents some additional data on party differences in Vietnam War attitudes during the 1965–1971 period. Two things are evident from that table. First, differences are not very large—never do they exceed 14 percent, and most frequently differences are in the 0 to 5 percent range. Second, in the period up to early 1969, Democrats quite consistently reported more support for the war than Republicans. But by late 1969, Republicans began to be

TABLE 5.2
SUPPORT FOR THE VIETNAM WAR BY PARTY

	SUPPORT		OPPOSE	
	Republicans	*Democrats*	*Republicans*	*Democrats*
May 1965	54%	54%	27%	25%
August 1965	57	62	28	22
November 1965	61	65	25	18
March 1966	56	60	27	24
May 1966	47	50	42	32
September 1966	43	49	42	32
November 1966	52	52	34	28
May 1967	45	55	43	31
July 1967	41	55	51	33
October 1967	37	48	54	41
Early February 1968	39	45	53	41
March 1968	39	46	53	43
April 1968	39	43	52	43
August 1968	31	37	58	50
Early October 1968	35	40	57	52
February 1969	36	44	54	47
September 1969	35	31	57	59
January 1970	36	32	53	56
March 1970	38	33	54	58
April 1970	38	33	49	49
January 1971	32	30	61	59
May 1971	31	27	58	64

Note: Samples of varying sizes.

Source: John E. Mueller, *War, Presidents and Public Opinion*, p. 271. Copyright © 1973. Reprinted by permission of John Wiley and Sons.

most supportive. A shift of opinion on the order of 10 percent apparently occurred as a result of the change in party identification of the president. Up to 1969, it was a Democratic president's war; then it became a Republican president's war, especially in view of the intensification of war criticism from Senate Democrats.

Table 5.3 provides further evidence of the importance of the president's party. That table reports on two questions asked about the Cambodian military operation in May 1970. In one question, respondents were merely asked whether "all in all, do you think the Cambodian military operation has been a mistake or not?" Twenty-seven percent of the Democrats said yes, and only 17 percent of the Republicans did the same. The other question was, "Taking everything into consideration, do you think President Nixon was right in ordering the military operation into Cambodia, or do you have serious doubts about his having done so?" The question is basically the same, but it identifies the decision as being Nixon's. In response to this question, 38 percent of Democrats expressed "serious doubts," but only 19 percent of Republicans did so. The gap between Republicans and Democrats increased by 9 percent (from 10 to 19 percent).

One of the conclusions of previous chapters was that Americans in general support their makers of foreign policy and that their attitudes frequently change to reflect government policy. This discussion lets us add a corollary: Many Americans also support their party; apparently they depend on the party (and especially on the leader of that party, if he is president) for cues as to what to believe. This should not be surprising. Nearly everyone who has typed him-

TABLE 5.3

PUBLIC REACTION TO THE CAMBODIAN OPERATIONS BY PARTY (JULY 1970)

	REPUBLICANS			DEMOCRATS		
	Support	Oppose	Not sure	Support	Oppose	Not sure
Question 1	66%	17	17	49%	27	24
Question 2	70%	19	11	45%	38	17

Question 1: "All in all, do you think the Cambodian military operation has been a mistake or not?"

Question 2: "Taking everything into consideration, do you think President Nixon was right in ordering the military operation into Cambodia, or do you have serious doubts about his having done this?"

Source: *Harris Survey Yearbook of Public Opinion, 1970,* (New York: Louis Harris and Associates, 1971, pp. 122–124).

self as liberal, conservative, middle-of-the-roader, or whatever has almost certainly had the experience, on reading or hearing a news event, of wondering what the appropriate position on that issue is.[3] There can be no better referent than the president, if he is of your party. Moreover, not only do the uninformed or politically naive react in that way—we shall see shortly how congressmen and senators also look to the president for cues.

Although evidence points overwhelmingly to insignificant party differences in the general population, there is clearly more to a party than its public adherents. Elected officials, as was shown earlier, do differ by party on major foreign issues. In the early part of the twentieth century, the Republicans were widely known as the party of protection (tariffs) and the Democrats as the party of free trade (although differences between presidents elected by the two parties have all but disappeared). The general images of the parties also differ in other respects. The Democrats have had the unfortunate luck to earn something of a public reputation as the party of war—they have managed to hold the White House during at least the early stages of both world wars, the Korean War, and the Vietnam War. Similarly, of course, the Republicans have been seen as the party of recession and unemployment by many, ever since the Great Depression. This association of the Democrats with war was greatly reduced during the 1964 campaign, in which Goldwater achieved a rather jingoistic reputation, and probably diminished further during Nixon's term of presiding over a deescalated, but continuing war in Indochina. Excerpts from the 1972 election party platforms illustrate both the existence of party differences on military issues and the greater militancy of Republicans in that year (see Table 5.4).

TABLE 5.4

CONTRASTED EXCERPTS ON VIETNAM AND DEFENSE, FROM THE PARTY PLATFORMS IN 1972

	Democratic platform	*Republican platform*
Vietnam	"We pledge, as the first order of business, an immediate and complete withdrawal of all U.S. forces in Indochina."	"We [support] the president ... in his refusal to accept terms which would dishonor this country."
Defense	"The military budget can be reduced substantially with no weakening of national security."	"We categorically reject this slash-now, beg-later approach to defense policy."

Source: *New York Times*, August 27, 1972.

Clearly, however, images of party leadership differences on foreign policy held by the general public are either not very clear or not very important to the public. If they were both clear and important, we would expect similar differences within the public. Although the public may not see important party differences on specific foreign policy issues, differences do exist, and in Congress they can be important. It is to that body that we now turn.

Parties in Congress

This section examines party voting in Congress over the post-World War II period.[4] Specifically, we will look at congressional voting on four issues: foreign aid, military aid, defense appropriations, and trade policy. The analysis primarily uses votes on amendments to measure attitudes in the issue areas.[5] Periodically it uses a motion to recommit a bill to committee with specific instructions to increase or decrease monies involved.

Underlying the procedure was a desire to select relatively close votes. Doing so focuses our attention on differences of opinion within Congress and allows us to ask whether those differences have a partisan base.[6] On a great many congressional votes, voting is near unanimous, or at least overwhelming. Such votes, however, frequently conceal a considerable amount of disagreement on issues. Much of the bargaining and compromising that is a part of all legislation occurs through amendment consideration and is finished before final votes are taken. Thus a "yes" vote on a measure may reflect some satisfaction with the final product (and recognition that some measure must be passed) but by no means indicates complete agreement with the policy. Similarly, some final votes reflect constituency pressure rather than individual preferences. Moreover, some votes even result from a desire to limit executive influence in an area that is felt to be under congressional prerogative. For instance, periodically a measure will be vetoed by the president, and Congress will pass the measure over the veto by a considerably larger vote than was obtained in first passage.

The graphs that follow separate not only Republicans from Democrats but also northern from southern Democrats. Levels of support (for foreign aid, military aid, defense expenditures, and freer trade) were calculated for each of the three groups. Support was indicated either by votes in favor of raising appropriations or votes against cuts in appropriations. On trade issues, support was indicated by votes to eliminate or reduce tariffs, quotas, or other trade barriers, and by votes against additional trade barriers.

The Senate

Nonmilitary Foreign Aid   Figure 5.1 shows the pattern of support, over time, for increased or maintained foreign aid in the Senate. Examination of the graph suggests several general statements. First, the Democrats have more often supported nonmilitary foreign aid than have the Republicans. During two periods, however, the parties differed little, or Republicans showed greater support. The first of these was between 1954 and 1960, while the second is the period since 1967. These two periods coincide quite well with the two eras of Republican administration since 1945. Thus the second generalization is that the president has a considerable impact on the voting behavior of congressmen in his party. All presidents in the post-World War II period, Democrat and Republican, have supported higher levels of spending for foreign aid than the Senate has been willing to allow. This then may explain the patterns in Figure 5.1. Between 1948 and 1951, during the years of the Truman administration, the northern Democrats consistently supported foreign aid,

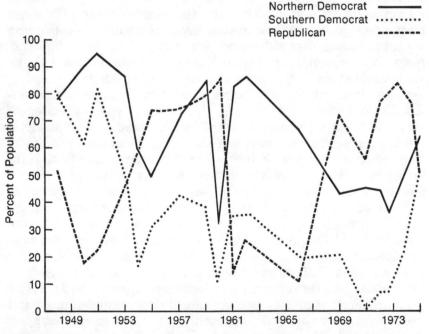

FIGURE **5.1**
SENATE VOTING TO INCREASE OR TO MAINTAIN ECONOMIC FOREIGN AID
EXPENDITURES

while the Republicans almost as consistently opposed increases or favored decreases. By 1954, however, a rather remarkable change occurred, and between then and 1961 Republicans markedly increased their support, while support among Democrats fell off. The first eight years of the 1960s, with Democratic administrations once again, saw a return to the pattern of the Truman years. In 1969, a Republican administration once again markedly changed the pattern. In short, there is a strong "presidential pull" factor working throughout the post-World War II period.

If we look at average support for foreign aid among northern Democrats and Republicans in Democratic and Republican administrations, we find that on the average 83 percent of northern Democrats supported foreign aid increases or opposed decreases in Democratic administrations, as opposed to 54 percent of northern Democrats under Republican administrations—an average pull factor of 29 percent. The Republicans appear even more responsive to the administration. They show only an average of 23 percent support for foreign aid under Democratic presidents, as opposed to 69 percent under Republicans—a switch of vote by 46 percent of Republicans on the average. Some other factors may explain part of this switching. For instance, it might be argued that there have been a few Democratic senators who did not support increases in foreign aid spending proposed by the Republicans because they were not as large as desired. There is no evidence for such an argument, however, and it would be illogical behavior in the context of most amendments examined here. Most of the votes forming the basis for Figure 5.1 were votes on amendments to reduce spending. Under Democratic presidents, the Republicans (and, to a lesser extent, southern Democrats) introduced these and pushed them. Under Republican presidents, the Democratic senators have been largely responsible for such amendments.

Up until this point there has been little mention of southern Democrats. They do appear, from the graph, to be a party unto themselves. Unlike the northern Democrats and the Republicans, their behavior does not appear to be cyclical and dependent on the party affiliation of the president.[7] Instead, there was a general trend throughout the post-World War II period for southern Democrats to increasingly oppose foreign aid, culminating in 1971 when all fifteen southern Democratic senators voted against an amendment by Senator Packwood (R-Oregon) to increase the economic and humanitarian aid authorization by $125 million for population control programs.[8] Whether the 1975 vote is an anomaly or a policy shift remains to be seen.

It might be expected that some of these same patterns would carry over to foreign policy voting on other issues. To a limited extent, they do. The interesting finding, however, is how different voting patterns have been for the different issues. We turn now to military aid.

Military Aid   Figure 5.2 presents the pattern of support for increased or maintained military aid among senators over time. There are similarities with Figure 5.1, but there are also substantial differences. It is impossible to say whether Republicans or northern Democrats have more often supported military aid. In the Truman years, the Democrats clearly did. In recent years, the Republicans clearly do. For a substantial interim period, however, the two parties and the southern democrats were quite similar.

Once again there appears to be a presidential pull factor, although it is not quite as strong as with nonmilitary foreign aid. In

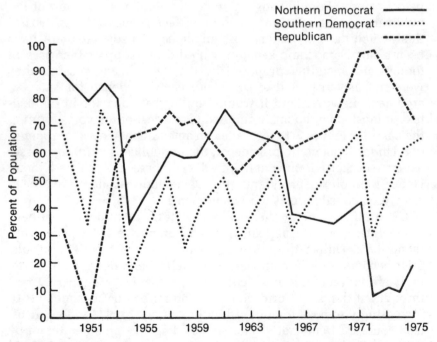

FIGURE 5.2
SENATE VOTING TO INCREASE OR TO MAINTAIN MILITARY FOREIGN AID
EXPENDITURES

Democratic administrations, 72 percent of northern Democratic senators voted in support of military aid, on the average, as opposed to 39 percent under Republican administrations—a difference of 33 percent. For Republicans, the difference is about the same. Under Republican administrations, 77 percent of Republican senators, on the average, supported increased or maintained military aid, compared to 43 percent in Democratic administrations—a difference of 34 percent.

Once again, southern Democrats appear relatively unaffected by the party affiliation of the president. In fact, they were more supportive of military aid under the Ford administration than they were in the Kennedy-Johnson period. It appears very likely that the southern Democrats have been affected more by wars than other factors. In 1954, their support for military aid dropped dramatically. This roughly coincides with both a change of administration and an end to the Korean War. In the late 1960s, however, their support for military aid climbed fairly substantially. The most obvious explanation for this lies in *relatively* greater southern Democratic support of the Vietnam War.

In fact, the war has had a major impact on the voting patterns of all three groups. The Republicans appeared quite supportive of military aid in 1965 and 1966, in spite of the Democratic administration. On the other hand, support among Democratic senators for military aid dropped in 1966, well before the election of Nixon. In this same period, of course, southern Democratic support increased. In general, the attitudes of senators toward the war apparently began to reduce and eventually eliminate the presidential pull. Although the Democrats have often been characterized as the "party of war," because of their uncanny ability to hold the presidency during the outbreak of war, Figure 5.2 might suggest somewhat greater militancy among Republicans and southern Democrats.

Turning briefly back to Figure 5.1, it appears possible that the war issue also affected voting on nonmilitary foreign aid in the late 1960s. Note that in 1967, prior to the election of Nixon, the Republicans increased their relative support for foreign aid and the Democrats decreased theirs. This probably reflected the general disaffection among many liberal northern Democrats with the policies of Johnson and with an active internationalist posture. The evidence is far too scanty in Figure 5.1 to dwell for long on such possibilities. The discussion of votes on defense spending and trade policy will again raise the same issue (of Vietnam War impact).

Defense Spending   Figure 5.3 shows support among senators for increased or maintained defense spending over time. Figure 5.3 is very different from the previous two.

For the bulk of the post-World War II period Democratic senators (northern and southern) were more likely to support defense spending than were Republican senators. By 1966 this had changed, and in recent years Republicans have been considerably more supportive. The most interesting aspect of party positions in Figure 5.3 is the dramatic reversal of Democratic and Republican positions.

Presidential pull is again a factor in Figure 5.3, at least in the period of the Truman and Eisenhower administrations. The graphic impact of the factor is, however, somewhat different in the case of defense spending from the case of foreign economic or military aid. While Eisenhower generally supported economic and military aid expenditures, as had his Democratic predecessor, he did not support attempts to increase the defense budget; in fact, he decreased it. The impact of this can be seen clearly for the years 1953 to 1956. In each of those years, a Democratic-sponsored amendment to increase defense appropriations met with presidential opposition. The results were overwhelming Republican votes against the increases and equally great Democratic votes in favor of the amendments. One could almost talk of a "presidential push" factor for the Democrats in this period. It would be unwise to attribute too much importance to the relative increase in Democratic support for defense during that period, compared to the Truman years, however, since the Republican administration was clearly introducing smaller defense budgets than Truman had, and some of the Democratic support for amendments to increase the spending must be attributed to that fact rather than to the stated position of a Republican president. The "pull factor" clearly operated on Republicans: They more often supported the defense requests of Truman than they did the Senate Democratic efforts to increase Eisenhower's defense budget.

The year 1957 appears in Figure 5.3 to stand as an exception to the "pull factor" argument. Here, however, is the oft-cited "exception that proves the rule." In 1957, the pattern of Democratic amendments to increase the budget (opposed by Eisenhower) was broken by a Republican amendment (Dvorshak, R-Idaho) to reduce the budget (Eisenhower also opposed). In this case, the Republicans rallied to the defense of their Republican president and voted to support the larger figure. The Democrats, perversely, were less willing to support Eisenhower's budget against a threatened cut in 1957 than they had been to increase it in 1956.

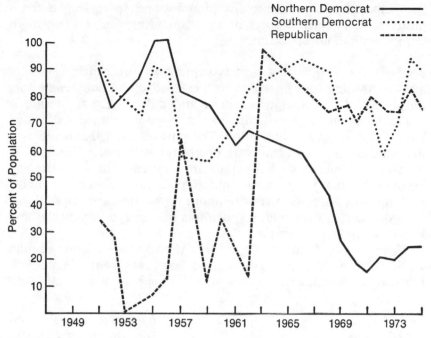

FIGURE 5.3
SENATE VOTING TO INCREASE OR TO MAINTAIN DOMESTIC DEFENSE
EXPENDITURES

Even before the end of Eisenhower's administration, however, other factors became important. One very important factor was the increasing disinclination of the Democrats to support military spending. The downward trend began as early as 1957, and, although arrested briefly in 1963, it has continued steadily since. There can be little doubt that the Vietnam War contributed to the pattern after 1963. The war must also lie behind the dramatic relative increase in Republican support for defense spending between 1963 and 1966. The president's party affiliation and presidential pull cannot explain voting in the 1960s. Although it is possible that voting behavior is cyclical here and that under a peacetime Democratic president voting patterns will again reverse, it may also be that a longer-term realignment of issue positions has occurred. In the framework of a military-industrial complex interpretation of politics, the present pattern has a certain economic logic that was lacking earlier. It makes more sense that the Republican party, tied as it is to business interests, and southern Democrats, representing the home of many defense installations and increasing defense production, should support defense spending and the northern Democrats should oppose it.

Trade Policy   Figure 5.4 reports support among senators for liberalized trading (or opposition to increased protection). Here, too, the nice cycles of foreign economic and military aid are absent.

For many years, the Republican party was defined in foreign policy as the party of protection. The gulf between Democrats and Republicans on this issue was deep and enduring. This gulf is evident in Figure 5.4—but things are changing. In 1965 the gap between northern Democrats and Republicans closed to almost nothing, and the positions of southern Democrats and Republicans reversed. In 1973 the relative positions of northern Democrats and Republicans finally reversed.

Three trends dominate Figure 5.4, with some variation around the trend lines. The most pronounced trends are for the Democrats, northern and southern, to become relatively more protectionist.[9]

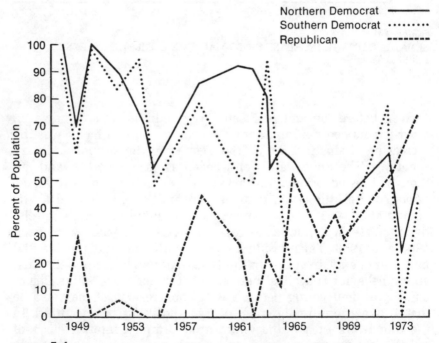

FIGURE 5.4
SENATE VOTING TO SUPPORT FREER TRADE OR TO OPPOSE ADDITIONAL
RESTRICTIONS

For the northern Democrats, this change undoubtedly derives from the increasing fear within the labor movement of free trade, which labor believes is undercutting many American industries and taking Americans' jobs, and from fear of the multinational corporation transfer of capital and technology out of the United States. The movement of southern Democrats toward protection may not result from the position of labor, but rather from the demands for protection by import-threatened southern industries, especially textiles and oil.

Perhaps the most interesting trend in Figure 5.4 is the small relative movement of Republicans toward free trade positions. It might have been expected that the long-continuing and worsening balance of payments problem and the threat posed by imports to such major northern industries as steel and automobiles would have reinforced Republicans in their protectionist sentiments, as well as converting Democrats. Yet Republicans were apparently not so affected. And, of course, big business (as represented by the National Association of Manufacturers and the U.S. Chamber of Commerce) has itself not turned protectionist, in spite of the threat to some in the business community. The important factor almost certainly is the rapid rise, in the post-World War II period, of the multinational corporation and of U.S. investment overseas. As a result, many business interests have become increasingly fearful of U.S. moves toward protection that might result in overseas retaliation. Although these interests do not dominate the Republican party, they are sufficiently important to affect it and to cause the movement of some Republican senators toward freer trade.

The House of Representatives

Rather than paralleling the Senate, party voting patterns in the House differ substantially. One difference, which affects the analysis to follow, is the lesser number of amendments to foreign policy bills in the House. More of the debate takes place in the committees, making it somewhat more difficult to analyze voting in the House.

Foreign Aid While the voting of the northern Democrats and Republicans in the Senate on foreign aid moved in cycles, largely in response to the party affiliation of the president, voting in the House has remained more stable. In particular, northern Democrats consistently supported foreign aid throughout the post-World War

II period, with only a partial exception in 1971. Republican representatives have been almost equally consistent in their opposition, but some "pull factor" is evident. During the period of the Eisenhower administration, characterized by Eisenhower's support for foreign aid, quite a number of Republicans moved into support. Their support of foreign aid ended abruptly in the Kennedy years but began again in 1972. Southern Democrats in the House have behaved very much like their counterparts in the Senate. Their voting has been characterized by a general trend toward opposition to foreign aid. As in the Senate, that trend seems to have been quite dramatically reversed since 1973, although it is too soon to make a judgement or to search for explanation.

The natural question raised by Figure 5.5 is why House members have responded less to presidential pull than have senators. Many reasonable but untested hypotheses can be suggested. One is that the president frequently concentrates his attention on the Senate when the struggle becomes intense and that he finds it easier to sway a few senators than to influence a larger number of represen-

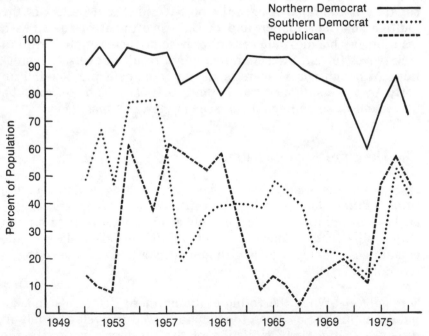

FIGURE 5.5
HOUSE VOTING TO INCREASE OR TO MAINTAIN ECONOMIC FOREIGN AID
EXPENDITURES

tatives. Another is that senators, with more fully developed presidential ambitions, feel more pressure to vote the party position as laid down by the president and leader of the party. Still another possible explanation is that representatives, with a smaller constituency, feel that they have less freedom to maneuver than have senators. The weakness in this last explanation is that this and other studies repeatedly show that foreign affairs lack salience among voters, and few constituents are likely to notice a vote by a representative on foreign aid. In fact, the public is more likely to observe a senator's vote. Other hypotheses might be proposed—and should be. The difference in voting between senators and representatives of the same parties are substantial enough to merit some attention.

Military Aid   The voting of parties in the House on military aid measures is similar to but not identical with that in the Senate. Under Truman, the northern Democrats in the House voted overwhelmingly in favor of military aid, while the Republicans were much less enthusiastic. With the incumbency of Eisenhower and his support for foreign aid (military and nonmilitary), the Republican support for military aid in the House increased markedly. Once again, Democratic representatives reacted in what might be called a "push effect," although their relatively decreased support for military aid more likely reflects the absence of Truman's pull. Southern Democrats, although less supportive in general of military aid than northern Democrats, exhibited voting behavior that basically paralleled that of their northern colleagues.

In the Kennedy regime of the early 1960s, House voting on military aid again changed substantially, with the northern Democrats nearly unanimous in their support for it and the Republicans quite strongly opposed. This, you will remember, also described the Senate, although the reversal from the Eisenhower era was not as marked there. Toward the middle and the end of the 1960s, a difference between House and Senate patterns emerges. In the Senate, Democratic support for military aid began dropping in the early 1960s (after a peak in 1961) and had dropped very noticeably by 1966. Similarly, Republican support in the Senate for military aid fell little with the Kennedy incumbency and began to climb again shortly. By 1965, the Republicans in the Senate were more supportive of military aid than were the Democrats. In the House, such a reversal of support also occurred, but not until 1969. Unfortunately, usable amendments concerning military aid in the House were not as numerous as those in the Senate, making it difficult to be confi-

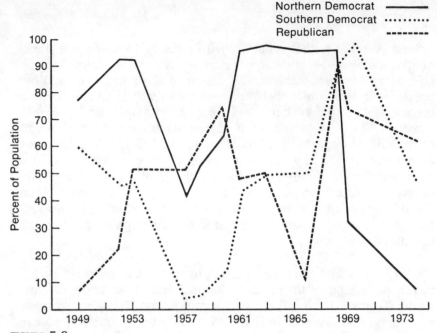

FIGURE 5.6
HOUSE VOTING TO INCREASE OR TO MAINTAIN MILITARY FOREIGN AID
EXPENDITURES

dent that 1969 was the turning point in the House. Nevertheless, it is clear from Figure 5.6 that the northern Democrats in the House were far more supportive of military aid in 1966 than were the Republicans—quite a different situation from the Senate.

Some tentative conclusions can be drawn concerning party voting in the Vietnam War period. In the Senate, opposition to the Vietnam War among Democrats arose early and affected their voting on military aid, defense spending, and possibly even foreign aid. Republicans and southern Democrats became relatively more supportive of military aid and defense spending. In the House, it appears from Figure 5.6, the same pattern may have developed, but did so two to four years later. In some sense, foreign policy voting by party members in the House has lagged behind that of their fellow party members in the Senate. In fact, in the House it is impossible to attribute the change to the war, since it came at the same time as a change in administration. The difference may reflect the lesser concern of the House with foreign policy and the closer ties of representatives to constituencies (which did not become generally antiwar until about 1968).

It is interesting to speculate that what we see in the House/Senate Democratic differences may again represent public official *leading*

of general public attitudes. While the Democratic president remained committed to a Vietnam role throughout the 1960s, Senate
Democratic criticism began by the mid-1960s, almost in parallel
with campus protests. The Fulbright hearings are the prime example. This disenchantment seems to appear in general Senate Democrat attitudes toward military foreign aid in the mid-1960s. The
House Democrats are more closely tied to Democrats (and Republicans) in the public, and their greater opposition to military aid did
not surface until 1969. In that same year, Democrats in the public
moved toward Vietnam War opposition in general and for the first
time became less supportive of the war than were Republicans in
the public (see Table 5.2).

Defense Spending   Figure 5.7 shows the support in the House for
maintained or increased spending on defense. Unfortunately, there
were relatively few amendments to defense measures in the House
as a whole. The pattern shown in Figure 5.7 is therefore not as
clearly developed as in earlier figures.

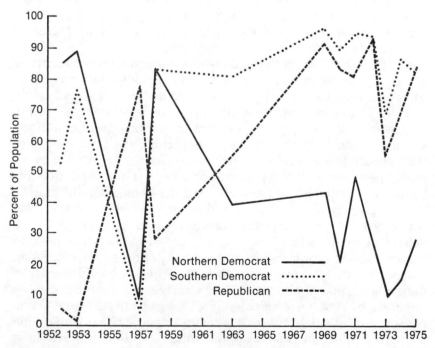

FIGURE 5.7

HOUSE VOTING TO INCREASE OR TO MAINTAIN DOMESTIC DEFENSE
EXPENDITURES

House voting on defense once again illustrates the potency of the president in foreign policy. Consider the two votes in 1957 and 1958. In 1957 Eisenhower supported a motion to recommit the defense appropriations bill with instructions to increase it by $313 million. Republican senators favored the motion by 78 percent, in spite of earlier opposition to defense spending. Northern Democrats provided only 7 percent of their votes toward passage of the motion. The following year, an amendment to provide an additional $99 million for the army was proposed in the House. Eisenhower opposed passage of the amendment. Only 29 percent of Republicans supported the amendment, while 83 percent of northern Democrats supported it. (It should be noted that the motion in 1957 was sponsored by a Republican, while the amendment in 1958 was proposed by a Democrat. This, however, is probably of substantially less importance than the expressed position of the president.)

Southern Democrats voted very much like northern Democrats through 1968. Thereafter, however, they resemble the Republicans more than their northern colleagues. Although the small number of data points makes exact dating of southern Democratic and Republican convergence impossible, it appears to have progressed steadily throughout the 1960s. Again the Vietnam War may have influenced the votes of the southern Democrats, who have most recently been very supportive of military spending.

By 1966 Republicans in the Senate had become more supportive of military spending than Democrats. In the House, this reversal of party positions had occurred by 1963. Although this would imply that the House led the Senate in this issue area, contrary to the discussion concerning party positions on military and nonmilitary aid, the evidence is ambiguous. In particular, the implications of the vote in the House in 1963 are unclear. The issue was an amendment *increasing* the president's request for the Air Force budget. Kennedy *opposed* passage, and the Democrats did provide less support for the amendment than did the Republicans. This contrasts with the vote in the Senate reported in Figure 5.3 (also defense spending). The Senate voted in 1964 on an *amendment to cut* the defense appropriation, and Kennedy *opposed* the cut. Again Democrats provided more support for the president's position than did Republicans. In short, the House and Senate votes on defense spending in 1963 were sufficiently different to thwart direct comparison. Presidential pull may be more important than any notion of party position in explaining the votes. It is thus impossible to state with certainty whether positions on defense spending were reversed in the House first or the Senate first. All that can be said with certainty is that by the late 1960s the parties had reversed their early post-World War II positions, and Republicans and southern Democrats have become the standard-bearers for increased or maintained defense spending.

Trade Policy   Figure 5.8 shows the support in the House for maintained or increased movement toward free trade until the 1970s. Northern Democrats quite consistently supported free trade, and Republicans generally supported protection. Southern Democrats fell somewhere in between, overall, but have exhibited considerable variation. This in general reflects increasingly protectionist stances on imports that threaten industries in the South, like textiles, combined with frequent free trade positions on items that do not threaten southern industry. For instance, southern Democrats strongly opposed in 1965 an increased tax on sugar imports—this shows up in Figure 5.8 for that year as a free trade position. Two years later, in 1967, southern Democrats strongly supported a protectionist measure that would have reassigned the cotton quotas of

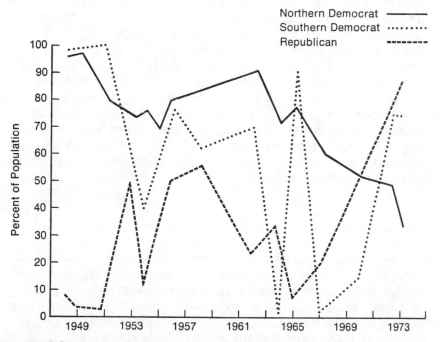

FIGURE 5.8
HOUSE VOTING TO SUPPORT FREER TRADE OR TO OPPOSE ADDITIONAL RESTRICTIONS

Egypt and the Sudan to the United States. Of course, the South has a much larger economic stake in cotton than in sugar, while the North has only sugar (from beets). In sum, while northern Democrats and Republicans voting generally appears to reflect consistent "ideological" positions on trade, the southern Democratic voting record shows an economically pragmatic base for voting.

In the Senate voting on trade (see Figure 5.4), there was a pronounced relative movement over time of northern (and southern) Democrats toward protection. There was a clear, although less major, relative movement of Republicans toward free trade. In House voting, we again see much the same pattern. It is not clear from Figure 5.8 whether there is a trend in the behavior of Republican representatives or if their behavior might once again reflect primarily the importance of presidential pull. In both the Eisenhower years and in the Nixon-Ford period, Republicans showed more support for the free trade positions of their president than they did in Democratic-dominated years.[10]

The best evidence for a basic realignment of party positions on trade policy in the House comes in 1972 and 1973. Earlier it was noted that the economic constituency of the parties can explain the trends in Senate voting. The growing protectionist sentiment in the labor movement is having its impact on traditionally free trade Democrats, just as in the post-World War II era support for freer trade from big business, especially the multinational corporations, is having its impact on Republican senators. It appears that the House has also been affected by those pressures. By the time of the 1970 Trade Act, which established quotas on a number of items, northern Democrats and Republicans in the House had nearly converged in their voting behavior, and by 1973 the Republicans took the lead on freer trade. Again the House seems to have lagged somewhat behind the Senate.

Summary of Congressional Party Analysis

The preceding data and analysis permit a number of general conclusions. First, the congressional parties differ considerably on foreign policy issues. Neither the popular notion of bipartisanship in foreign policy nor the overwhelming votes on many final measures should be allowed to conceal basic party differences.

Second, these party differences have been changing throughout the post-World War II period. It would not, however, be accurate to summarize these changes in terms of new Democratic isolation or an increased Republican internationalism. If one were to examine only the period since the early 1960s, it would appear that Democrats in both the House and Senate had become relatively less supportive than the Republicans of most internationalist policies. However, the longer period that we have looked at makes clear the considerable impact of short-term factors and makes us reluctant to conclude that there has been a long-term realignment.

This brings us to the third conclusion: Many of the changes in Republican and Democratic voting can be explained by the party affiliation of the president and the president's position on foreign policy. There is clearly a strong presidential pull on his own party and perhaps even a presidential push on the opposing party. These are the strongest of the short-run factors.

Fourth, the Vietnam War was another short-term factor that had substantial impact on congressional voting. The opposition to the war among northern Democrats drove the northern and southern Democrats apart and led the northern Democrats, especially in the Senate, to oppose much spending related to foreign policy. This began to be clear in the late years of the Johnson administration. The graphs presented, however, suggest that the relative support for foreign aid by Democrats and Republicans in the Nixon-Ford period was not all that different from their *relative* support under the Eisenhower administration (see Figure 5.1 especially). In other words, there is some reason to believe that the greater internationalism of Republicans in the early 1970s combines two short-term effects—presidential pull and the reaction of Democrats to the Vietnam War.

We saw in Chapters 2 and 3 that there has also been a recent restructuring among the more educated and some others near the center of society, in which support for military internationalism has waned. The two phenomena may be related and result from the same short-term factors. If so, we would expect that, under a new Democratic administration and with the passage of time since Vietnam, congressional voting patterns would shift again toward greater Democratic internationalism, and the educated would again begin to support a broad range of internationalist measures.

The fifth conclusion we can draw is that there most likely is.one long-term trend, that in trade policy. Here the realignment of Republicans and northern Democrats probably does result from more than the short-run impact of the president's partisan affiliation or of the Vietnam War. Potentially, there could be a short-term factor at work here—namely, the continuing negative balance of payments situation of the United States and the shift in the 1970s to a negative balance of trade. This has certainly had an impact on American labor and industries, which have felt threatened. Yet there is at least one factor in the international economic situation that will not change, even with an improved U.S. balance of payments. The post-World War II period has been marked by a dramatic growth of the multinational corporation and its investment overseas. An increasingly large segment of the business community sees this as a boon that it might lose if international trade barriers arose again. Labor sees it as a threat that might become less salient but that will hardly disappear as the balance of trade improves. Given the considerable strength of these two economic sectors in the Republican and Democratic parties, respectively, the trends may well not be reversed.

A clarifying point should be made. Other long-term trends exist and are changing the voting patterns of *both* Democrats and Republicans. For instance, the level of support for foreign aid on Capitol Hill, as around the nation, has declined throughout the last two decades. Similarly, the Vietnam War has led to an intensification of desires to scale down the worldwide U.S. military presence. These long-term trends, affecting both Democrats and Republicans, were traced in Chapter 4. This discussion has looked only at the patterns of *relative* support and opposition for various foreign policy issues by Democrats and Republicans and at the changes in that relative support. It is in that context that we can conclude that long-term trends (in relative support) clearly exist only on trade policy issues.

Demographic Factors Affecting Congressional Voting

In view of our earlier discussion of the relationship between sociological characteristics and attitudes in the public, it is an interesting digression to ask whether similar relationships hold within Congress. Apparently they do, but prove much weaker there than within the general public. Leroy Rieselbach looked in depth at congressional foreign policy voting in the post-World War II period. He found that "on foreign aid, but not foreign trade matters, Catholic congressmen are more internationalist and less isolationist than Protestant representatives."[11] The relationship, however, was not strong. He found that older congressmen with more seniority do not differ significantly from younger ones. Most surprisingly, Rieselbach uncovered no relationship between education and internationalism. Perhaps this is because the overall education level of congressmen is so high.

More recently there has been some evidence of generational differences in Senate voting on U.S. troops overseas. The youngest members of the Senate most strongly supported the Mansfield Amendment to various foreign policy bills, calling for a 40 percent reduction in the U.S. troop level in Europe. The oldest members of the Senate, those who built the containment policy, most frequently opposed the amendment.[12] Recent studies of the House have also found that younger congressmen, those born after 1920 or elected after the McCarthy era, are clearly more dovish than their older colleagues.[13]

George Grassmuck examined regional voting differences over time.[14] His general conclusion was that party differences were more important than sectional ones. He did find, however, some regional voting patterns. For instance, congressmen on both coasts have (not at all surprisingly) been more supportive of navy legislation than have congressmen in the Great Plains states. In an analysis of support for foreign fiscal programs, Grassmuck found that southern voting (prior to World War II) was markedly affected by the party affiliation of the president. But he found that voting in the Great Plains area and the New England and North Atlantic area was quite consistent, with congressmen from the latter area showing considerably more support for the measures.

Grassmuck also suggests the importance on some issues of the urban-rural distinction. He found congressmen from urban areas to be most supportive of foreign fiscal measures. And in a struggle over immigration during the 1930s, he reports that the northern Democrats representing urban areas found themselves almost alone in opposing immigration restriction.

Thus demographic characteristics of senators and representatives may have some importance in shaping their voting. On the whole, however, analyses have not shown the importance of *congressmen* characteristics such as age, religion, education, or occupational background. In large part this results from the relative sociological homogeneity of congressmen. Instead, they more often show, as did the Grassmuck study, the importance of *constituency* characteristics such as region of the country and urban-rural location. Rieselbach found that other demographic characteristics of the congressional district are also important. He reported that[15]

> The representative of eastern, urban, high ethnic, high socio-economic status districts who had emerged during the Eisenhower era as the leading proponents of foreign aid continued (during the Kennedy administration) as the major backers of the program.

The importance of demographic factors, either those of the congressmen or his constituency, should not be overestimated. Party identification is a much better predictor of vote.

Party and the President

After the discussion of this chapter, it is hardly necessary to comment at length on the president. Throughout the post-World War II period, no matter who has been president, internationalist policies have characterized the White House. It seems that the U.S. governmental structure, giving primary responsibility for foreign affairs to the executive, places considerable pressure on a man, whatever his party affiliation, to pursue an active policy.[16] This is especially true during a generally internationalist period like the postwar era. The president, no matter what his party or personal beliefs, is greatly constrained by obligations and promises of previous administrations.

All the presidents of the last forty years have supported the Reciprocal Trade Agreements Act and its use to create freer international trade. Nixon and Ford were perhaps less active advocates of free trade than earlier presidents, but this may be primarily a result of their having obtained the presidency during a period in which the U.S. trade balance became negative. They thus felt it necessary to use the U.S. trade power as a weapon to obtain some concessions from major trading partners, especially Japan. They were also exposed to very intense pressure for protective quotas from some quite severely trade-threatened industries.

All of the post-World War II presidents have supported foreign aid. Congress has so repeatedly cut their requests that it has become something of a ritual. During the 1960s and early 1970s, disillusionment with aid led to somewhat decreasing support by the presidents for the program, but again this is not peculiar to presidents of either party.

Presidents of neither party have been adverse to using military forces abroad. Although Eisenhower worked to end the Korean conflict, he used troops to further U.S. interests in Lebanon in 1958. It was in his administration that the CIA supported a small invasion of Guatemala and planned support for one of Cuba. Kennedy used military force or displays thereof in Berlin and Cuba and placed military "advisors" in Indochina. Johnson will always have the Vietnam War as well as the Dominican invasion, associated with his presidency. Nixon maintained forces in Indochina for four years in spite of considerable congressional opposition. Ford has been accused of using unnecessary force in the Mayaguez incident, and he pushed for a more active role in Angola than the Senate was willing to support.

The possibility of detente with the communists has been explored and apparently actively desired by all postwar presidents. Eisenhower's administration made many efforts to improve relations, especially in the summit periods of 1956 and 1960, and in spite of the hard-line positions and rhetoric of his strong secretary of state, John Foster Dulles. Kennedy and Johnson similarly pursued agreement on various issues, ranging from a hot line and test ban to some arms limitations, even throughout the Vietnam War. Nixon, the man with the anticommunist reputation from the McCarthy era, had more meetings with communist leaders and signed more far-reaching agreements than any other postwar president. Ford backed continued detente policy so strongly that it nearly cost him the 1976 presidential nomination.

Conclusions

The impact of parties on the foreign policy process is clearly mixed. There are rather insignificant foreign policy attitude differences between party members in the general public. And although presidents of different parties may hold different attitudes about international relations, their behavior has not been strongly tied to party affiliation. Congressmen and the more educated within the general public do, however, differ by party. This has important implications in congressional voting. Bipartisanship in foreign policy is accurate in broad outlines: Members of both parties have cooperated in the general maintenance of an active international position. Yet the veneer of bipartisanship that we have seen on many major postwar votes (the Marshall Plan, NATO, etc.) covers a broader voting pattern with significant party differences. These differences show up most clearly when amendments such as those we have examined in this chapter come to a vote. On three of the four issues we examined—economic foreign aid, military foreign aid, and trade policy—differences between parties have also shown up most clearly when Democrats controlled the White House, leaving Republican congressmen free to vote the somewhat more isolationist positions that have been deemphasized under internationalist Republican presidents.

Parties, of course, are not the only type of group with political influence. Interest groups, although they often have additional reasons for being, also seek to shape policy. We turn now to a discussion of interest groups and foreign policy.

Notes

1. The more educated in the general public also exhibit partisan differences. See George Belknap and Angus Campbell, "Political Party Identification and Attitudes Toward Foreign Policy," *Public Opinion Quarterly*, 15 (Winter, 1951–1952): 601–623.

2. J. S. Robinson et al., *Measures of Political Attitudes* (Ann Arbor, MI: Survey Research Center, Institute for Social Research, University of Michigan, 1969), p. 561.

3. My wife has labeled this the Whippoorwillian effect.

4. A considerable number of other studies have done this for earlier time periods, or for fewer issues. See Robert A. Dahl, *Congress and Foreign Policy* (New York: Harcourt Brace Jovanovich, 1950); David Truman, *The Congressional Party* (New York: John Wiley, 1959); Bradford H. Westerfield, *Foreign Policy and Party Politics: Pearl Harbor to Korea* (New Haven, CT: Yale University Press, 1955); Kenneth Waltz, *Foreign Policy and Democratic Politics* (Boston: Little, Brown, 1967); Julius Turner, *Party and Constituency: Pressures on Congress*, revised edition, Edward Schneier, Jr., ed. (Baltimore: Johns Hopkins University Press, 1970); Malcolm E. Jewell, *Senatorial Politics and Foreign Policy* (Lexington: University of Kentucky Press, 1962); George Grassmuck, *Sectional Biases in Congress on Foreign Policy* (Baltimore: Johns Hopkins University Press, 1954); Leroy N. Rieselbach, *Roots of Isolationism: Congressional Voting and Presidential Leadership in Foreign Policy* (Indianapolis: Bobbs Merrill, 1966); Mark Kesselman, "Presidential Leadership in Congress on Foreign Policy," in Leroy N. Rieselbach, ed., *The Congressional System* (Belmont, CA: Wadsworth, 1970), pp. 280–285; William Keefe and Morris Ogul, *The American Legislative Process* (Englewood Cliffs, NJ: Prentice-Hall, 1964), pp. 270–275.

5. Malcolm Jewell, *op. cit.*, has said, "At times, particularly after a foreign aid program has been generally accepted, a key vote on an amendment cutting the aid funds has given a clearer picture of foreign aid sentiment than has the final vote on passage of the bill" (p. 12).

6. Turner and Schneier, *op. cit.*, followed a similar procedure. They excluded votes where 90 percent of both parties were on the same side of the issue. Criteria here have been less formal—the closest votes were sought. Samuel Huntington found that these were most likely to occur on amendments: *The Common Defense* (New York: Columbia Univer-

sity, 1961), pp. 180–181. Craig Liske notes that, regardless of substantive issue, votes on amendments tend to be more partisan than votes on final passage—"Changing Patterns of Partisanship in Senate Voting on Defense and Foreign Policy, 1946–1969," in Patrick J. McGowan, ed., *Sage International Yearbook of Foreign Policy Studies*, Vol. 3 (Beverly Hills, CA: Sage, 1975), p. 140.

7. This behavior of southern Democrats is quite different than that reported by Grassmuck, *op. cit.*, p. 99. He found that the southern Democrats were particularly responsive to the president, voting against Republican-sponsored measures in the 1920s with near unanimity and voting for similar measures with equal cohesion under Roosevelt in the 1930s.

8. Malcolm Jewell has discussed the decline of southern internationalism, at least for the 1950s period. He suggests a number of reasons, including (1) a fear that international economic policies were negatively affecting the southern economy and (2) opposition to discretionary powers of the president. See Malcolm Jewell, "Evaluating the Decline of Southern Internationalism Through Senatorial Roll Call Votes," *Journal of Politics*, 21 (November 1959): 624–646.

9. For a discussion of this in the early postwar period, see Holbert Carroll, *The House of Representatives and Foreign Affairs* (Pittsburgh: University of Pittsburgh Press, 1958), p. 51.

10. Lewis Anthony Dexter discusses the importance of Eisenhower to Republican congressmen on trade. He quotes opposition to free trade as saying about two Republican leaders (Joseph Martin and Charles Halleck): "Joe and Charlie are worth at least twenty-five votes to reciprocal trade, but in their hearts they know it's wrong. They're just doing it for the White House." See Lewis Anthony Dexter, *The Sociology and Politics of Congress* (Chicago: Rand McNally, 1969), pp. 43–44.

11. Reiselbach, *op. cit.*, p. 66.

12. "Troop Cuts: The Senate Guard is Changing," *The New York Times*, September 29, 1973.

13. Wayne Moyer, "House Voting on Defense: An Ideological Explanation," in Bruce Russett and Alfred Stepan, *Military Force and American Society* (New York: Harper & Row, 1973), pp. 106–142.

14. Grassmuck, *op. cit.*, p. 15.

15. Rieselbach, *op. cit.*, p. 196. This study is also reported in Leroy N. Rieselbach, "The Demography of the Congressional Vote on Foreign Aid, 1939–1958," *American Political Science Review*, 58, No. 3 (September 1964): 577–588.

16. Grassmuck, *op. cit.*, p. 92, has said "Indeed it may be said that, by its assignment of duties and powers, our Constitution, as drafted in 1787, makes the executive relatively internationalist and the legislature nationalist."

6

Interest Groups

Political interest groups are identifiable segments of the general population *who share some common attitudes and orientation toward the political process*, generally because some aspect of that process affects the members in similar fashion. For example, businessmen, laborers, the military, consumers, farmers, people against abortion, and thousands of other segments of the population can be labeled *interest groups*. Interest groups may be unorganized and generally latent or potential elements in the foreign policy process, or they may have an organizational structure and be active current participants. For instance, businessmen as a whole constitute a relatively identifiable latent or potential grouping, and a number of formal organizations represent large segments of the business community. Consumers make up another potential group, and in the last few years some consumer organization has appeared, although without the staff or budgets of business groups.

Some political scientists argue that all of politics can and *should* be explained as the interaction of groups.[1] They argue that even the unorganized groups are important, because either decision makers recognize their existence and act to avoid their displeasure, or the groups will in fact organize when their interests are threatened.[2] This chapter will focus overwhelmingly on the formal organizations that have represented various groups in the post-World War II period, because it generally requires a structure and budget to have influence in the policy process. The major exception will be a discussion of the military-industrial complex and the press—neither has a formal headquarters or membership list, and the extent of influence on policy of both is hotly debated.

As in past chapters, both attitudinal and behavioral evidence can contribute to greater understanding of foreign policy positions taken by interest groups. The bulk of group behavior lies in providing information to the public and decision makers, thus attempting to sway the policy process. Often the information is a simple statement of policy preference and the importance of the policy to the group. Thus a direct procedure for discovering a great deal about both group behavior and attitudes is to examine the content of group publications. Such informal content analysis will constitute the major approach of the chapter.

Attitudinal Surveys of Groups

There have been, however, some direct studies of group attitudes, using questionnaires and surveys, and these merit our attention. Two of the most informative were carried out in 1971–1972 by Allen Barton of Columbia and his colleagues and a year and a half later by Bruce Russett of Yale.[3] Chapter 3 noted these studies, and Table 3.8 reported responses to the foreign policy questions asked military, political, business, mass media, and civil servant elites. If you look back at that table it should become obvious why it is important to study interest groups. There exist some very considerable differences of opinion between the groups on several issues. The primary example is the issue of reducing defense spending— only 12 percent of military men wished to do so, in contrast with 79 percent of the representatives from various media. A similar split appeared on another issue affecting the military men directly, namely whether or not to dismantle our alliance system. Sixty-two percent of media officials said yes; only 22 percent of military leaders did. On other issues, however, differences among the groups were much less major. For instance, 84 percent of the military men thought the Third World was nationalistic, and 91 percent of media leaders agreed. In this case, labor leaders contrasted most sharply with the media—only 60 percent felt the Third World was nationalistic.

Aside from simply recording isolated responses to various foreign policy issue questions, however, the studies sought to answer some questions about the overall structure of elite attitudes. For example, is there a "military mind" sufficiently different from the "civilian mind" to threaten civil-military relations? Do business and military men have a common interest in and desire for active and hawkish international policy to open and maintain markets for the businessmen and to "employ" the military? Is there a "media mind," markedly more liberal and dovish than that of other elites?

Interestingly, except for those issues such as defense spending and alliances directly touching the military, Russett found no "military mind." Instead he found that the domestic ideology (conservatism/liberalism) of military men and businessmen more often could "explain" their foreign policy issue positions than could their professions.[4] He did find, however, considerably greater "hawkishness" among the military than among businessmen, surprising no one.

Russett and Hanson found "only weak and rather fragmentary evidence in favor of theories attributing war to economic interests."[5] Businessmen were not found to be as hawkish or aggressive as the military, but were more so than other elites except Republican politicians. Executives from foreign-oriented firms did prove somewhat more hawkish than other businessmen. Interestingly, executives of defense-oriented industries were *not* more hawkish than other executives.

The mass media executives and professionals do exhibit a very noticeably more liberal and dovish set of mind than other group leaders, except perhaps the leadership of voluntary organizations. And there can be little doubt that the foreign policy issue positions taken by the media officials lie much closer to those of Democratic politicians than to those of Republican politicians. The hostility of the Nixon administration to the press appears to have been based on more than personality alone.

Once again, however, formal organizations constitute our primary interest here. Let us turn to an examination of those groups and the positions they take.

Formal Interest Groups

Many thousands of interest groups concern themselves with foreign policy. The State Department once estimated that more than half of the about 6500 national organizations in the United States are interested in foreign policy.[6] Moreover, about 300 operate foreign policy educational and information programs.[7] The rest of this chapter has two aims: to note some major categories of groups and to discuss briefly the most important members of those categories.[8] We shall look first at economic interest groups, since these are generally (and rightfully) credited with being the most influential groups in the making of foreign policy. We will look also at ethnic associations, veterans' groupings, women's organizations, religious interests, and citizens' groups. Finally, we shall touch briefly on the press.

Although both business and labor have economic stakes in foreign policy, the business organizations have historically spent more time and money in attempting to influence governmental decisions. Businesses frequently have immediate and clearly identifiable international interests. Perhaps the offer of a million dollars to the CIA by ITT for some not too clearly specified actions in Chile[9] is an unusually dramatic reminder of the international interests of U.S. business, especially of multinational corporation concerns. Yet the post-World War II period has provided many situations of similar salience to elements of the business community.

At one time, the primary business interest in foreign policy was the protection of the domestic market; desire for foreign markets was largely a secondary concern. Some industries, notably textiles, shoes, and to a lesser extent steel and autos, are still primarily concerned with restricting foreign competition. The pendulum is now swinging in the other direction. The rise of industrial empires and giant multinational corporations in electronics, petroleum, and aerospace has given most of American business an outward-looking orientation. The economic internationalism of these groups now dominates American business lobbying.

American labor also has economic interests in American foreign policy. Yet the government policies most likely to aid or damage those interests, basically jobs and wages, are often difficult to identify. Whereas the corporate interests of Anaconda and Kennecott copper in Chile, the interest of IBM and Ford in Germany, and the interests of Gulf and Exxon in the Mid-East are clear, the impact of those corporate interests on jobs in the United States is less than clear. It is not surprising, then, that business groupings exert relatively greater and more effective influence in foreign affairs than does labor.

Business

When an American president declares that "the business of America is business" and a nominee for secretary of defense states that "what is good for our country is good for General Motors and vice versa,"[10] it becomes obvious that business interests influence American domestic and foreign policy. Some would go much further than "influence," as this statement by A. William Domhoff indicates:[11]

> American foreign policy during the postwar era was initiated, planned and carried out by the richest, most powerful and most international-minded owners and managers of major corporations and financial institutions. None of the factors that are often of importance on domestic issues—Congress, labor, public opinion—had anything but an occasional and minor effect on foreign policy.

Even a more temperate view has to recognize the pervasive impact of business on all aspects of American life and politics. The material benefits of this society derive from corporate institutions, and that fact shapes many basic and untested premises. The expansion of private U.S. investment abroad, from $19 billion in 1950 to $165 billion in 1973, committed U.S. business to an active international role (see Table 6.1). That commitment accounts for much of the internationalism of the societal center groups that Chapter 3 documents. It constitutes the most powerful single argument that the United States will not again become an isolationist nation.

The internationalism of business, although it does much to shape the general American approach to foreign policy and should not be underestimated as a factor in that foreign policy, leaves considerable latitude for specific foreign behavior. Specific corporations, industries, or business as a whole cannot, as Domhoff argues, initiate, plan, and carry out foreign policy. There exists no single and identifiable "business" view on all international issues. On the contrary, business groups are frequently either immobilized by internal divisions or counteracted by other business groups.

Trade and Tariff Issues Lobbying on trade barriers, *the major business interest group concern and activity*, repeatedly and most graphically illustrates the intrabusiness divisions. Prior to the 1934

TABLE 6.1

FOREIGN INVESTMENTS OF AND IN THE UNITED STATES, IN BILLIONS OF DOLLARS

	1950	1955	1960	1965	1970	1973
Total U.S. assets and investments abroad	$54.4	$65.1	$85.6	$120.4	$166.6	$218.5
Private	19.0	29.1	49.3	81.5	119.9	165.3
Government	11.1	13.1	16.9	23.4	32.2	38.8
Monetary	24.3	22.8	19.4	15.5	14.5	14.4
Foreign assets and investments in the United States	17.6	27.8	40.9	58.8	97.5	163.1

Source: Adapted from U.S. Department of Commerce *The Multinational Corporation: Studies on U.S. Foreign Investment*, Vol. 1 (March 1972), p. 11, Table 2; data for 1973 from U.S. Department of Commerce, *Statistical Abstract of the United States, 1975* (Washington, DC: U.S. Government Printing Office, 1976), p. 802.

passage of the Reciprocal Trade Agreements Act, giving trade regulation power to the president, interest groups besieged Congress.[12] In fact, the pressure from all sides of the tariff issue made it increasingly difficult for Congress to deal effectively with trade, and executive action became necessary.

Some corporations and industries consistently favor higher tariffs, import quotas, or other trade barriers to protect them from the competition of foreign firms. Others support fewer restraints on imports, generally in anticipation of reciprocal action in other nations and thus of increased sales in foreign markets. The divisions within the business community over trade barriers have made it nearly impossible for groups representing a wide spectrum of business interests (such as the National Association of Manufacturers or the even broader U.S. Chamber of Commerce) to take a firm position on trade policy. Every year the Chamber of Commerce appoints a body such as the Committee on International Political and Social Problems to formulate international policy for the organization. When the committee develops a policy statement on trade, the statement is sent out to members prior to the annual meeting. The annual meeting accepts or rejects the policy position, and throughout the post-World War II period has consistently supported administration movements toward freer trade. The support has been less than unanimous, however. In 1962 protectionist forces initially defeated the committee statement, and only in a subsequent vote, when protectionists allege that many delegates had left the floor, did the assembly pass the official resolution. Because of a division within the organization, its lobbying efforts on behalf of the official policy have been quite limited. One study reports the statement of a lobbyist that he would never again testify on behalf of the Chamber of Commerce. According to him, all he could do was to state the official resolution. When asked questions, his reply had to be, "The chamber has no position on that."[13]

The problem of mixed interest plagues not only the peak organizations of business, but also many specific industries. For instance, in the wool industry, manufacturers and growers have urged higher tariffs and quota restrictions on wool fabrics; the growers want protection on raw wool, while the fabric and clothing producers do not; wool importers prefer freer trade of raw and finished products. Even within a large diversified corporation, interests differ. A 1954 study found that eight departments of General Electric took protectionist positions while the chairman of the board testified before a House committee in support of freer trade.

Although the mixed interests of businessmen in trade policy often mean that lobbyists cancel each other out, this is not always the case. In some industries, such as maritime shipping and fishing, there exists no organized counterinterest. In these cases, pressure is frequently effective. For instance, U.S. shipping interests have traditionally been strong, because labor and management team up to back regulations such as the one that requires 50 percent of all U.S. foreign aid shipments to be carried in American ships.[14] In 1964 the International Longshoremen's Association refused to load wheat for Russia until the government agreed that one-half of future grain sales would be carried in U.S. ships.[15]

Although in the postwar period there has been general and growing support within the business community for fewer trade restrictions (as expressed in U.S. Chamber of Commerce and National Association of Manufacturers policy positions),[16] considerable business lobbying for protection persists. This occurs because a corporation or industry tends to ask for protection of its products quite fervently, while those who support freer trade have less motivation to push their case. Thus while a poll in 1954 showed that 38 percent of businessmen favored reduction in tariff levels and only 5 percent favored increases, an examination of their letter-writing habits in the 1952–1954 period suggested that from every hundred businessmen in the study, Congress received about twenty-six letters asking for protection and only sixteen from liberal traders.[17]

Not surprisingly, principal business support for protectionism originates in industries that were once strong domestically and internationally and that now face severe competition. Thus in the debate on the 1970 trade bill, protectionist stances were taken by the American Textile Manufacturer's Association, the National Cotton Council, the American Footwear Manufacturer's Association, and the National Machine Tool Builders' Association.[18] Besides textiles and shoes, perhaps the most significant postwar exceptions to business support for free trade are in the energy industries. Domestic oil and coal producers were influential for fourteen years in maintaining an oil import quota system. The American Petroleum Institute had $17 million income in 1971 (although it reported only $38,656 lobbying expense the following year).[19] It spends widely on public campaigns ("oil is the heartbeat of America") and election campaigns. The quotas prevented for years the entry of significant amounts of lower-priced Mideastern oil and cost consumers as much as $5 billion annually.[20]

The prevailing support among businessmen for freer trade is, of course, largely a perception of self-interest and by no means constitutes a policy position that they have always taken or always will hold. It was pressure from business that forced interwar tariffs up and up, culminating in the Hawley-Smoot Tariff of 1930. Chapter 5 documented the fact that the Republican party, which generally represents business interests better than the Democrats, maintained a basically protectionist orientation into the post-World War II period. The present support among businessmen and most Republicans for freer trade and internationalist policies more generally clearly is influenced by the success the United States has had in penetrating the outside world with capital investment and exports. The most active support for free trade comes quite naturally from the growing phenomenon of the multinational corporation.[21] Markedly increased capital investment by Europeans and the Japanese in the United States or further negative shift in the balance of trade could influence business lobbying again.

Trading with the Communists   Another aspect of trade policy, the issue of trading with the communists, has also divided business. Although the overwhelming majority of businessmen quite naturally oppose communism on ideological grounds, many members of the business community have found potential sales to the communists very enticing. In fact, pressure from business interests was a factor in the U.S. recognition of the Soviet Union in 1934, a fact that led Will Rogers to state that we would recognize the devil if we could sell him pitchforks.[22] More recently, the prospect of large purchases of wheat and other Western exports led many businessmen to oppose continuation of the embargo imposed on trade with the communists early in the cold war. The Committee for Economic Development (a group of liberal businessmen) urged the removal of restrictions on all but military items, proposed long-term credits to the communist nations, and suggested a governmental effort to overcome the currency convertibility difficulties that hinder East-West trade.[23] The more conservative National Foreign Trade Council has also said that it "welcomes the continuing efforts of the U.S. Department of Commerce to remove controls on products of nonmilitary character which are readily available to the communist countries of eastern Europe, the Soviet Union, and China."[24] The attraction to American business of imports from the communist countries, especially of natural gas and oil from the Soviet Union, is also a factor in recent business support for expanded East-West trade. And, of course, the ability of the Soviet Union to pay its bills with gold when its exports are inadequate has a certain attraction.

Most recently, some businessmen have acted with amazing speed to formalize relationships with the new government of South Vietnam. The existence of prior investment and the discovery of offshore oil have spurred commercial liaisons well in advance of political ones.[25]

Other Foreign Policy Issues Business groups do, of course, take positions and urge policies on issues other than trade. Many, for instance, have been concerned with foreign aid and have expressed a desire to see greater control over the uses to which aid is put; there has been frequent reference to "giveaways." There has also been some desire to use aid as a stick. For instance, at the inception of the Marshall Plan, the National Association of Manufacturers (NAM) urged that receiving nations be prohibited from any further nationalizations of industry—a requirement that would have contradicted the Marshall Plan policy of nonintervention internally in Europe.[26]

Two business-dominated organizations, the Council on Foreign Relations and the Committee for Economic Development (CED) routinely prepare studies on a variety of foreign policy issues. The Council on Foreign Relations publishes the prestigious journal *Foreign Affairs*. The CED distributes its studies and proposals very widely. Those who have seen American corporations as the dictators of American foreign policy frequently point to the consistent internationalism of those two organizations as evidence. No one can deny that the Korean and Vietnam Wars, as well as the cold war, had roots in such internationalism. Moreover, no one can deny the influential positions that many of the organizational members hold in Washington. One can question whether these facts allow us to attribute sole or even primary responsibility for American foreign policy decisions to American business.

International Political Activity of Business   Many business critics do not attack the general positions and influence of the community but focus instead on the situations in which one corporation or one industry has a clear and strong foreign interest and feels it important to act. There may be no strong group with a counterinterest; there may, in fact, be no national government capable of withstanding the economic power of the corporation. For instance, multinational corporations (MNCs) frequently find themselves threatened by expropriation or less drastic but no more desirable means of control by host countries. It is within the power of some of these corporations to make their own foreign policy in such situations. Chile's economy under Allende was plagued by worldwide seizures of copper shipments and suits against it by the copper companies around the world. The same sort of thing happened to Mexico after it nationalized the oil industry there. Robert Engler described the consequences:[27]

> The nationalized industry in Mexico . . . found itself boycotted by the international companies who were determined to cut off Mexican oil from world markets. . . . . The major tanker fleets avoided her ports, drilling equipment from the United States became difficult to obtain because of the relationship between big oil and the supply companies. At least one oil company used its travel services to discourage tourists from entering "dangerous" Mexico.

The oil companies have more recently tried the same techniques against Libya, but with little success.[28]

There is no question that the MNCs are strong enough to markedly affect economic and political conditions around the world. Their impact in the international monetary crises of 1973 leading to dollar devaluation was substantial. Simply by shifting surplus funds to strong currencies and by leading and lagging (paying bills in strong currencies early and letting bills in weak currencies stand), the MNCs emerged as major "speculators." Their part in toppling the dollar, although protective of their interests rather than malicious, was significant. The power of MNCs is especially great in the underdeveloped world, where they are larger than many governments. A major reason for the formation of the Organization of Petroleum Exporting Countries (OPEC) by Mideastern and North African nations in 1960 was to create a countervailing power against the oil companies. The most dramatic episodes involve direct interference in the politics or administration of foreign countries. Although the CIA did not accept ITT's 1970 offer of money for interference in Chile, the CIA did respond a short time later by suggesting actions that ITT could take to create a deteriorating economic situation so as to undermine then President Allende.[29] The public record does not tell us whether or not such interference occurred. The post-Watergate era has clearly documented, however, quite widespread corporate international bribery. The Securities and Exchange Commission disclosed that the Gulf Oil Corporation alone delivered $4.2 million in bribes to foreign politicians in fifteen countries.[30]

Business Involvement in U.S. Foreign Policy   Most disconcerting, and the constant target of business critics, are covert and frequently illegal efforts to influence U.S. policy. The ITT and CIA actions were almost certainly the exception rather than the rule, but they will provide support for conspiracy theory accusations for years. The same $10.3 million Gulf Oil Corporation fund that provided $4.2 million in foreign bribes underwrote $5.4 million in domestic political "gifts."

The normal interaction of business and government is more public. There have been many cases in which the U.S. government had aided American business. Examples abound in U.S.-Latin American relations, and we need not go back to the days of dollar diplomacy to find them. In early 1962, a Brazilian subsidiary of ITT was expropriated. Senator Bourke Hickenlooper introduced a successful amendment to the 1962 Foreign Assistance Act, requiring the president to suspend all economic aid to any country "that expropriated the property of a U.S. company, repudiated a contract with a U.S. company, or made a U.S. company subject to discriminatory taxation or administration."[31] The Hickenlooper Amendment was an important factor in resolving the ITT case to the satisfaction of the company. It was also applied in 1963 to Peru as a result of a dispute between that government and a subsidiary of Standard Oil of New Jersey. The amendment is still law. Although the Hickenlooper Amendment was resisted initially by Kennedy and although Nixon was reticent to apply it (for instance, in Peru, again), its mere existence and potential for use is a boon to business.

American business has special power in Latin American relations. There has even been a business group called the Council for

Latin America, headed by David Rockefeller and representing 224 corporations. This group has area subcommittees corresponding to the State Department and Agency for International Development (AID) desk organizations, and the subcommittees meet two or three times a year with those government agencies.

The government also aids business through the Export-Import Bank, which provides long-term and fairly low-interest credits (loans) to nations wishing to buy from U.S. companies. A major recent debate has raged over the extent of such credits to communist countries. Another debate has focused on the Overseas Private Investment Corporation (OPIC). This government body offers insurance against expropriation, inconvertibility, and war. The primary original purpose in 1948 was to encourage private investment in less-developed countries—a goal supported by the United States and such countries alike. More recently, MNCs have come under attack in many countries, and the fear has grown in the United States that the existence of such insurance would increase the probability of U.S. intervention on behalf of business. ITT did draw OPIC's potential $339 million liability to the attention of government officials after Allende's expropriations in Chile.[32]

The reader should keep these business-government ties in some international perspective. The Japanese government and, for that matter, many European nations have significantly closer ties to business; American corporations have recently complained about the inroads of the Japanese ("Japan, Incorporated") into the traditionally American territory of South America. And, as East-West trade increases, the government-economic unity of the communist nations may well provide the largest challenge to U.S. multinational corporations.

In summary, the business community as a whole does participate in setting the general internationalist framework within which American foreign policy is made. It has been an especially powerful force underlying U.S. determination to move the world toward lower tariffs and freer trade. Yet neither the general business community nor specific industries can dictate the details of foreign policy, even foreign economic policy on trade and aid. There is insufficient consensus among industries to do so. Some individual corporations or industries do influence U.S. policy toward countries in which they have a major interest and can even be powerful international political actors in their own right. We will return in the next chapter to discussion of the situations in which business influence is particularly strong.

Labor

Labor leadership has traditionally been internationalist. Although U.S. unions have never adopted the international labor solidarity theme of European socialist labor, they have tried to maintain international contracts. The American Federation of Labor (AFL) helped in the formation of the Pan-American Federation of Labor in 1916, and, working with the Congress of Industrial Organizations (CIO) in 1960, it created the American Institute for Free Labor Development (AIFLD) in Latin America.[33] Naturally, labor very frequently benefits from the same international policies, especially those establishing foreign markets, that serve the interests of management. As we shall see later, American agriculture similarly profits from foreign markets. This post-World War II consensus of American economic interests on the benefits of internationalism makes questionable the argument that business alone shapes policy.

Labor, like business, is far from unified on foreign policy issues. In the early post-World War II period, before the AFL and the CIO merged in 1955, they supported fairly different foreign policies. The CIO had a relatively powerful communist faction until 1948 and did not accept the growing national perception of a communist threat as early as did the AFL.[34]

Labor and Jobs   Not surprisingly, many labor positions on foreign policy issues flow from a desire to protect the jobs of the American working force. In fact, American labor's activity in the free trade union movement abroad is in part tied to fears of "cheap" labor abroad.[35] Fear of competition for scarce jobs has also periodically caused some antiimmigration sentiment to rise. Prior to World War II, labor was influential in the maintenance of the Chinese Exclusion Law.[36] The Democratic Party, with which labor has been associated fairly closely since the Depression, has also been the party of the immigrants, and has generally supported liberalized trade and immigration policies. Thus there has existed a potential conflict between the policies of the Democratic party and the labor unions. In the post-World War II period, union leadership (particularly in the CIO) has often taken positions on immigration, trade, and race relation issues consistent with party leaders, even when such positions have been contrary to the feelings of most in the rank and file. Of course, legal immigration is now relatively limited, and the issue arises infrequently. The more important issue now is illegal immigration, especially from Mexico and other Latin American nations. The AFL-CIO has strongly supported legislation and executive action to halt "the employment of illegal aliens and bring under control the existing widespread use of Mexican commuters."[37]

In the post-World War II period, the AFL-CIO accepted the movement toward freer trade and supported the reciprocal trade legislation authorizing the president to negotiate tariff reductions. This support was often with some reservations, however. By 1970 the AFL-CIO had shifted away from its earlier, generally free trade stance toward favoring restrictions on imports that were shown to damage U.S. industries. The *AFL-CIO American Federationist* argued in 1971 that[38]

> We can no longer afford unregulated international trade any more than we can afford unregulated security markets or drug manufacturing or food packaging. Regulation of trade, designed to soften the impact of concentrated imports from other nations with lower wage standards, has become an absolute necessity if we are to avoid growing disruption, loss of job opportunities, and sharp rises in our costs of job training and public assistance.

The late 1960s and early 1970s brought labor recognition of another and related threat to job security: the multinational corporation. Many U.S. corporations have established affiliates or divisions overseas because of less expensive labor, more ready access to markets, tax savings, and other economic advantages. Labor has strongly attacked this tendency and feels it has led to a loss of jobs. Since 1972 labor has actively lobbied for passage of the Burke-Hartke Foreign Trade and Investment Act (or a variant) to establish quotas on all imports on a category by category basis and to make it less profitable for large MNCs to invest overseas by eliminating foreign tax credits.[39] The AFL-CIO has also attacked the Export-Import Bank, through which the "U.S. taxpayers are being forced to subsidize the export of American technology, production and jobs,"[40] and the Overseas Private Investment Corporation (OPIC). Although labor has had little or no success to date in harnessing American multinational corporations, with the possible exception of new restrictions on OPIC, it remains very critical of large-scale investment overseas by MNCs.[41] The material, energy, and food shortages of 1973–1974 led the AFL-CIO even one step further into protectionist policy advocacy—they argued for export controls on "agricultural products and raw materials."[42] So far, the new protectionist stance of labor has been overriden by businessmen and many others who fear retaliation against the United States for both import- and export-oriented protectionist measures. The strength of the American economy and the balance of trade will probably determine the ultimate victor in the struggle. If unemployment continues to decline, labor's argument will be less stringent and less convincing. If not, the pendulum of U.S. policy could conceivably swing toward protection. Interestingly, already by early 1976 the demands of labor appeared to be shifting toward partial import controls and piecemeal revision of taxes on multinational corporations, and away from the omnibus approach of Burke-Hartke.

Labor and Other Issues Labor less frequently than business takes and strongly advocates positions on foreign policy without a clear impact on jobs. In 1974, 1975, and 1976, the AFL-CIO supported the reimposition of the boycott on Rhodesian chrome, the funding of Radio Free Europe and Radio Liberty, and defeat of most-favored-nation treatment for Romania. They also maintained their strong support for defense spending and new weapons systems such as the Trident submarine program and mounted a major attack on what they perceived to be a very one-sided detente.[43] These stands reflect both the anticommunism of labor and, once again, an economic interest. Few have stated the economic motivation quite as bluntly as Joseph Berne, president of the Communications Workers of America, immediately after Nixon's invasion of Cambodia in May 1970:[44]

> Suppose last night, instead of escalating into Cambodia, President Nixon [had] said we are pulling every man out in the quickest manner—This morning the Pentagon would have notified thousands of corporations and said "your contract is cancelled"—by tomorrow millions would be laid off.

Labor positions and activity in 1975 and 1976 also began to suggest a broader disillusionment with international organizations, as well as continuing earlier attacks on multinational corporations and detente. In 1975, the AFL-CIO fought against U.S. funds for the International Labor Organization (ILO), an organization it once supported, in large part because the ILO extended observer status to the Palestine Liberation Organization (PLO). The AFL-CIO also urged termination of funds to the United Nations Educational, Scientific and Cultural Organization (UNESCO) and the United Nations Development Program (UNDP).[45] In general, however, with the exception of recent trade issues, labor has less often than business directed its resources toward the shaping of foreign policy.

Agriculture

Another category of economic interest with involvement in and influence on foreign policy is the agricultural organization. Throughout U.S. history, farmers and agricultural organizations have maintained an important role in making U.S. foreign policy, even while their numbers waned from 80 to 6 percent of the total population.

Agriculture's Historical Role   During the early nineteenth century, agriculture *was* big business, not just *a* big business. William Appleman Williams documented the influence of agricultural interests on foreign policy. For instance, the conflict with Britain over the Oregon Territory up to 54 degrees, 40 minutes, latitude was settled in part by British moves to open up its agricultural market to foreign competition. Farmers also influenced tariff policies strongly, pushing for reciprocally lowered tariffs during some periods. By the late part of the nineteenth century, American agricultural exports had grown to the point that foreign, especially European, governments were raising barriers to the products on the ground that American meats were diseased. Finally at the turn of the century, agricultural interests wanted intervention in Cuba, an important market. Appleman argues that[46]

> The primary force producing the war against Spain was the market place expansionist outlook generated by the agricultural majority of the country during the generation after the firing on Fort Sumter. The agricultural businessman played a smaller, but by no means insignificant, part in the crucial definition of the war as an instrument of American expansion in Asia.

Agriculture has remained big business in the United States and an important contributor to total exports. Before World War II, however, the United States competed with Latin America and even eastern Europe and the Soviet Union in the world grain market. The world has increased its dependence on the United States markedly since that time. By 1973, U.S. grain exports reached approximately 66 million metric tons, more than twelve times the level of the 1930s and about 70 percent of total world exports. In 1974, they increased further, to a value of $22 billion, about the magnitude of oil imports. In that year, the United States exported 21.5 percent of its corn crop and 41.8 percent of its soybean production.[47] Every indication is that export volume and its monetary value will hold or rise through the end of the century.

Not surprisingly, potential economic benefit underlies many of the international positions taken by the agricultural organizations. For instance, in 1927 the secretary of agriculture prohibited the import of fresh meats from regions where rinderpest or hoof-and-mouth disease existed, including Argentina, an action reminiscent of those taken against American agriculture in the nineteenth century. In 1935, the Argentine Sanitary Convention was signed, modifying the prohibition so that it would not apply to regions of Argentina known to be free from hoof-and-mouth disease. That treaty was opposed by the American Farm Bureau Federation, the National Grange, the American Livestock Association, the National Livestock Marketing Association of Swine Records, the American Shorthorn Breeders' Association, the National Wool Growers' Association, and still others. Only one group, the National Foreign Trade Council, went on record in favor of the convention.[48]

On some issues—for instance, on the issue of increasing foreign agricultural sales—farmers share a clear economic interest. On other issues, policy positions frequently represent noneconomic factors and consequently divide farm organizations. For instance, the foreign policy positions of the National Farmers Union and the American Farm Bureau Federation very frequently differ. The positions of the National Grange (the third largest agricultural organization) generally fall between those of the other two groups, although it probably finds itself more often in agreement with the Farm Bureau than with the National Farmers Union. The policy position differences are interesting enough and substantial enough to merit a closer look.[49]

The American Farm Bureau Federation   The Farm Bureau is a semigovernmental organization with its power lying largely in the county farm bureaus. It is a conservative organization, has its major strength in the South and Midwest, and is the most powerful of the farm groups. The Farm Bureau has often found itself closely identified with business and in opposition to labor. For instance, it actively supported the legalized importation of braceros (Mexican farm laborers), which liberal groups and labor opposed.[50] The policies proposed in recent years by the bureau support, as do those of all farm organizations, the principle of expanded U.S. agricultural exports. The bureau opposes barriers to trade, including nontariff barriers. It protests the Common Market policies that have made that area more difficult for American agricultural products to penetrate. It proposes a more flexible government credit program in support of agricultural exports.

On issues other than agricultural trade, the American Farm Bureau Federation's positions show a combination of isolationism and nationalism. It supported President Nixon's efforts to "bring an honorable and early settlement in Vietnam."[51] It favors complete ownership and control by the United States of the Panama Canal. Except for the Food for Peace program, in which it has an economic interest, it has severe doubts about our foreign aid program. It favors a reappraisal of aid programs and a "termination of these programs where no conflict with the interest of our national security is involved." It is also very negative toward the United Nations. It feels that communists are using the United Nations as a base of espionage and propaganda in New York, and it would like to see us reduce our contribution.

The National Grange The Grange (Order of Patrons of Husbandry) has a different geographical base than the National Farm Bureau: the Mid-Atlantic states, New England, and the Pacific Northwest. Perhaps as a result of this base, it does not show the same isolationism in policy positions as the Farm Bureau. The Grange now supports the admission of Communist China to the United Nations (the Farm Bureau suggests the reinstatement of Nationalist China). The Grange also calls for a reevaluation of our aid program but has expressed no opposition to its continuation. The Grange also supported the president's paced withdrawal program in Vietnam.[52]

On trading policy, the international issue of greatest concern for the Grange, a fairly strong economic nationalism comes through. This is perhaps not surprising, given a Grange history of economic nationalism, including one-time support for high tariffs. The Grange, in common with the Farm Bureau, supports expanded agricultural trade, including the grain sale to the Soviet Union, which others have characterized as the "Great Grain Robbery." In contrast with the Farm Bureau, however, the Grange is not totally consistent in its support for free international trade. It supports lower tariffs but manages to maintain support for quotas "at such level as to reserve to domestic producers such portion of the market for any agricultural commodity as they are able to supply at a fair and reasonable price level."[53] It also supported the Nixon administration's efforts to limit textile imports.

The National Farmers Union The policies of the Farmers Union contrast quite markedly with the two other major farm organizations.[54] This is an organization largely of the wheat-producing

Great Plains states. The Farmers Union supported immediate withdrawal from Vietnam and criticized Nixon's pace. It also criticized the administration's handling of the wheat sales to the Soviet Union, the benefit of which, it argued, fell less to farmers than to grain traders in "windfall profits."[55] The Farmers Union not only supports the United Nations but even urges its strengthening. For instance, it suggests the eventual integration of the Peace Corps (which it supports) into a United Nations Volunteer Corps. The internationalism of the National Farmers Union has even led it to establish an organization (the International Assistance Corporation) that conducts agricultural technical assistance programs in fourteen countries.[56]

The position of the Farmers Union on agricultural trade policy is also rather different from that of the other farm organizations. The Farmers Union argues that, given managed economies and multinational corporations, it is no longer meaningful to talk in terms of *free* and *competitive* trade. This does not, however, lead the farmers to a position of support for trade barriers of any kind. Instead, they argue in opposition to the operating patterns of multinational agricultural trading corporations and in favor of international agreements on commodity pricing.

In summary, some generalizations can be made about agricultural interest groups. They all favor what is in their economic interest: expanded exports of agricultural products. In general, they oppose restrictions on international trading, although with differing fervor and alternative suggestions concerning the most effective procedures for expanding exports. Beyond this rather narrow (albeit important) ground of agreement, their international policy positions differ remarkably. It would be surprising, then, if their impact on foreign relations extended beyond their lobbying for expanded agricultural exports, and apparently it does not.

Veterans and Military Associations

Aside from business, labor, and agriculture, few economic groups have an identifiable interest in foreign policy. Some of the professional associations—such as the American Bar Association, the Federation of American Scientists, or the National Education Association—are very peripherally involved in foreign affairs. For instance, the National Education Association holds a contract with the Agency for International Development for the Teachers' Corps. In spite of considerable access to government leaders by leaders of professional organizations, they seldom take positions on foreign policy issues or try to influence the making of foreign policy.[57] In this section, we begin looking at groups defined on bases other than mutual economic interest.

Veterans' Organizations   Although noneconomic groups often have a less direct interest (or stake) in foreign affairs, many groups feel very strongly about U.S. foreign policy. Among these are veterans' associations. Some of the older associations, such as the Veterans of Foreign Wars (formed after the Spanish-American War) and the American Legion (established in 1919) have been intensely nationalistic. They have consistently supported a strong military posture. Their nationalism has at times shown up in support of immigration restriction.[58] Both of these groups supported Nixon's actions toward China and in the Strategic Arms Limitation Talks (SALT) agreements, but it was partial and almost grudging support. Both oppose any diplomatic recognition of China or any action that hints at abandoning Taiwan. Both stress that in the SALT agreement the United States should be extremely watchful of the Soviets' actions and distrustful of their intentions.[59]

Although the policy positions of the two organizations are very similar, the smaller Veterans of Foreign Wars (VFW) is probably more ardent in its nationalism. The organization has passed resolutions, for instance, condemning world government and has supported very considerable and broad strengthening of U.S. forces. The VFW has also felt it desirable to condemn in advance "no win" policies in future military involvements. It also decries any concessions to Panama on the canal treaty issue, strongly opposes amnesty for draft dodgers and deserters, and eagerly supports increased defense spending.

There appears to be something of a generation gap among veterans' groups, however. Two groups that are restricted to veterans of World War II, American Veterans of World War II (AMVETS) and the American Veterans' Committee, have taken somewhat more liberal and internationalist positions. Moreover, one of the most politically active groups coming out of the Vietnam War was Vietnam Veterans Against the War, a decidedly antimilitaristic group. It may be that even the American Legion and the VFW are changing somewhat as a result of the attitudes of their younger members and as a result of the antiwar sentiment in the society. In early 1973, the American Legion announced an effort to seek a "friendly dialogue" with war veterans behind the Iron Curtain—a decision that was admitted to be "slightly traumatic" for some of the older members.[60] And, in mid-1973, a VFW newsletter discussing the continuing presidential bombing in Cambodia in spite of growing congressional opposition was weighted slightly to the congressional side.[61]

Although the members of many of the veterans' organizations feel quite strongly about foreign policy issues, the vast bulk of their attention is directed, as with other interest groups, to issues of more immediate concern for their members. For veterans' groups, this means that most lobbying time and money is spent working for more aid to disabled veterans, higher pensions, and wider veterans' benefits. The American Legion, the most politically active group, has also been greatly concerned with domestic issues, such as flag desecration. The veterans' groups have been very influential on domestic policy, especially veterans' benefits. They have not done nearly as well on international issues. One detailed study of the American Legion and its positions on foreign affairs is a study of repeated failure to influence external policy.[62]

Military Support Associations   In addition to the veterans' associations, there is another class of organization with fairly close ties to the military world and whose members provide active support for military programs and positions. Groups such as the Navy League (founded originally in 1902 to counteract reaction against the Spanish-American War), the Air Force Association (founded in 1946), and the Association for the U.S. Army (the most recent of the military organizations, established in 1950) have for years tied together military men, businessmen, and others interested in military policy.[63] The Air Force Association, which has been described as the largest and most influential of the associations (its strength derives in part from the very heavy dependence of the aircraft industry on military spending) has 300 "affiliates" or industrial firms, which each pay $350 annual dues.[64]

The military associations provide a linkage also from the military to the public, especially former members of the military. For instance, the Navy League publishes a magazine called *Sea Power* with a circulation of 55,000, provides speakers for public meetings, conducts "sea power seminars," and aids the Navy recruitment program. Although the Navy League prohibits membership by those on active duty, it is clearly dominated by those who once were. Close contacts are maintained between the service organizations and the veterans' associations such as the American Legion.

Another variety of military support organization has its deepest roots in the business community but again brings together industry, the military, and others interested in military policy, especially armaments. The American Ordnance Association, the National Security Industrial Association, and the Aerospace Industries Association are three.[65] It is not too surprising that the major concerns of these organizations center on the maintenance of a large and well-equipped military and the development and purchase of new weapons systems. They do so by providing a constituency of support for the military and by supplying "experts" who share the view of the military that major weapons expenditures are necessary for national defense. The experts can be useful to the military either within the executive (including support during intraservice disputes) or before Congress.

The American Ordnance Association was founded in 1919 and describes itself as "a membership society of American citizens dedicated to armament progress and industrial preparedness for the United States."[66] Its membership of 40,000 includes, according to its description, "executives, engineers, scientists, military and defense-minded citizens." Unless it is very different from similar organizations, its membership, in particular its leadership, is predominantly military officers (active or retired) and businessmen (predominantly those connected with armaments production), with a sprinkling of journalists, academics, and politicians. A self-description of the American Ordnance Association objectives stresses that the organization does not attempt to influence legislation or to promote the commercial interests of members. It says, however, that it will "Cooperate with all agencies of the Government in planning the mobilization and utilization of the nation's scientific and industrial resources for the national security."[67] There can be no question that such cooperation would be difficult without influencing legislation concerning the size and nature of the defense budget and without some impact on purchases from major armaments producers. The association fields about ninety "technical advisory groups," and, as all lobbyists know, information is their primary tool.

The American Ordnance Association and the other military support organizations may sound to some like the backbone of a military-industrial complex. The notion of such a powerful complex is so widespread that it merits separate discussion.

The Military-Industrial Complex

On January 17, 1961, Dwight Eisenhower delivered his farewell address to the nation. In that address, he warned Americans of two threats. The first was government domination of research. The second threat is the one that most have remembered:[68]

Until the last of our world conflicts, the United States had no armaments industry. American makers of plowshares could, with time and as required, make swords as well. But we can no longer risk emergency improvisation of national defense. We have been compelled to create a permanent armaments industry of vast proportions. Added to this, three-and-a-half million men and women are directly engaged in the defense establishment. We annually spend on military security alone more than the net income of all United States corporations.

Now this conjunction of an immense military establishment and a large arms industry is new in the American experience. The total influence—economic, political, even spiritual—is felt in every city, every state house, every office of the federal government.

We recognize the imperative need for this development. Yet we must not fail to comprehend its grave implications. Our toil, resources, and livelihood are all involved; so is the very structure of our society.

In the councils of government, we must guard against the acquisition of unwarranted influence, whether sought or unsought, by the military-industrial complex. The potential for the disastrous rise of misplaced power exists and will persist.

Since that address, the phrase *military-industrial complex* (MIC) has become almost universally known.[69] In part because the MIC provided a target for anti-Vietnam activists, its supposed influence has also become widely feared. Much of the discussion of the military-industrial complex has been so emotional, however, that it is difficult to separate facts from assumptions and accusations. The facts do not speak for themselves.

Collusion on Contracts   William Proxmire has reported some of the facts.[70] In 1968 there were $38.8 billion of prime military contracts. Of this amount, 67 percent went to one hundred companies. These same companies employed "some 2072 retired military officers of the rank of colonel or Navy captain and above." This is an increase from 751 in 1959, about the time of Eisenhower's warning. Overall defense spending directly generates employment for about 7.5 million people.[71] About 90 percent of military contracts are negotiated, not competitively bid. Cost overruns are very frequent. Profits of the defense industry are high and risks are relatively low, in spite of protestations to the contrary by the industry.

Conclusions drawn from these facts vary widely. Some are almost certainly justified. For instance, the hiring of former military men, who retain friendships and contacts in the military, aids corporations in obtaining contracts, in negotiating good terms, and in obtaining favorable responses to cost overruns. The extent of money mismanagement and corruption is unknown, but with nearly $40 billion available annually some crime in the executive suites is inevitable. The 1975 disclosure of and controversy over the lavish entertainment of military men by Northrup, a major military contractor, is almost certainly touching only the bottom rung on the ladder of unethical and illegal behavior.

More General Defense Policy Influence   The real issue, however, is not favoritism in contracts, but potential policy influence. It is here that interpretations vary wildly. Most frightening are the conspiracy, power-elite theories. These are by their nature, of course, impossible to disprove—a conspiracy theorist can always explain all the facts with an interpretation of hidden and devious action. There are, however, pieces of evidence that suggest that the MICs' power is frequently overestimated.

First, many studies have examined the relationship between concentrations of defense spending (in states or districts) and congressional foreign policy voting.[72] None of these have found more than a weak relationship. This implies that defense industries are not able to influence that voting in any major way. Second, defense spending since the early 1950s has declined as a percentage share of GNP and the federal budget (review Figure 3.1). In fact, in constant dollars, non-Vietnam defense spending has declined in absolute terms since 1964.[73] Military pay raises (recently used to build an all-volunteer army) have taken an increasingly large share of the military budget at the expense of weapons spending. These facts do not support overwhelming influence on the *size* of the pie or on the size of the weapons spending slice. Clearly the MIC does wield power on the *division* of that slice. Third, the aerospace industry, the heart of the complex, is ailing and finds it easier to try to survive by expanding foreign military sales than by increasing domestic ones. Military sales abroad in great volume are beginning to raise doubts among many Americans, however, and so far the MIC has been successful on that issue.

The outcome of the 1971 debate on the supersonic transport (SST) plane might illustrate the inability of the MIC to carry the day on many issues important to it. Supporting a governmental program to build the SST were the National Committee for the SST, Industry and Labor for the SST, and of course the Nixon administration itself. SST contractors, subcontractors, and aircraft industry labor worked hard for governmental support. A coalition against building the SST, led by Friends of the Earth and primarily containing other environmental groups, helped defeat the proposal. Similarly, in the 1969 struggle over the antiballistic missile (ABM) program, a coalition of peace groups, church groups, and general citizens organizations prevented another coalition, containing General Electric and Lockheed, from obtaining more than a limited deployment. In fact, the public image of the MIC is so bad that pro-ABM industry groups avoided open lobbying.[74]

These arguments do not deny that military and industrial organizations have played a role in the maintenance of massive defense spending; they do suggest significant limits on that role. Those in the MIC certainly also contribute to the continuation of general public animosities and fears related to the cold war. Yet other organizations operate to present alternative views, and there is nothing magically persuasive about the viewpoints (or propaganda) of the MIC. Eisenhower's warning is still appropriate (as is his other warning on the dangers of government sponsorship and control of research), but the MIC does not dominate foreign policy.

Women's Organizations

Many women's organizations also take positions on foreign policy issues. Most often women's groups actively support internationalist and peace positions on issues. This should not be taken to mean that they have been entirely pacifistic, however. Women's organizations did support U.S. entry into the North Atlantic Pact in 1949, even though they expressed misgivings.[75]

By far the most politically active women's group is the League of Women Voters. This women's group, as its name suggests, is a highly politicized one, unlike some of the more social groupings such as the General Federation of Women's Clubs. The League is very active in community-level work and in national lobbying. One of the League's most active and persistent campaigns has been in support of liberalized trading. For forty years it has championed liberal trade policies, including reduced tariffs and elimination of trade barriers such as quotas. It is probably the most active single lobby on trade bills. This, of course, does not mean that it is the most effective lobby—an issue to which we will return in the next chapter.

The League has also taken strong internationalist stands on a variety of issues.[76] It supports foreign aid for development and also the application in trade policy of "preferential treatment to all LDCs" (less developed countries). It worked for improved relations with China even before Nixon's trip there. It advocates considerable strengthening of the United Nations. It is interesting, however, that the League has generally not taken positions on issues involving the military. These include the number of troops stationed in Europe, the level of defense spending, and even the Vietnam War.

Other women's organizations have flowered periodically. In 1943 a Women's Action Committee for a Lasting Peace was established and pursued a very internationalist foreign policy. A more conservative group is the National Federation of Business and Professional Women's Clubs, which has close ties with the NAM and Chamber of Commerce. It, too, has supported the Reciprocal Trade Agreements Act, but with protectionist restrictions. It seldom adopts a position on what it considers "partisan issues," including those of foreign policy.

Religious Organizations

Religious organizations, like women's groups, are often liberal and internationalist, with a touch of religious pacifism.[77] This is, of course, a source of weakness, since it often misrepresents church members. Interestingly, also, the most active church goers and supporters are frequently those least likely to be permissive toward church involvement in public issues.

Various churches have their own organizations. The National Council of Churches of Christ in America (earlier known as the Federal Council) represents Protestants. A more recent Protestant group, the American Council of Christian Churches, is more conservative and nationalist. This latter group has been intensely anticommunist and has strongly attacked the position taken by the National Council of Churches (as early as 1958) in favor of diplomatic recognition of Red China.[78] Neither group engages in much lobbying, although both have substantial budgets for publications.

Among religious groupings, Jewish organizations have been the most active in foreign policy. Groups such as the Zionist Organization of America have been actively involved in promoting pro-Israel policy. Currently, the American-Israel Public Affairs Committee (AIPAC) spearheads the pro-Israel lobby. Jewish groups have, moreover, been very influential. The nearly immediate recognition of the new state of Israel by Truman in 1948 was an early indication of their importance. Sherman Adams, an assistant to President Eisenhower, gave further evidence of their influence in his memoirs:[79]

> Any attempt to give aid to the Arabs always met with opposition behind the scenes in Washington, where the members of Congress were acutely aware of the strong popular sentiment in this country for Israel. Had the members of Congress either underestimated or overlooked the strength of such feeling they would have been quickly reminded of it by the alert representatives of the many well-organized pro-Israel lobbies that were always effective and influential in the Capitol. Consideration for the great body of private opinion in the United States favoring Israel was a large factor in every government decision on the Middle East issues, especially in the [Suez] crisis.

In 1956 the American Zionist Committee for Public Affairs displayed an endorsement by 153 members of the House of Representatives of a statement on Israel favoring armament assistance and a security guarantee.[80] More recently, in 1974, Congress balked on providing most-favored-nation trade status to the Soviet Union, as agreed to by Nixon in his Moscow visit, largely because of the Soviet exit tax on educated Jews.

Jewish organizations have wielded special influence because of the concentration of the Jewish vote in the major urban centers and the resulting strategic importance of the vote in large urban states such as New York. Widespread public support of Israel has been another important factor. Certainly of no small importance is the persistence and skill of the Jewish lobby: State Department officials have suggested that only on questions involving Israel is there a public that directly approaches and seeks to influence the department, rather than working through Congress.[81]

It should not be assumed that all Jewish organizations are intensely Zionist. Certainly the Jewish Defense League does fit that characterization. Although not as militant, the American Jewish Committee is also concerned with Jews overseas, in Israel and the rest of the Mid-East, and of course in the Soviet Union. The committee would like to see the United States work through the United Nations and other channels to bring pressure on Syria and the Soviet Union. The American Council for Judaism, however, is non-Zionist and opposes some of the activities of the Zionist groups. It would prefer that the diversity within the Jewish community be recognized, rather than have that community project an image of unanimity. In fact, a recurrent argument of the council is that there is no "Jewish voting bloc."[82]

Ethnics

Ethnic groups are, of course, always important in American politics, and many have been concerned with foreign policy. Ironically, two of the largest minority groups in this country, the Irish and the Germans, have been generally hostile toward England. In spite of a policy of Anglo-American friendship, pursued and desired by the dominant ethnic group (WASPs), these groups have made it difficult to create as close a relationship with England as desired by many presidents and secretaries of state. The groups were, of course, in large part responsible for our delayed entry into two world wars on the side of the British, and a large concentration of German-Americans in the Midwest helped give that area its earlier reputation for isolationist sentiment. At the time of the sinking of the Lusitania by a German submarine in 1916, one newspaper catering to those of German descent in Milwaukee and St. Louis defended the action.[83] The WASPs were always able, however, to move our policy toward support of Britain, as in the case of 1940–1941 aid to England.

Since the uniting of the West by the cold war, opposition to Britain by the Irish and Germans has not been of any particular importance. More important have been the groups originating in the nations of eastern Europe—those nations that became communist in the post-World War II period. A number of minorities from that area formed the Federation of Americans of Central and East European Descent. Not surprisingly, this organization of individuals who largely immigrated before or at the time of the installation of communist regimes in eastern Europe has maintained a very strong anticommunist orientation. They have also advocated liberal immigration quotas for the area. The number of Americans of East European descent is considerably lower than those of German or Irish descent, however, and this is one reason such groups have lacked significant political impact.

Another group that has ethnic foundations, although it has made a conscious effort to avoid the appearance of an ethnic group, is the Committee of One Million Against the Admission of Communist China to the United Nations. This group strove for years for the goal specified in its name. It had, needless to say, success for many years. In 1956 it boasted that ninety-seven members of the House of Representatives were members of this organization. Nearly one-third of the members of the lower house signed a nonpartisan position to have both parties include a platform plank in opposition to China's U.N. membership.[84] A member of the Senate from California was referred to by some in his state as the "Senator from Formosa."[85] The successor of the Committee of One Million, the Committee for a Free China, continues to support the Republic of China on Taiwan and to attack the mainland government. Recently it has publicized, for instance, charges that the mainland government is growing massive amounts of opium for export—much of it eventually arriving in the United States.[86]

Many other ethnic groups have an interest in foreign policy. One such group, Arab Americans, has faced considerable public and governmental opposition. Unlike Jews, who have the American Israel Public Affairs Committee (AIPAC), Arabs have had no single well-organized umbrella organization. The National Association of Arab Americans, founded in 1972, has moved in that direction. Other important groups supporting the Arab Mid-East countries are Americans for Middle East Understanding, Inc., American Near East Refugee Aid, Inc., Action Committee on American-Arab Relations and American Friends of the Middle East. All of the organizations are underfunded, by AIPAC standards, although the oil companies have provided most of what they do receive.[87] These groups work under the very considerable burden of American popular support for Israel. Consider, for instance, the American Friends of the Middle East. It began as a political action group but decided (as have other groups) that a long-term education campaign would be more profitable. It faces not only the problem of widespread Israeli sympathy, but Arab suspicions as well. It does not officially submit positions to the State Department because it does not wish to be accused by the Arabs of being associated with the department.[88]

Foreign Policy Groups

A variety of groups in the United States are not founded on the basis of a shared economic or demographic characteristic, but on the basis of shared beliefs. There are a number of foreign policy organizations, overwhelmingly with an emphasis on support for international organizations, international law, and an active non-military U.S. foreign policy. Many of these organizations, including the most active ones, characterize themselves as "peace" groups. Such groups existed prior to the Vietnam War and continue to be active after it—they should not be confused with antiwar groups. Peace groups go back at least to 1828 when the American Peace Society was formed.[89] Many foreign policy organizations grew out of the defeat of the League of Nations Treaty by the U.S. Senate and the belief of some Americans that the United States should take an active international role designed to create a more peaceful world. Among these, the Foreign Policy Association, formed in 1918, and the Council on Foreign Relations, established in 1921, are still active.

One fairly well-known peace group is SANE, a citizens' organization "for a sane world." SANE is interested in seeing substantial cuts in arms spending with the transfer of resources to civilian programs, disarmament agreements, and strengthened international organizations.[90] The peace organizations generally desire to deemphasize nationalism and to strengthen international organizations (groups such as the American Security Council might characterize this as eroding national sovereignty). This desire is greatest among groups such as the World Federalists, U.S.A. The World Federalists urge strengthening of the United Nations. Realizing that world unity is hardly likely to be accomplished by a diplomatic masterstroke (not even one of Henry Kissinger's), they urge U.S. support for existing international organizations and less dramatic actions such as international agreements on the use of the sea bed.[91]

Most of the foreign policy groups have strong academic ties. Quite frequently one sees full-page newspaper ads sponsored by these groups with endorsements of professors across the country. The Carnegie Endowment for International Peace (with an endowment of $10 million) is run by scholars. As in the case of the Carnegie Endowment, a considerable portion of peace group effort is directed toward the study of international relations more generally. Much emphasis is placed on public education. The Foreign Policy Association is perhaps best known for its large-scale adult education programs.

Most of the foreign policy groups forego substantial lobbying, although they take positions on international issue and provide legislative testimony. An exception is a foreign policy organization within Congress itself, called Members of Congress for Peace Through Law. In 1975, the membership list of this bicameral and bipartisan group contained names of 35 senators and 121 representatives. The group even boasts its own staff and a variety of committees.[92] Its policy concerns are nonmilitary internationalism: international food, resource, trade, development, and arms control problems. The creation of the organization in 1966 and its rapid growth since then illustrate in Congress the new liberal/nonmilitary internationalism attitude realignment discussed in previous chapters.

Citizens' Groups

In addition to the foreign policy and/or peace organizations, there exist a number of more general ideological groups, concerned with domestic programs and international policies. These include the Americans for Constitutional Action (ACA) on the right and the Americans for Democratic Action (ADA) on the left. Since the organizations on the right differ most dramatically from the peace organizations, it is interesting to look at some of the issue positions of the Americans for Constitutional Action. In their periodic report on the voting records of members of Congress,[93] they report that a number of particular votes represented positions compatible with "strengthening national sovereignty," a major concern of the ACA. These included votes to defeat amendments proposing cuts in the defense budget for B-1 bombers and Indochina military appropriations and votes to require the president to bypass a U.N. embargo against importing chromium from Southern Rhodesia if chromium ore were being imported from any communist nation (the two principal sources of chromium in the world are the Soviet Union and Southern Rhodesia). The bulk of the concerns of the ACA are, however, domestic.

The Americans for Democratic Action, in contrast, are intensely concerned with a large number of foreign policy issues.[94] They actively support major cuts in the defense budget. Unlike the ACA, they seek U.S. adherence to stronger trade sanctions against Southern Rhodesia (which they call Zimbabwe). Further, the ADA has continually opposed U.S. involvement in Vietnam and has supported pressure on Portugal, South Africa, and Greece for changes in policy. Although the ADA is opposed to the reestablishment of tariff barriers or drastic limitations on overseas investment, it does suggest strong measures to aid American workers who are adversely affected by present politics. Like the ACA, however, the ADA lobbies little, and devotes most of its efforts to publications for its members and to public information.

Common Cause fits into a category by itself. This self-described "citizens'" lobby normally directs its attention to consumer issues and issues of political accountability. It has, however, taken positions on such foreign policy issues as supersonic transport, which it opposed, and the anti-Vietnam War amendments of 1970, which it favored. It also reacted to the post-Watergate disclosures of foreign and covert CIA activities by backing proposals to redefine CIA and FBI mandates.[95] If Common Cause were ever to turn its major attention to a foreign policy issue, it could be much more effective than most citizen groups, because it has a well-organized and well-financed Washington lobbying effort.

In 1976, Russell Peterson organized a group called New Directions, somewhat modeled after Common Cause but explicitly concerned with global problems, such as hunger, unemployment, energy shortage, pollution, and nuclear proliferation. It is something of a peak organization (an organization of organizations) for other generally liberal and internationalist groups. Among officers are John Gardner, the chairman and founder of Common Cause, Norman Cousins, and the president of the League of Women Voters. It works and lobbies in Washington but seeks to establish a global network of like-minded groups.

Another type of citizen's group is the ad hoc group that grows up around a single issue for a specific period of time. Fred Riggs calls these "catalytic groups."[96] It is a catchy term, although perhaps inappropriate in a chemical sense, since the completion of the policy reaction (in contrast to the chemical reaction) usually means the end of the catalyst. An example of this kind of group is the Committee for the Marshall Plan (a grouping of bankers, lawyers, trade unionists, editors, and others), which was formed to back that proposal.[97] Before World War II, two organizations, the Committee to Defend America by Aiding the Allies and the American First Committee, were established to work for and oppose, respectively, U.S. entry into the war.[98] Even earlier, in 1935, a group opposed to U.S. adherence to the World Court formed quickly around the issue and helped defeat the proposal.[99] More recently, the National Mobilization Committee grew up as a peak organization for anti-Vietnam groups. Often less formal is the temporary multiple-group alliance. For instance, during much of Johnson's administration an alliance existed among the AFL-CIO, National Farmers Union, National Education Association, and several other liberal groups. It was dubbed the "Coalition."

Foreign Lobbies

Although foreign governments and nongovernmental groups must be extremely wary of backlash in any influence attempts, some 400 foreign employers with active representatives in the United States were identified under the Foreign Agents Registration Act in the early 1970s.[100] The registration act itself is a result of the reaction against Nazi and fascist propaganda in the United States before World War II.

The most important lobbying in the United States by foreign countries has often been associated with the sugar quotas. The United States allows only a certain amount of sugar to enter the United States annually, and that amount is split among many foreign producers. Most of the producers are less-developed nations with limited export goods, and the sugar quota is of considerable importance. In 1963 a major battle shaped up because of the elimination of the Cuban quota share and its redistribution to other producers. It is customary for foreign countries to hire American citizens for the lobbying effort, and many excongressmen became involved. Again, however, foreign nations can hardly expect to exert significant influence.

Recently the Japanese have done considerable lobbying. A few lobbyists are registered as foreign agents with the Justice Department to represent Japanese businesses, especially in steel and textiles, which have come under considerable criticism in the United States, as they compete with American firms.[101] The United States-Japan Trade Council also represents about 900 U.S. and Japanese firms. The lobbying however, remains low key, since the congressmen have little to gain by identification with foreign interests.

Most recently the lobbying activities of various South Koreans in both the United States and Japan have begun to surface. The South Koreans seem to have been more successful than any other foreign group in reaching a broad range of government officials, including many members of Congress. As of this writing, investigations are proceeding concerning the possible illegality and probable impropriety of gift acceptance by congressmen. The press reports considerable anxiety in Washington.

The Press

Although it is not strictly an interest group, the press has often been credited with being a major shaper of foreign policy, and merits a short discussion here. It has been given credit (or blame) for U.S. belligerency in the Spanish-American War and for much of the interventionist sentiment prior to World War II.[102] Less spectacularly, the press has been credited with mobilizing support for the Marshall Plan and through the favorable *New York Times* articles on Castro in 1957, with aiding him to obtain followers and funds for his revolution.[103] More recently, many in the Nixon administration attacked the press as partial on foreign issues. Quite naturally, when the press is perceived by an administration as having its own position, that position is counter to the policy of the administration.[104]

The perhaps most important part that the press plays in the policy process has been well described by Walter Lippman: "It is like the beam of a searchlight that moves restlessly about, bringing one episode and then another out of darkness into vision."[105] It is not just the vision of the general public that is affected by the beam, but also, and most importantly, the vision of those making foreign policy or those in a position to influence decision makers. Members of the process that makes foreign policy, from the president down through the desk officer in the State Department, rely very heavily on papers such as the *New York Times* and the *Washington Post*. Information and commentary from these papers may shape their daily activities as much as or more than internal reports and governmental information services.

The manner in which those making foreign policy are most influenced by the press is explicit in the searchlight analogy. The press is important in two ways in determining where policy makers direct their attention. First, by presenting an image of the outside world that inevitably is selective in its highlights, the press influences the decision makers' image of which problems—of all those out there—merit their concern. Second, the press works indirectly through the general public to force its concerns on the decision makers. Bernard Cohen has suggested that there are four *participant* roles of the press: representing the public, criticizing the government, advocating policy, and sometimes even making policy (through the generation of ideas that are accepted).[106]

Given the impact of the press on policy makers' images and priorities, it is instructive to look at some of the biases that are often attributed to the press. First, the press is frequently guilty of a focus on Europe and the industrialized nations at the expense of the underdeveloped world. While 50 percent of foreign correspondents are assigned in Europe, only 25 percent are in Latin America, Africa, and the Middle East combined.[107] This type of emphasis certainly reflects that of much of the public, the decision makers, and perhaps even the security interests of the United States. Nevertheless, it makes shifts in attention to Latin America or Africa by policy makers more difficult.

Second, the press places a heavy emphasis on the spectacular, especially the conflictual, as opposed to the more routine and cooperative. It is frequently noted that the press draws the attention of the public, and therein those making foreign policy, to conflicts and crises. One newspaperman went so far as to claim that the

Lebanese civil war of 1958 was created by the United Press International (UPI).[108] These are, of course, again events more important to the security of the United States than nonconflictual events. Yet it is justifiable to question the deemphasis of opportunities for cooperation and even of currently quiet situations with crisis potential. It has often been noted that the U.S. government does fairly little long-term planning, moving instead from crisis to crisis and responding as best as possible. It may be that the press is in part responsible for this behavior pattern.

Third, and related to the emphasis on crisis and conflict, is the tendency to stretch a crisis out. The action remains (or it does so in the press) at the scene of a recent crisis.[109] This is in part because of an increased sensitivity to the region by journalists and presumably also by decision makers. It is also in part a result of still having reporters in the area and of the press's use of them to feed the heightened public interest in the area. It is common after a crisis to have a period of weeks during which follow-up stories continue to be written. At this point, policy makers might be better directed toward other areas of the world.

Finally, ideological biases have been attributed to the press. Foreign reporters may overrepresent a liberal internationalist position, although editors seem to balance this somewhat with a conservative bias.[110] The major eastern prestige newspapers, such as the *Times* and the *Post,* do in fact overrepresent liberal and internationalist positions. Although local and noneastern papers probably balance this by overrepresenting conservative and nationalist positions, the critics of the press in the Nixon administration had a valid complaint—it is the prestige newspapers that are dominant in decision-making circles, and they may represent a kind of fifth column in a conservative administration.

Conclusions

This chapter has been largely descriptive. The major interest groups active in the foreign policy process have been noted and their positions delineated. We have also argued, however, that the influence of interest groups is less extensive than frequently thought. This is even true of the notorious military-industrial complex. There are a number of reasons for the limited role of groups. First, many are primarily concerned either with domestic issues or with a fairly narrow range of foreign policy issues. Second, there is frequently (although by no means always) a group with countervailing influence. Third, the congressional role in the foreign policy process is more limited than in domestic policy, and the executive branch is more difficult to influence. Also, lobbying has a rather negative image, and most public officials would resent blatant pressure, so that groups must be careful in their approach.

There are situations, however, in which groups can be very important in the shaping of foreign policy. It is to an analysis of the circumstances under which they are important that we now move.

Notes

1. For a short review of the group theorist literature, see R. Joseph Monsen and Mark W. Cannon, *The Makers of Public Policy: American Power Groups and Their Ideologies* (New York: McGraw-Hill, 1965), pp. 2–10.

2. This "anticipated reaction" argument was, of course, also suggested in the previous chapter as one of the mechanisms for more general public control of foreign policy. For a general statement of the argument, see C. J. Friedrich, *Man and His Government* (New York: McGraw-Hill, 1963).

3. Allen H. Barton, "Conflict and Consensus Among American Leaders," *Public Opinion Quarterly*, *38*, No. 4 (Winter 1974–1975): 507–530; Bruce M. Russett, "Political Prospective of U.S. Military and Business Elites," *Armed Forces and Society*, *1*, No. 1 (November 1974): 79–108; Bruce M. Russett and Elizabeth C. Hanson, *Interest and Ideology* (San Francisco: W. H. Freeman, 1975).

4. Russett, *op. cit.*, p. 93.

5. Russett and Hanson, *op. cit.*, p. 249.

6. The department has about 300 names in the files of its Organization Liaison Branch, according to John S. Dickey, "The Secretary of State and the American Public," in Don K. Price, ed., *The Secretary of State* (Englewood Cliffs, NJ: Prentice-Hall, 1960), p. 156.

7. William O. Chittick, *State Department, Press and Pressure Groups* (New York: John Wiley, 1970), p. 222.

8. Although this chapter relies heavily for specific information on recent group literature, it owes a debt also to some of the early group studies. Among these are Arthur Bentley, *The Process of Government* (Chicago: University of Chicago Press, 1908); E. Pendleton Herring, *Group Representation Before Congress: Public Administration and the Public Interest* (New York: Alfred Knopf, 1951).

9. *Multinational Corporations and the United States Foreign Policy,* Hearings Before the Subcommittee on Multinational Corporations of the U.S. Senate Committee on Foreign Relations (Washington, DC: U.S. Government Printing Office, 1973), pp. 101–102.

10. Quoted in Marian Irish and Elke Frank, *U.S. Foreign Policy* (New York: Harcourt Brace Jovanovich, 1975), p. 158.

11. G. William Domhoff, "Who Made American Foreign Policy 1945–1963?" in David Horowitz, ed., *Corporations and the Cold War* (New York: Monthly Review Press, 1969), p. 25.

12. For a discussion of the earlier period, see E. E. Schattschneider, *Politics, Pressures, and the Tariff* (Englewood Cliffs, NJ: Prentice-Hall, 1935). For a review of American tariff history and a study of more recent years, see Raymond A. Bauer, Ithiel de Sola Pool, and Lewis Anthony Dexter, *American Business and Public Policy: The Politics of Foreign Trade* (Chicago: Aldine-Atherton, 1973), second edition.

13. Raymond Bauer et al., "Pressure Groups and the Politics of Foreign Trade," in Stephen Monsma and Jack R. Van Der Slik, eds., *American Politics: Research and Readings* (New York: Holt, Rinehart and Winston, 1970), p. 620.

14. Samuel A. Lawrence, *United States Merchant Shipping Policies and Politics* (Washington, DC: Brookings Institution, 1966), p. 296; see also Paul M. Zeis, *American Shipping Policy* (Princeton, NJ: Princeton University Press, 1938).

15. Chittick, *op. cit.*, p. 36.

16. See "The Many Faces of Nontariff Barriers, Export Inventives" (National Association of Manufacturers, 277 Park Avenue, New York, NY 10017, undated).

17. Raymond Bauer et al., *American Business and Public Policy, op. cit.*, p. 113 and 210.

18. Marian Irish and Elke Frank, *U.S. Foreign Policy* (New York: Harcourt Brace Jovanovich, 1975).

19. "Oil Import Quotas Due to Fall, Despite Energy Lobby," *New York Times,* April 18, 1973, p. 20.

20. Robert Engler, *The Politics of Oil* (Chicago: University of Chicago Press, 1961).

21. *U.S. Stake in World Trade and Investment: The Role of Multinational Corporation* (National Association of Manufacturers, undated); see also the periodic bulletins of the NAM.

22. Donald C. Blaisdell, *American Democracy Under Pressure* (New York: Ronald Press, 1957), p. 255; see also Paul F. Boller, Jr., "The Great Conspiracy of 1933: A Study in Short Memories," in Richard M. Abrams and Lawrence W. Levine, eds., *The Shaping of the Twentieth-Century America* (Boston: Little, Brown, 1965), pp. 482–501; Robert

Paul Browder, *The Origins of Soviet-American Diplomacy* (Princeton, NJ: Princeton University Press, 1953). Bernard Cohen provides a different and very credible interpretation of the recognition, arguing that Roosevelt orchestrated the public providing the economic argument, in support of a *Realpolitik* policy. *The Public's Impact on Foreign Policy* (Boston: Little, Brown, 1973), pp. 179–180.

23. "Business Panel Asks Trade with Reds," *Cleveland Plain Dealer*, September 11, 1972, p. 11-A.

24. "Declaration of the 58th National Foreign Trade Convention" (National Foreign Trade Council, 10 Rockefeller Plaza, New York, NY 10020, November 15–17, 1971), p. 10.

25. "Yankee Come Back," *Forbes*, January 15, 1976, p. 17.

26. Gabriel A. Almond, *The American People and Foreign Policy* (New York: Praeger, 1960), p. 162.

27. Engler, *op. cit.*, p. 195.

28. For instance, an ad was published on page 59 of the September 27, 1973, edition of the *New York Times* by Esso Standard Libya Inc. and Esso Sinte Inc., announcing that "Each country intends to take such action as it deems appropriate to protect and enforce its rights against those who" purchased or contracted for oil that the companies insisted still legally belonged to them.

29. *New York Times*, March 29, 1973, p. 1.

30. *New York Times*, May 3, 1975, p. 15.

31. Jerome Levinson and Juan de Onis, *The Alliance That Lost Its Way* (Chicago: Quadrangle Books, 1970), p. 144. For a discussion of the million dollar offer by ITT to the CIA, see *Hearings Before the Subcommittee on Multinational Corporations of the Committee on Foreign Relations*, United States Senate, 93rd Congress, U.S. Government Printing Office, SN 5270-01929, pp. 63–65.

32. For a good discussion of these issues, see "The Overseas Private Investment Corporation, a Report to the Senate Committee on Foreign Relations by the Subcommittee on Multinational Corporations" Washington, DC: U.S. Government Printing Office, 1973.

33. George Meany, "The International Role of the AFL-CIO," in Herbert I. Schiller and Joseph D. Phillips, eds., *Super State: Readings in the Military-Industrial Complex* (Urbana: University of Illinois Press, 1972).

34. Almond, *op cit.*

35. Chittick, *op. cit.*, p. 14.

36. Fred W. Riggs, *Pressures on Congress: A Study of the Repeal of Chinese Exclusion* (New York: King's Crown Press, 1950), p. 22.

37. *Labor Looks at the 93rd Congress*, AFL-CIO Legislative Report, Publication No. 77O (AFL-CIO, 815 Sixteenth St., N.W., Washington, DC 20006, January 1974).

38. Howard Samuel, "A New Perspective on World Trade," *AFL-CIO American Federation* (June 1971) reprint.

39. "What Labor Wants on Trade," *New York Times*, March 4, 1973, Section 3, p. 1; *Labor Looks at 93rd Congress*, AFL-CIO Legislative Report, Publication No. 77P, February 1975, pp. 22–27; *Labor Looks at Congress, 1975*, AFL-CIO Legislative Report, Publication No. 77Q (March 1976).

40. *Labor Looks at Congress, 1975*, AFL-CIO Legislative Report, Publication No. 77Q (March 1976), pp. 27, 28.

41. Among recent discussions of the merits of MNCs are George W. Ball, ed., *Global Companies* (Englewood Cliffs, NJ: Prentice-Hall, 1975); Abdul A. Said and Luiz R. Simmons, eds., *The New Sovereigns* (Englewood Cliffs, NJ: Prentice-Hall, 1975); Richard Barnet and Ronald E. Mueller, *Global Reach* (New York: Simon & Schuster, 1974).

42. *Labor Looks at the 93rd Congress*, p. 31.

43. *Labor Looks at Congress, 1973*, an AFL-CIO Legislative Report, January 1974, pp. 104–110; *Labor Looks at the 93rd Congress*, pp. 137–147; *Solzhenitsyn: The Voice of Freedom*, American Federation of Labor and Congress of Industrial Organizations (Washington, DC: AFL-CIO, 1975); *AFL-CIO Free Trade Union News*, October 1974, pp. 1–8.

44. Quoted in James Clotfelter, *The Military in American Politics* (New York: Harper & Row, 1973), p. 64.

45. *Labor Looks at Congress, 1975*, pp. 110–113.

46. William Appleman Williams, *The Roots of the Modern American Empire* (New York: Random House, 1969), pp. 408–409.

47. Data for 1973 from Lester R. Brown, *By Bread Alone* (New York: Praeger, 1975), p. 61; for 1974 from Wayne Moyer, "Iowa Dateline: A View From the Cornfields," *Foreign Policy*, 19 (Summer 1975): 184.

48. Donald C. Blaisdell, *Economic Power and Political Pressures*, Temporary National Economic Committee Monograph No. 26 (Washington, DC: U.S. Government Printing Office, 1941), p. 60.

49. See also Lauren K. Soth, "Farm Policy, Foreign Policy, and Farm Opinion," *The Annals*, 331 (September 1960): 103–109; Charles M. Hardin, "Congressional Farm Policies and Economic Foreign Policy," *The Annals*, 331 (September 1960): viii–x.

50. Richard B. Craig, *The Bracero Program* (Austin: University of Texas Press, 1971).

51. *Farm Bureau Policies for 1972* (Chicago: American Farm Bureau Federation, December 1971), pp. 38–42.

52. *Legislative Policies 1972* (National Grange, 1616 H Street, N.W., Washington, DC 20006; undated), p. 9.

53. *Ibid.*

54. *1972 Policy of National Farmers Union* (Farmers Union, Suite 1200, 1012 14th St. N.W., Washington, DC 20005; undated).

55. Statement of Weldon Barton, Assistant Legislative Director of Farmers Union before the Subcommittee on Livestock and Grains, House Committee on Agriculture, Washington, DC, September 18, 1972).

56. Chittick, *op. cit.,* p. 75.

57. Chittick, *op. cit.,* p. 77.

58. Riggs, *op. cit.*

59. *The American Legion Foreign Relations Program* (National Foreign Relations Commission, December 1970); various bulletins of the American Legion (American Legion, 1608 K St. N.W., Washington, DC 20006); *VFW Priority Goals for 1975: Legislative and Security* (Veterans of Foreign Wars, Broadway at 34th Street, Kansas City, MO 64111; undated); see also issues of *VFW American Security Reporter* (monthly); the director for national security and foreign affairs of the VFW has been kind enough over the last three years to mail me these publications plus the near-weekly bulletins to VFW officers.

60. "Leaders of American Legion, in a Major Shift, Seeking 'Friendly Dialogue' with Soviet War Veterans," *New York Times.*

61. Bulletin released on May 24, 1973, by Phelps Jones, Col. (Ret.), Director of National Security and Foreign Affairs for the VFW (Washington Memorial Building, 200 Maryland Ave., N.E., Washington, DC 20002).

62. See Roscoe Baker, *The American Legion and American Foreign Policy* (New York: Bookman Associates, 1954); the same impression comes from Raymond Moley, Jr., *The American Legion Story* (New York: Duell, Sloan, and Pearce, 1968).

63. Hanson Baldwin, "When the Big Guns Speak," in Lester Markel, ed., *Public Opinion and Foreign Policy* (New York: Harper and Bros., 1949), pp. 97–120.

64. Morris Janowitz, *The Professional Soldier: A Social and Political Portrait* (New York: Free Press, 1960), p. 383.

65. Donald R. Hall, *Cooperative Lobbying—The Power of Pressure* (Tucson: University of Arizona Press, 1969), p. 53.

66. *Ordnance,* 57, No. 313 (July–August 1972), p. 4.

67. "Objectives of the American Ordnance Association," *Mimeo,* May 14, 1969 (Transportation Building, Washington, DC 20006).

68. Eisenhower's farewell address, in Schiller and Phillips, eds., *op. cit.,* p. 31.

69. There also is a large and rapidly growing literature on the complex. See Schiller and Phillips, eds., *op. cit.*; Steven Rosen, ed., *Testing the Theory of the Military Industrial Complex* (Lexington, MA: D. C. Heath, 1973); Omer L. Carey, ed., *The Military-Industrial Complex and U.S. Foreign Policy* (Pullman: Washington State University Press, 1969); Sidney Lens, *The Military-Industrial Complex* (Philadelphia: Pilgrim Press, 1970). See also James Clotfelter, *The Military in American Politics* (New York: Harper & Row, 1973); Adam Yarmolinsky, *The Military Establishment* (New York: Harper & Row, 1973).

70. William Proxmire, "Retired High-Ranking Military Officers Employed by Large Contractors," in Schiller and Phillips, eds., *op. cit.*, pp. 65–74.

71. Carey, *op. cit.*, p. 58.

72. Charles Gray and Glen Gregory, "Military Spending and Senate Voting," *Journal of Peace Research*, 5 (1968): 44–54; Bruce Russett, *What Price Vigilance?* (New Haven, CT: Yale University Press, 1970); Stephen A. Cobb, "Defense Spending and Foreign Policy in the House of Representatives," *Journal of Conflict Resolution*, 13, No. 3 (September 1969): 358–69; Stephen Cobb, "The United States Senate and the Impact of Defense Spending Concentrations," in Rosen, *op. cit.*, pp. 197–224.

73. Barry Blechman, *et al.*, *Setting National Priorities: The 1975 Budget* (Washington, DC: Brookings Institution, 1974), p. 72. See also Jerome Slate and Terry Nardin, "The Concept of a Military-Industrial Complex," in Rosen, *op. cit.*, p. 44.

74. For information on both the ABM and SST battles, see *The Washington Lobby*, second edition (Washington, DC: *Congressional Quarterly*, 1974), pp. 12, 14.

75. Almond, *op. cit.*, p. 179.

76. *Study and Action: 1972–74 National Program* (Washington, DC: League of Women Voters, undated).

77. Alfred O. Hero, Jr., *American Religious Groups View Foreign Policy* (Durham, NC: Duke University Press, 1973), p. 226, Note 13; for a general discussion that suggests the general ineffectiveness of church lobbying, see James Adams, *The Growing Church Lobby in Washington* (Grand Rapids, MI: William B. Eerdmans, 1970).

78. See, for instance, The American Council of Christian Churches, *Christian Accent*, 2, No. 1 (Winter 1973), p. 12. Even more politically right-wing and nationalist sentiment is expressed by the Christian Echoes National Ministry, *Christian Crusade Weekly*.

79. Quoted in Sheldon Appleton, *United States Foreign Policy* (Boston: Little, Brown, 1968), p. 296.

80. Holbert Carroll, *The House of Representatives and Foreign Affairs* (Pittsburgh: University of Pittsburgh Press, 1958), p. 252.

81. Bernard C. Cohen, *The Public's Impact on Foreign Policy* (Boston: Little, Brown, 1973), p. 54.

82. This argument is made repeatedly in the bimonthly newsletter, *Brief.* For an interesting discussion of Jewish organizations, see Robert Silverberg, *If I Forget Thee O Jerusalem: American Jews and the State of Israel* (New York: William Morrow, 1970).

83. Lawrence H. Fuchs, "Minority Groups and Foreign Policy," in Lawrence H. Fuchs, ed., *American Ethnic Politics* (New York: Harper & Row, 1968), p. 149.

84. Carroll, *op. cit.,* p. 252. We shall evaluate claims of success made for this and other groups in the next chapter. Some such claims, however, remind the author of an elephant joke. A man was becoming annoyed at the incessant finger clicking of another man. Finally he asked the reason for it. The answer was that "It keeps the elephants away." The first man pointed out that there were no elephants within 100 miles of them. The obvious response: "See, it works!"

85. Hanna Fenichel Pitkin, *The Concept of Representation* (Berkeley: University of California Press, 1967), p. 115.

86. The Committee for a Free China (Institute of International Relations, Republic of China) commissioned a study by Allan C. Brownfeld called, "The Peking Connection: Communist China and the Narcotics Trade," published in *Issues and Studies,* 8, No. 6 (March 1972); see also their more general publication, *China Report* (Spring 1974), p. 5.

87. *The Washington Lobby,* second edition (Washington, DC: *Congressional Quarterly,* 1974), pp. 117–122. This probably accounts for the emphasis of the Americans for Middle East Understanding, Inc. (AMEU) and the National Association of Arab Americans on the deleterious effects of the oil embargo of 1973–1974. Almost certainly such emphasis contributes more to anti-Arab sentiment than it does to reevaluation of aid in Israel. See AMEU's newsletters of November 1 and 13, 1973 (AMEU, Rm. 538, 475 Riverside Drive, New York, NY 10027).

88. Chittick, *op. cit.,* p. 79.

89. Herring, *op. cit.,* p. 238.

90. See their newsletter, *Sane World.*

91. Resolutions on current issues and policy statement, adopted at the 25th General Assembly. See also monthly editions of *The World Citizen/Federalist Letter* (2029 K Street, N.W., Washington, DC 20006).

92. Members of Congress for Peace Through Law, *MCPL Report* (September 1975), Washington, DC, and MCPL self-description pamphlet.

93. *ACA Index: An Analysis of the Voting Record of Each Member in the Congress of the United States: 1st Session, 92nd Congress, 1971*

(Washington, DC: Americans for Constitutional Action, 1971); *Congressional Record: Digest and Tally of Roll Call Votes in the 93rd Congress of the United States, First and Second Sessions* (Washington, DC: Americans for Constitutional Action, 1973 and 1974).

94. See Leon Shull and Stina Santiestevan, *ADA Now, What Do We Want Right Now* reprinted from *Dissent* (December 1971), *ADA: Where It's Been, Where It's At* (undated); proposals adopted at the annual conventions of Americans for Democratic Action (1424 Sixteenth St., N.W., Washington, DC 20036).

95. "An Executive Branch that Protects Individual Liberties," In *Common, 7*, No. 1 (Winter 1976), pp. 12–16.

96. Fred Riggs, *op. cit.*, p. 44.

97. Richard Neustadt, *Presidential Power: The Politics of Leadership* (New York: John Wiley, 1960); for case studies, see Harry Bayard Price, *The Marshall Plan and Its Meaning* (Ithaca, NY: Cornell University, 1955); Joseph M. Jones, *The Fifteen Weeks* (New York: Viking Press, 1955).

98. Blaisdell, *American Democracy Under Pressure*, p. 256; for case studies of the organizations, see Wayne S. Cole, *America First: The Battle Against Intervention, 1940–41* (Madison: University of Wisconsin Press, 1953); Walter Johnson, *The Battle Against Isolation* (Chicago: University of Chicago Press, 1955).

99. Robert Dahl, *Congress and Foreign Policy* (New York: Harcourt Brace Jovanovich, 1950), p. 54.

100. *The Washington Lobby.*

101. *The Washington Lobby*, pp. 92–96.

102. Harry Elmer Barnes, "The World War of 1914–18," in Gerald N. Grob and George Athan Billias, eds., *Interpretations of American History* (New York: Free Press, 1972).

103. Bernard Cohen, *The Press and Foreign Policy* (Princeton, NJ: Princeton University Press, 1963), pp. 44–45. This is a comprehensive book on the subject.

104. For an argument that the press is not only an ineffective interest group but has even been muzzled by the government in the name of national security, see Dale Minor, *The Information War* (New York: Hawthorn Books, 1970).

105. Walter Lippmann, *Public Opinion* (New York: Macmillan, 1922), p. 275.

106. Cohen, *op. cit.*, p. 38.

107. Bernard Cohen, "Mass Communication and Foreign Policy," in James Rosenau, ed., *Domestic Sources of Foreign Policy* (New York: Free Press, 1967), p. 208. Besides his work on the press, Cohen has written

excellent material on interest groups, including *The Influence of Non-Government Groups on Foreign Policy-Making* (Boston: World Peace Foundation, 1959).

108. Cohen, *The Press and Foreign Policy*, pp. 56–57.

109. Bernard C. Cohen, "The Foreign Policy Reporter," in Douglas Fox, *The Politics of U.S. Foreign Policy Making* (Pacific Palisades, CA: Goodyear, 1971), p. 72.

110. Cohen, *The Press and Foreign Policy*, p. 75. Also on the press and foreign policy, see James Reston, *The Artillery of the Press: Its Influence on American Foreign Policy* (New York: Harper & Row, 1967).

7

The Variability
of Public Influence

A segment of the general American public has sufficient interest in and adequate knowledge about foreign policy that the individuals within that segment can maintain considerable control over foreign policy. We have seen that as much as 30 percent of the public (although generally a smaller percentage) fits into such a category. These people are sometimes called *opinion leaders*, because they frequently influence the attitudes of another and still larger group of people attentive to the most major foreign policy issues.[1] Opinion leaders and—to a lesser degree—the attentive public, do influence foreign policy in a number of ways—through sharing similar attitudes with those placed in decision-making positions, through electoral coercion or the anticipation of it by decision makers, and through party and interest group organizations.

The last five chapters of this book detailed the attitudes of opinion leaders and the attentive public and discussed the issue positions of the two major parties and various interest groups. They have thus tried to answer the first of the two questions that underlie this book: What does the public think about foreign policy? Those chapters have not, however, really grappled with the relative applicability of the various models of foreign policy decision making discussed in Chapter 1. That is, they have not answered this book's second question: What does it matter what the public thinks? As noted in Chapter 1, there is every reason to expect that no single model is completely appropriate in describing how the United States makes foreign policy. Advocates of different models generally illustrate their models with different examples. What we want to learn is whether there are clusters of issues with which we can identify the various models of decision making. The logical approach is first to try to discover the issues on which opinion leaders in general, parties, and various interest groups are relatively more important or less important. This chapter will undertake that exploration. Then we can generalize about the circumstances in which the various models are more or less appropriate, a task that is left for the next and last chapter.

Factors Underlying Public Influence

Three major factors interact to determine the extent and nature of general public and group influence on foreign policy decision making: the issue type, the focus of decision-making activity within the government, and the speed with which the decision is made. These three factors are by no means independent of each other. For instance, Congress has relatively more control over economic decisions than over diplomatic ones; and when decisions are made in Congress rather than in the executive branch, they almost always require more time to make. Nevertheless, it will be useful to comment on each of the factors individually before turning to their joint impact.

Of the political scientists who have attempted to identify the conditions under which the public and various interest groups are particularly effective or ineffective in the foreign policy process, Lester Milbrath was one of the most successful. Among his generalizations is the following:[2]

> Decisions on foreign policies that involve direct, visible (usually economic) rewards and/or punishment to different sectors of the society generally tend to be shared by Congress and the president . . . and to stimulate more lobbying activities by groups at many points of access.

Many have argued that interest groups more frequently affect decisions on domestic than do foreign affairs. Milbrath identifies the major reason: Foreign affairs less often have a direct and identifiable impact on any segment of the population.

Within the general area of foreign affairs, we can identify at least three specific issue areas: economic, security, and diplomatic. A given issue frequently falls into more than one issue area. For instance, the Marshall Plan was undertaken in the name of national security, but much debate raged over the nation's ability to afford the program, and many individuals and groups such as maritime interests saw an immediate economic impact on themselves. On the basis of the logic suggested above—identifiability of impact—we would expect groups within the public to become most active on foreign policy issues related to economics and least on diplomatic ones. Security issues clearly can have the most dramatic impact on lives, but the impact is frequently unpredictable and uncertain, so that groups less often see rewards or punishments in any one action.

The quotation from Milbrath also suggests the importance of the decision-making body in determining the extent of public influence in foreign policy. In addition to the identifiability of rewards from government economic decisions, another reason that groups become active in the making of economic decisions is the fact that Congress holds the constitutionally defined power of the purse. The public and various interest groups have more access to congressmen than to those in the executive branch because of the district system and the larger number of elected officials in Congress. Interest groups frequently have a regional base of strength even when they have a national organization, so that the regional representation of Congress becomes a benefit.

The arm of the executive branch in control of foreign relations, the State Department, is unlike the Departments of Commerce or Labor or the regulatory agencies, in that it has a much less identifiable clientele. Other agencies involved in foreign policy, like the Agency for International Development, are similarly free from pressure group influence, compared to Congress or domestic policy components of the executive. This is not to say that the executive is free from group influence. Prior to World War II, for example, antiwar groups forced strict administration of the neutrality laws,[3] and in 1968 antiwar groups helped force the winding down of the Vietnam War.

Another reason that Congress is the locus of decision making that is better suited to group influence is that Congress takes longer to make decisions and thus provides groups time to marshal forces. In general, the longer the period of decision making, the greater the opportunity for group participation, either in congressional or executive decision making. Much of the executive branch policy making in foreign policy takes place in a crisis atmosphere that gives groups little access.

A Typology of Decision Cases for Analysis of Group Influence

Table 7.1 uses two of the three factors discussed above (issue area and decision time) to establish an eight-category decision typology.[4] The locus of decision making was not used explicitly, because it is in very large part implicitly determined by the other two factors: Congress becomes increasingly involved in decisions when they have a greater economic component and when the time for decision making is longer.

Three dichotomies form the base of Table 7.1. The first is the length of time available for a decision. Time available was simply divided into short (not exceeding a month or two and often involving only days) and long. Many of the issues classified in Table 7.1 as involving long decision time are issues that recur frequently, such as decisions on the extent of trade we should have with communist countries. Two of the three dimensions in Table 7.1 come from the issues area factor. Economic considerations can either be important or *relatively* unimportant in decisions—they are hardly ever completely absent.[5] Issues that are debated in terms of the economic cost clearly fall into the first category. Those issues include some in which the economic cost or benefit is debated for the nation as a whole (e.g., the Marshall Plan or the defense budget) and others for which the economic impact is restricted to a population subgroup (e.g., Chile's nationalization of copper mines). The second dichotomy derived from the issue area factor separates issues on which national security is a paramount concern from those in which no major security issue is at stake. Those issues for which neither economic nor security concerns are paramount (see Columns 7 and 8 of Table 7.1) are primarily diplomatic issues. Again it should be stressed that the three issue areas, economic, security, and diplomatic, are not mutually exclusive.

Two or more examples illustrate each of the eight categories of Table 7.1. The next section of this chapter will use the typology of issues and the example issues in an effort to generalize about public involvement and influence in the foreign policy process. Insofar

TABLE 7.1
A TYPOLOGY OF FOREIGN POLICY DECISIONS, WITH EXAMPLES

ECONOMIC CONSIDERATIONS IMPORTANT				ECONOMIC CONSIDERATIONS RELATIVELY UNIMPORTANT			
Security issue		Nonsecurity issue		Security issue		Nonsecurity issue	
Decision time long (1)	Decision time short (2)	Decision time long (3)	Decision time short (4)	Decision time long (5)	Decision time short (6)	Decision time long (7)	Decision time short (8)
Size of defense budget	Marshall Plan	Tariff structure	Chile's copper nationalization	NATO formation	Korean invasion	Recognition of Biafra	U.N. vote to oust South Africa
Vietnam War deescalation	Foreign oil embargo	Weapons system choice	Peru's fishing extension	Arms Limitation Treaty	Cuban missile crisis	Admission of China to United Nations	
Extent of trade with communists		Japanese Fisheries Agreement			U-2 shot down	Japanese Peace Settlement	Arrest of prominent American citizen
ABM deployment					Berlin Airlift	Adherence to World Court	

as possible, the examples were chosen from the case study literature; that is, we know something about how decisions were or are made for many of these issues.

Examining the
Variability of Public Impact

It is extremely difficult to judge a group's impact on the decision process. Within the political science literature, statements of interest group influence become widely accepted through constant quotation, no matter how flimsy their initial basis.[6] Influence, the ability to elicit desired behavior from others, is the core of this chapter's discussion. Unfortunately, and not for lack of trying, political scientists still find it exceptionally difficult to measure influence. This failing has plagued all analyses of the domestic sources of government policy. Bernard Cohen has provided an excellent discussion of the long literature relying on "nonevidential assertions or implication of influence."[7] The end result of Cohen's review is not a new technique for influence determination. It is, instead, a resolve to proceed cautiously and analytically and to be as scientific as possible in a situation where we lack basic scientific tools. That must be the resolve of this study, too. And, since this analysis will rely heavily on earlier studies, it must also proceed skeptically, reevaluating assertions of influence that seem poorly documented and separating statements of *activity* from conclusions of *influence*.

The General Public (Opinion Leaders
and the Attentive Public)

The power of specific interest groups and the general attentive public to influence policy has three bases: the size of the group desiring to influence policy, the intensity of the group members' feelings, and access by the group to the decision process. When economically, ethnically, religiously, or ideologically identifiable segments of the public feel intensely about an issue, they often form an interest group. Some issues, however, affect a fairly wide stratum of people, represented by no single interest group. Frequently in such cases, coalitions of interest groups form in Washington to jointly lobby for their respective positions. For instance, in 1969 about twenty organizations, including the National Committee for a Sane

Nuclear Policy, Americans for Democratic Action, the Southern Christian Leadership Conference, and United World Federalists formed the *formal* Coalition on National Priorities to oppose ABM deployment.[8]

Such coalitions clearly provide the first base of power for the attentive public and opinion leaders: a large group. They also provide one means of access to decision makers, namely lobbying. Public opinion polls, the press, and the electoral process provide others, when time is adequate. The intensity of public interest depends on the issue. Specifically, we would expect the attentive public and opinion makers to hold relatively intense opinions about issues that combined security and economic concerns, less intense opinions about issues involving either security or economic matters, and very little interest in primarily diplomatic issues.

In sum, we would hypothesize that the public has the greatest potential influence in foreign policy when the issues are economic, security is relevant, and decision time is long. In short, the public should have greatest potential influence over those issues in Column 1 of Table 7.1. The public should have less influence when only economic or security matters are important but there is considerable time for decisions (Columns 3 and 5) or when both issue areas are relevant but time is short (Column 2).

A glance at the example issues in Table 7.1 confirms this judgment about potential influence, because the public has clearly had actual influence on many of the issues in Columns 1, 2, 3, and 5. The deescalation of the Vietnam War after 1968 has been cited several times in this book to illustrate public influence on foreign policy. Had we been trying to argue that the classical democratic model of making foreign policy was the most appropriate of the foreign policy models, we would certainly have focused on that issue and on others in Column 1. As always, it is impossible to definitely prove causality. Yet the strong temporal association between the movement of the public from support to opposition of the war and the change in administration policies from escalation to deescalation provides bases for a conclusion of causality.[9] Most important, the shift of public opinion, as evidenced by polls and demonstrations, was quite dramatic *prior to* deescalation.

The size of the defense budget also illustrates public influence. Between 1945 and the early 1960s, majorities of 60 percent and more of those with an opinion generally favored maintenance or increase in the defense budget size[10] (review Figure 4.3). Only the personal standing of Dwight Eisenhower was able to hold the line on budget increases. Moreover, by the end of the Eisenhower administration widespread pressure was building for the significant and expensive rebuilding of forces.[11] During the Kennedy years, a major expansion of strategic (nuclear) capability did begin, although the defense budget as a percentage of the GNP did not grow, a result of belt tightening for conventional forces in McNamara's Pentagon. By 1968, a majority of the public thought we were spending too much. Since then, considerable decreases in the defense budget as a proportion of the total budget and the GNP have been made. Clearly, the actual resistance to executive defense spending in the 1970s has come from the Senate, not from public opinion polls, but this does not deny the importance of the wider public in setting the climate of opinion within which the Senate works.

On the issues of ABM deployment and trade with the communists, there has not been the same breadth of public concern and interest, but there has been, nevertheless, a fairly intense concern extending beyond a handful of special interests. During both the Johnson and Nixon administrations, this stratum of the public retarded deployment of ABMs.

The public has played a smaller role on security issues without major economic components, like the formation of NATO and the Strategic Arms Limitations Talks (SALT) agreements (Column 5 in Table 7.1). In these two cases, the generally internationalist orientation of the center groups (opinion leaders) may well have been extremely important in Senate approval of the two actions, quite possibly against majority sentiment in the periphery of the public. On the economic but nonsecurity issues of Column 3, there is little evidence of general public interest, much less involvement. We have already discussed, for instance, how various specific economic interests dominate tariff deliberations, with more general public groups such as the League of Women Voters taking positions, but with comparatively little intensity or influence. Clearly, when it comes to decisions among weapons systems (e.g., between two bombers), the general public has no interest. (Weapons system choice might well have been labeled a security issue; it was not so labeled because the reference here is to choice among generally acceptable weapons, e.g., planes, after the decision to acquire some system has been made.) Bernard Cohen has extensively documented the negotiations over the Japanese Fisheries Agreement in 1952, and finds little awareness of it or even of the more general Japanese Peace Settlement.[12]

On the issues in Column 2 of Table 7.1, those with security and economic components but short decision times, there can be no question of public awareness and interest. Both the Marshall Plan and the oil embargo by the Mid-East in the winter of 1973–1974 had massive press coverage. For instance, the Marshall Plan merited 11,740 column inches in the New York Times versus 1124 column inches for the 1949 Reciprocal Trade Act.[13] In both cases, however, the decision period was *relatively* short, when compared to those containing the sequences of decisions on the defense budget or the ABM. In the fifteen weeks of deliberations leading up to the Marshall Plan and in the comparable period of the oil embargo, the public *learned* about the two situations and provided general support for governmental action but never really became involved in decision making. In both of these situations, however, and most clearly in the case of the Marshall Plan,[14] the government did look to the public for support and, to a lesser degree, even for guidance. In both cases, the press became very important in educating the public and in providing the government with a surrogate measure of public opinion. We will return to this role played by the press in a moment.

If the issues discussed above could be used to support the applicability of a classical democratic model of policy making, modified somewhat to recognize the relative importance of the opinion leaders and the unimportance of the mass public, the other issue categories of Table 7.1 could equally well support nondemocratic models of decision making. On some of those issues, however, specific groups within the public have considerable influence; in others, only elements within the executive branch appear important. Subsequent sections will comment on decision making on those issues.

The Press's Role

The last chapter treated the press as an interest group. Seldom, if ever, however, does the press have the unified and consistent point of view that characterizes interest groups. It is generally more appropriate to look at the press as a two-way channel of communication between government and opinion leaders.

There are, however, some instances in which a press viewpoint, rather than its function as an information conduit, does influence policy. For example, an editorial of one of the most respected newspapers or, more often, the report of a widely known columnist, might now and then focus governmental attention on a previously unconsidered alternative. Walter Lippmann apparently provided this service periodically. Another situation in which the press may have impact on policy beyond that gained by conveying the opinions of others is when the press spotlights a particular foreign policy issue or facet of government foreign policy. Some of the surprise revelations concerning decision making in the government are of particular importance here. Consider, for instance, the publication of the report, prepared in the Defense Department for McNamara, that came to be known as the Pentagon Papers. This action, taken first by the *New York Times,* and later by other papers, may not have had a significant immediate impact on government policy in Vietnam, but it sparked a large series of public debates over the war. Similarly, Jack Anderson's revelations of the reluctance of many in the State Department to support Pakistan against India in the conflict over Bangladesh gave additional encouragement to those groups internal and external to the government that opposed the Nixon policy.[15]

Primarily, however, the press is important as a conduit of opinion. It can serve the government in mobilizing public and group opinion in support of policy, or it can serve to bring pressure on the government from the domestic environment. We can hypothesize two conditions underlying the greatest press role. First, it is natural that the role of the press be greatest when its coverage is broadest. It will not be able to convey opinion or pressure in either direction if coverage is significantly limited. In terms of Table 7.1, then, the press role should be greatest when the public is attentive—an attentiveness in part created by the press but in part an independent phenomenon to which the press responds. Those issues involving both security and economy should receive greatest press attention; those involving only one of the two should receive less attention; those involving primarily diplomacy should merit the least coverage. The second condition under which we would expect the press to be most important is when the time available to the government for a decision is substantial. The communications process takes time, especially if instead of a mere information flow there is to be a dialogue between the government and those it represents.

This would lead us to expect that the issues in Table 7.1 for which the role of the press has been most important would be those in Columns 1 and 5: the general size of the defense budget, the decision to deescalate the Vietnam War, the formation of NATO, and the agreements on arms limitations following the SALT negotiations. There is substantial reason to accept this generalization. For example, the press's role throughout the Vietnam War, with a very lengthy ongoing decision-making process and a large attentive public, was substantial. The press aided communication in two directions. Especially in the early phases of the war, the press consistently reported information about the war provided by the government. As a result, it was a major factor in successful governmental efforts to build support for its policies. Later in the war, when considerable doubt was cast on the accuracy (or credibility) or government information and analyses, the press was less helpful to the government. The press also carried the message of the dissidents within the public to the rest of the public and the government. Although the press focus on the violent and the disruptive element of dissent very early in the 1960s did little to encourage a dialogue, the depth of press coverage grew as the movement against the war grew. During the crucial period, between 1966 and 1968, when public opinion began to shift away from support for the military effort, the press not only provided a very important dialogue between the two positions but also served as a major battlefield.

Press importance in other situations, such as the decision to create NATO or the decision to limit ABM deployments and missile number, may not have seemed quite as great, because a large, active opposition to the policies was absent. Yet the press provided a channel for communication by the government to the public in those situations and for whatever opposition that did exist. This can be contrasted fairly dramatically to such situations as crises in which time does not permit two-way communication. During the Cuban missile crisis of 1962, the press was provided no information from the government. The *New York Times* was specifically asked not to publish anything concerning the events when it uncovered the story.

The case studies of the issues and policies listed in Table 7.1 suggest an important press role in at least two other of the situations listed: U.S. reaction to the Korean invasion and the origination of the Marshall Plan. Although Truman's reaction to the North Korean invasion of South Korea was too swift for the press to serve as a channel for public discussion, a detailed case study of the Truman reaction concludes that it was in fact a sequence of actions and that subsequent actions were affected by the response in the press to earlier ones.[16] Immediately after news of the invasion reached Washington on June 24, 1950, Truman established a small decision-making body. On June 25 this group agreed that strong resistance was necessary. Editorials in respected papers on the same day reinforced this agreement. The commitment on June 26 of air and sea forces (without combat troops) was also reinforced by reaction from the press and Congress. The positions taken by the press in the first three days of the crisis were certainly very important in the decisions made on June 29 and 30 to commit combat troops. Had the initial reaction of the press to the invasion been less strong and less supportive of government action, the government might have limited action.

The development of both the Truman Doctrine and the Marshall Plan were other situations in which press response to potential government policy proved very important. The pattern established by press reporting of reaction encouraged the government. The press generally focused on the highly favorable reactions of the European governments and of the eastern seaboard area. The press did not focus on the less enthusiastic sentiment in the Midwest. The Marshall Plan took much longer to develop, of course, than a reaction to the North Korean invasion. As events unfolded, public opinion could be and was tapped more directly than by looking at press reaction; it proved highly favorable.[17]

Both the reaction to the Korean invasion and the Marshall Plan were situations in which decision time was somewhat limited. Thus, contrary to our earlier generalization that press impact is greatest when decision time is long and the public attentive, the press may be especially important in some cases when decision time is moderate. In these two cases, the press reaction was used by decision makers in part as a surrogate measure of general public reaction. James Reston suggested this role when he said: "The influence of the American press on American foreign policy, in my view, is usually exaggerated. Its influence is exercised primarily through the Congress, which confuses press opinion with public opinion."[18]

Two general statements may summarize the press role. First, the press is most important as a channel for a government/domestic opinion dialogue when press coverage is extensive (so that the public's attention is engaged) and when decision time is considerable. Second, the press may serve in an important role as an indicator of public reaction to potential or actual government policies, especially when coverage is substantial (the event is important) and when decision time is moderate.

The Parties

The press provides one mechanism by which some elements in the public communicate policy desires to the government and have some influence over policy. Political parties provide another. The motivation of this chapter is not to conclude that parties either work or do not work as a policy control mechanism. As in our discussion of the press and in the discussion to follow on interest groups, this chapter begins with an assumption that parties have *some* influence over policy but that party differences do not dictate policy. Data from previous chapters strongly support an attribution of effectiveness to all the mechanisms for public influence on policy that we have discussed. The motivation of this chapter is to begin to more closely define the role of parties (and of the press and interest groups) by making *relative* statements and to do so specifically by suggesting the circumstances under which parties are more or less useful in bringing public sentiment into the decision arena.

Chapter 5 noted that the partisan affiliation of postwar presidents has not markedly affected their foreign policy behavior. The office almost seems to demand a broadly internationalist orientation—a willingness to support foreign aid, to support freer trade, and to intervene militarily and/or covertly outside of the United States. Postwar presidents have differed in foreign policies but not perceptibly in partisan fashion. Chapter 5 also discussed a relative absence of partisan disagreements over foreign policy among party identifiers in the general public. In contrast, however, congressmen were shown in Chapter 5 to differ quite consistently on four different foreign policy issues: foreign economic and military aid, trade, and defense spending. Thus party differences can be important in the foreign policy process.

Although there exist clear party differences in Congress on foreign policy issues, these should be kept in perspective. A recent study of congressional party differences between 1953 and 1964 found that the extent of these differences varied considerably by the issue involved. On three clusters of issues the differences were considerable: social welfare, government management (i.e., management of the economy and national resources), and agricultural assistance. On international involvement issues, the differences were much less substantial, and on civil liberties issues the differences disappeared almost completely.[19]

The impact of partisanship on foreign policy will depend on two factors. First, given the greater importance of partisanship on foreign issues to congressmen than to the president, the party factor will be most important for issues requiring and allowing congressional action: those with a larger economic component and those with a fairly long period for decision. Second, the impact of partisanship on foreign policy should be greatest when the parties are most different. The study of congressional party voting noted above discovered greatest party differences on basically economic issues: social welfare, government management, and agricultural assistance. We would logically expect the foreign economic issues to again arouse greatest partisanship. Foreign security issues probably call forth something more nearly approximating a bipartisan reaction, and there is no reason to expect major partisan struggles over largely diplomatic issues.

The graphs of Chapter 5 support these hypotheses about congressional party differences. The most purely economic of the four issues examined in that chapter is trade policy. On trade issues votes throughout the postwar period, Senate and House Democrats and Republicans maintained clear (if diminishing) party positions. Almost never did the Democrats give less support for a free trade position than Republicans. The second issue with high economic content was foreign aid. In the House, Democrats almost always provided more support for foreign aid than Republicans, and in the Senate the Republicans infrequently and marginally surpassed Democrats in foreign aid support. The remaining two issues, military foreign aid and defense spending are frequently debated in economic terms but clearly touch on more general national security concerns. On these two issues, Democrats and Republicans in both houses of Congress alternated frequently in providing greatest support.

In general, then, we would expect partisanship to be most important on economic issues allowing considerable decision time (Columns 1 and 3 of Table 7.1) and least important on diplomatic issues or noneconomic issues with little decision time (Columns 6, 7, and 8 of Table 7.1). Moreover, of course, we would expect the parties to take positions primarily on those economic-based foreign policy issues involving the economic interest of large segments of the population (e.g., labor versus business) and major expenditures, rather than those involving only a single or limited set of industries. Table 7.1 confirms these judgements. Major foreign policy crises (security issues with short decision times), such as the Korean invasion, allow little or no congressional involvement and do not become partisan issues. If the conflict stretches on, however, and especially if the economic impact becomes an issue, as it did in the Korean and Vietnam Wars, parties do begin to be important.

Party identification is related to the foreign policy issue positions of a relatively small number of people in the general public. For these people, however, partisanship becomes one mechanism for an input into the foreign policy process.

Interest Groups: Economic

This section will focus on economic groups, and we will return to other types of interests in the next section. Several general statements can be made about the influence of economic interest groups. First, economic interest groups should quite naturally be most effective on issues that are in large part economic. Clearly they will be most interested in such issues. They will thus devote more time and money to attempts to influence policy. Another important factor is that the government is likely to see their interest in economic issues as legitimate and their expertise as useful. In short, the groups not only are very likely going to be concerned with issues that affect their interest, but the government is likely to be receptive to that concern. Second, time should aid the interest groups. The longer the decision process, the longer groups will have to become aware of the implications of an issue for them, to make a case for their position, and to convince decision makers to side with them. And finally, as Milbrath has suggested, issues on which there is only a small attentive public are most likely to be those on which economic interests are free to act. Since the public's attentiveness is increased when an issue has both economic *and* security components, economic interest groups should be hampered in influencing that set of issues, in spite of their interest and their expertise.

Turning again to Table 7.1, we can suggest on the basis of the generalizations in the previous paragraph that the influence of economic interest groups would be greatest in Column 3. That is, economic interest groups are most likely to be influential when there is decision making over a long period of time, when economic considerations are paramount, and when the issue has no major security component. The sample issues in that category are the tariff structure, a choice between two competing weapons systems, and a more specific issue, the agreement in 1952 with Japan on fishing in the North Pacific area. Decisions on all of these took or take form over a long period of time, public attention to all was or is low, and they have been *very* important to some economic interests.

There are important case studies of these issues. Bernard Cohen has looked in detail at the Japanese Fisheries Agreement and has uncovered intensive group activity and extensive group influence. West Coast fishing interests began to work as early as 1947 for a favorable fishing agreement, as soon as there was prospect of a peace treaty with Japan. They were active toward the State Department and toward West Coast senators; they were able to obtain the support of West Coast newspapers. The U.S. delegation that eventually went to Tokyo for final negotiations took with them a set of proposals drafted in such a way as to be satisfactory to the fishermen. The delegation also included advisors from the industry. In short, the North Pacific Fisheries Convention negotiation indicates how strong economic interests can be.[20]

Debates within Congress over tariff policy, and in particular, over the renewal of the Reciprocal Trade Agreement Act show the same intensive activity of economic interests but not the same extensiveness of influence. The major reason for lesser influence is competing interests. In spite of the considerable support within the business community for freer trade (especially among peak organizations like the National Association of Manufacturers), Bauer, Pool, and Dexter discovered that those who want protection are more likely to be active, since economic advantage is usually clearer in higher tariffs than in lower ones.[21] Although the balance of economic interest group activity is thus opposed to free trade, U.S. trade policy since the 1930s has been to steadily reduce trade barriers.[22]

At least three reasons can be given for the lesser importance of economic interest groups in tariffs than in the Japanese Fisheries Agreement. The first reason is that the economic interest groups themselves have been internally divided on the tariff issue. Although most letters to congressmen from businessmen may be protectionist, much testimony, especially that of the National Association of Manufacturers, the U.S. Chamber of Commerce, and other peak organizations has been for fewer trade barriers. This disagreement can be contrasted with that on the fisheries issue, where there was little disagreement among the major lobbyists, West Coast fishermen. The importance of opposition or lack of it in determining interest group pressure should be stressed. The second reason for less economic interest group influence on the tariff issue may be the extent of interest among the public. Although the public was listed in Table 5.1 as unattentive to the tariff issue, some segments have been very interested. For instance, the League of Women Voters has carried on massive campaigns for freer trade. More importantly, we already noted that the tariff issue affects such a wide variety of economic interests that the political parties have become very involved in tariff policy. Party involvement would limit the influence of specific economic interests. Finally, economic group influence on tariff policy has undoubtedly decreased because of the shift from Congress in the making of that policy to the executive.

Bauer, Pool, and Dexter note how much more important Schattschneider found pressure groups to be in the 1929–1930 negotiations, before the Reciprocal Trade Act of 1934 moved most tariff-setting power to the president.[23]

The above discussion should not lead us to conclude that economic interest groups are ineffective in tariff and trade policy. Pressure is frequently rewarded. Quotas (limits on the total annual imports of a commodity) can be used to circumvent for an industry the tariff levels set by the government in negotiation with other governments. Oil and sugar interests benefitted in this way for years, even in the face of growing shortages of petroleum and most recently of sugar products. In the last few years, "voluntary" quotas or restrictions on imports of Japanese steel and textiles have served the same purpose. Other kinds of restrictions on trade can also be noted; for example, one particularly resourceful interest managed to have a bill passed through the House requiring restaurants selling foreign trout to label it as such.[24]

In short, there is ample evidence in the tariff and Japanese fisheries issue to support the contention that interest groups are very active and often effective on economic issues in which the public is not highly involved and for which decision time is considerable. There can be little question that on the third issue in Column 3 of Table 7.1, choice among weapons systems, affected industries lobby intensively at all levels. The movement of military officers into executive suites, the log-rolling behavior of congressmen, and the other activities that indicate the working of a military-industrial complex all surface on issues of weapon system choice.

Going back to Table 7.1, we would also expect interest groups to have considerable concern about issues in Column 4, even if a necessity for rapid decision making precluded much participation. The two sample issues in that category, U.S. reaction to Chile's nationalization of copper and to Peru's extension of fishing limits from 12 to 200 miles suggest two further hypotheses. The first is that initial government action may be based less on anticipated desires of economic interest groups than on more general foreign policy considerations. Specifically, the government took no significant action to defend American business interests in either case. The second hypothesis is that groups may continue to exert pressure for a change in government policy or for a basic reversal of the initial decision, sometimes with delayed success. The continuing interest of fishing interests in Peru's action, as well as the State Department's sympathy for that interest, were documented in a film made by the State Department entitled "From Where I Sit." Kennecott and Anaconda Copper never gave up pushing claims against Chile or in their desire for U.S. support. Neither did ITT. The persistence of interest groups is considerable. Dayton McKean reports how the sugar interests, including the United States Beet Sugar Association, strove for years to obtain independence for the Philippines, since this would put up trade barriers against sugar from those islands (an interesting example also of how economic groups can benefit from U.S. overseas withdrawal rather than from colonial expansion).[25]

Economic interest groups may also have some influence in the first column of Table 7.1. The decision to deescalate the Vietnam War can hardly be attributed primarily to economic interest, unless that were so broadly interpreted as to include groups such as the poor and the aged, who were disadvantaged by military expenditures and war-related inflation. But economic interests were important in the eventual decision to deescalate, and they have also taken an active role in debates on both ABM deployment and trade with the communists. Again, these issues indicate the *limits* on special interest group influence when the issue also has a security component and therefore attracts the attention of a wider public. Those industries that could have benefitted from a massive ABM program faced the opposition of economics-oriented domestic interests and the argument that an ABM race would *threaten* national security by making first-strike capabilities credible. Economic interests only began to have an impact on policy regulating communist trade as detente grew, making the issue one decreasingly related to security.

It is interesting also to look at the economic foreign aid issue. Foreign aid policy reflects some security concerns but is largely an economic issue. The program has in part been shaped by a moderately attentive public. For instance, the general reluctance of many in the public to support "giveaways" has kept expenditures down and has also contributed to the increasing emphasis on loans rather than grants. But many characteristics of the program indicate the strength of particular group interests. For instance, the tying of loans and grants to purchases in the United States and the requirement that much of the materials shipped overseas travel in American merchant ships are in large part attributable to effective group lobbying in Congress and the executive. The U.S. merchant marine managed to obtain a requirement that 50 percent of all Marshall Plan shipments to Europe, including those to Norway, which had an important and depressed shipping industry, go in American ships. At the same time, some farm interests wanted to sell surplus agricultural products to Europe rather than to give them. In a related display of merchant marine strength, during February 1964, the International Longshoremen's Association refused to load wheat for Russia and other communist bloc countries until the government agreed that in the future 50 percent of all such grain would be carried in U.S. flagships.[26]

In summary, the following general statements can be made about economic interest groups. First, they are most influential in making policy with clear economic implications, with which the general public is not particularly concerned and for which the government has considerable decision-making time. Such policy will be strongly influenced by economic interests, especially when the decisions are made by Congress. An absence of opposition by other key economic or noneconomic groups will further increase influence. The ability of economic interest groups to make frequent and quite large campaign contributions to many candidates certainly underlies much of that strength. Second, economic interests are very active and have considerable staying power. Thus they will act to reverse or to modify government policy affecting them and may have considerable impact over the long run, even if initial decisions are adverse to them.

Interest Groups: Noneconomic

Although business, labor, and agricultural groups are generally more influential in the foreign policy arena than other special interest groups, there are a number of very active noneconomic groups. Veterans groups, women's organizations, and world peace groups frequently testify before congressional committees. Because of the wide variety of interests represented in this category, it is difficult to generalize about the types of issues that they are most likely to try to influence or about their likely success. Perhaps the most valid generalization is that some noneconomic groups are likely to be active on nearly every issue but that in general they are infrequently effective.

There are a number of reasons for their generally low level of impact. One of these is a relative disadvantage in comparison with economic groups or the general public. For instance, consider the tariff structure issue. Many groups, other than those with direct economic interests, testify whenever it is time to consider renewal of the Reciprocal Trade Agreements Act. Among these is the League of Women Voters. It has frequently been noted that the testimony of the League, and of other noneconomic groups is at a disadvantage because the League lacks a specific economic interest in the bill— its interest does not have the same legitimacy. Few presidents or congressmen would say today as did Calvin Coolidge, that "The man who builds a factory builds a temple." Yet economic groups, especially business groups, are thought by many politicians to be more important to the country than noneconomic groups. Moreover, the economic group that can argue with credibility that X jobs will be created or lost by a particular action will be assured an audience among legislators.[27]

Consider, for instance the relative impact of peace groups, who for years worked for an easing of tensions with the Soviet Union and China, and of the business interests whose desire for trade was a more important pressure behind an improvement of relations. One student of interest groups says[28]

> While important on occasion, the staying power, resources, and plausibility of program of these peace groups are hardly in the same class as those of the business groups with an economic stake in shipping policy. The peace groups by and large are considered either radical or unrealistic; the business groups, on the other hand, are generally regarded as "sound."

And just as noneconomic groups may be at a competitive disadvantage *vis-à-vis* economic groups, they are again when the general public becomes interested in an issue. The American Legion, for instance, has often found itself arrayed against the majority of the public, and this is one reason it has suffered defeat after defeat.[29] This argument must be qualified, however, since "the public" is in essence an amalgam of specific groups. Rather than rely exclusively on opinion polls or the press for a measure of public sentiment, decision makers are likely to see the position represented by the majority of lobbying groups as that of the majority of the public. In this sense, noneconomic groups clearly do wield influence. Yet it is qualitatively different from that of economic groups, which, singly or in small groups, can influence significant aspects of policy. Noneconomic groups are much more likely to require the massive coalition that makes them appear to represent "the public."

To summarize these arguments about when noneconomic groups are least likely to be effective (singly, that is), they will infrequently influence policy when either economic interest groups or a larger public has an interest in the issue. That is, neither economic nor security, but perhaps diplomatic issues are best suited for influence by noneconomic interest groups. These groups, too, are apt to benefit from longer decision periods. Thus our attention is drawn to Column 7 of Table 7.1. In fact, case studies of two of the issues in that column suggest the importance of noneconomic interest groups. Robert Dahl looked at the issue of U.S. adherence to the World Court:[30]

> In the last days of 1934 ... passage of a resolution of adherence to the World Court during the forthcoming session seemed almost certain. After polling their members, the majority and minority leaders of the Senate estimated that all but seven or eight Democrats and eight or ten Republicans would support the measure. Discussions began in the Senate on January 14, 1935. William Randolph Hearst and other "isolationists" immediately undertook a huge campaign in opposition to the court proposal. With a staff in the Mayflower Hotel they telephoned influential people throughout the country, and soon telegrams in opposition began to pour into the Senate. On January 29, thirty-six senators voted against the measure rather than the fifteen to eighteen originally anticipated. This was more than enough to prevent the necessary two-thirds majority, and the measure went down to another of its long series of defeats.

Similarly, the Committee of One Million, better known as the China Lobby, was formed to prevent U.S. recognition of The People's Republic of China and its admission to the United Nations. This group had a remarkable impact on our policy for many years. Because most diplomatic issues are handled by the executive, and accepted without question in the Congress, another barrier is placed in the way of noneconomic interest groups influence.

The example of the World Court issue illustrates the power of ad hoc groups that grow up in a short time, mobilize considerable sentiment, and then disintegrate. Holbert Carroll ascribed the influence of another ad hoc group:[31]

> In the spring of 1951, church groups actively backed the proposal to send American grain to India. Hundreds of letters from bishops and missionaries poured in upon Congress. Ministers mailed their sermons on the subject to their representative. In the final vote, dozens of members normally hostile to foreign aid proposals, particularly those of a relief nature, were lined up with the yeas.

Other examples of important ad hoc groups include the Committee to Defend America by Aiding the Allies and the America First Committee, which advocated and opposed, respectively, American participation in World War II. Another was the Citizens Committee for the Marshall Plan. It may be that the surge of an ad hoc group is respected because it, once again, provides some indication, however inadequate, of public opinion.[32]

In summary, the following generalizations can be made about the influence of noneconomic groups. First, these groups are not particularly effective. This is a result of competition with other groups and the public and of their frequent lack of legitimacy, and because the locus of decision making for many issues in which they are most interested is in the executive rather than in Congress. Second, individually they are most likely to be influential when economic considerations are not particularly important, when the public in general is not particularly concerned, and when decision time is substantial. Finally, in coalitions they can be influential, under the same circumstances in which the public is likely to be influential, and because they serve as an indicator of public sentiment to policy makers. This means that rapidly growing and large ad hoc groups can be especially effective.

The Public and Groups
in Foreign Policy Decision Making

This chapter has tried to answer the second of our two questions: What does it matter what the public thinks about foreign policy? The answer provided here is that it depends on the type of foreign policy decision. The general public, or at least the largest fraction of the general public ever involved in foreign policy decisions, most often has a role in decisions that involve both economic and security concerns and that allow relatively leisurely decision making. Since this category clearly contains very important decisions, our democratic instincts may cause that conclusion to cheer us somewhat. Remember, however, that the public involved in such decisions will still be a minority and that it has been a minority with a fairly strong internationalist bias throughout most of the postwar period. We have also seen in this chapter that the public can have a smaller but significant role in three other categories of decisions: in economic and security issues with little decision time and in both predominantly security and predominantly economic issues with much decision time. (In sum, the public is important in Column 1 of Table 7.1 and to a lesser degree in Columns 2, 3, and 5.)

The press's role appears to be maximized in two decision categories: economic and security decisions with long decision time and predominantly security issues with long decision time. In both of these types of decisions, the press can operate as a two-way conduit of information and an independent force in the decision process. (That is, influence of the press is concentrated in Columns 1 and 5.)

The role of parties becomes stronger when economic issues are involved and when decision time allows use of the congressional process. (Look at Columns 1 and 3.) Economic interest groups have their greatest policy impact when the issues affect them most and when a more general public fails to be involved. This means that economic but nonsecurity issues with long decision times are most conducive to such influence, and the groups will also seek influence on the same type of issues with more limited decision time. (See Columns 3 and 4.) Noneconomic interest groups have difficulty competing with economic groups and frequently, of course, have noneconomic interests. Thus their impact is maintained in predominantly diplomatic issues with considerable decision time. (Specifically, they play a large role in decisions in Column 7.)

Note that none of the domestic groupings discussed here proved important in Columns 6 and 8 of Table 7.1. That is, for decisions that are not predominantly economic and for which decision time is short, domestic factors do not seem to be involved. Column 8 contains decisions that are largely diplomatic and for which we would expect and perhaps want a largely diplomatic and standardized response. Column 6, however, contains those types of issues normally considered "crises." Here there is a very important set of decisions that are made largely without public input. This may not be surprising or even disconcerting—except through the "anticipated reaction" of the public, how could domestic factors have a role? What is especially interesting, however, is that a very large portion of the foreign policy decision-making literature concentrates on this category, in large part because of its drama. The bias that such case study selection would introduce into an evaluation of the public's role in decision making is obvious. For instance, one recent and very good set of case studies was analyzed specifically to evaluate the social context of foreign policy decisions.[33] Of eleven case studies, five fall into Column 6 of Table 7.1. None fall into Column 1, the category allowing greatest general public, press, and party influence, although the other six do belong in Columns 2, 3, and 5. Although the authors conclude on a relatively optimistic note concerning the role of domestic groupings, their case studies repeatedly point to a very limited role. In fact, one receives from the book a strong impression of presidential orchestration of public opinion, a pattern that is not surprising after action is taken in a crisis.

The issue categorization and the case study analyses in this chapter could very usefully be pursued much further. Nevertheless, the reader now has the background to move further into our general portrayal of domestic forces in foreign policy decision making.

Notes

1. This classification of the public differs from that of James Rosenau, *Public Opinion and Foreign Policy* (New York: Random House, 1961), pp. 27–31, even though the same terminology is used. Rosenau puts 70 to 90 percent of the population in a mass public category, only 1 to 2 percent in the opinion maker category, and puts the remaining individuals in the attentive public category.

2. Lester Milbrath, "Interest Groups and Foreign Policy," in James Rosenau, ed., *Domestic Sources of Foreign Policy* (New York: Free Press, 1967), p. 249.

3. Donald C. Blaisdell, *American Democracy Under Pressure* (New York: Ronald Press, 1957), p. 256.

4. This typology approach owes a conscious debt to James N. Rosenau, "Pre-Theories and Theories of Foreign Policy," in R. Barry Farrell, ed., *Approaches to Comparative and International Politics* (Evanston, IL: Northwestern University Press, 1966), pp. 27–92.

5. Arguments that the United States has entered wars in order to guarantee a present or potential economic interest are common, as are arguments that nearly all of U.S. foreign policy is economically motivated. For an interesting discussion of such arguments see Harry Elmer Barnes, "The World War of 1914–1918" in Gerald N. Grob and George Athan Billias, eds., *Interpretations of American History* (New York: Free Press, 1972), pp. 232–243.

6. Bernard Cohen has shown how widespread this problem is. See "The Relationship Between Public Opinion and Foreign Policy Maker," in Melvin Small, ed., *Public Opinion and Historians: Interdisciplinary Perspectives* (Detroit: Wayne State University Press, 1970), pp. 65–80.

7. Bernard Cohen, *The Public's Impact on Foreign Policy* (Boston: Little, Brown, 1973), pp. 8–13.

8. *The Washington Lobby*, second edition (Washington, DC: Congressional Quarterly, 1974), p. 12.

9. For some details of one study of the relationship, see the discussion by Barry R. McCaffery, "The Policy Process—United States Disengagement in Vietnam: The Role of Public Opinion and Congress," an unpublished graduate seminar paper, American University, School of International Service, December 5, 1970, as cited in Marian Irish and Elke Frank, *U.S. Foreign Policy* (New York: Harcourt Brace Jovanovich, 1975), p. 157.

10. See also Leslie H. Gelb, "Domestic Change and National Security Policy," in Henry Owen, ed., *The Next Phase in Foreign Policy* (Washington, DC: Brookings Institution, 1973), p. 251.

11. The report of the Gaither Committee was the tip of the iceberg. See John Donovan, *The Cold Warriors* (Lexington, MA: D. C. Heath, 1974.)

12. Bernard Cohen, *The Political Process and Foreign Policy: The Making of the Japanese Peace Settlement* (Princeton, NJ: Princeton University Press, 1957.)

13. *Ibid.*, p. 113.

14. Joseph M. Jones, *The Fifteen Weeks* (New York: Viking, 1955).

15. Jack Anderson, *The Anderson Papers* (New York: Random House, 1973).

16. Glen D. Paige, "The Korean Decision" in James Rosenau, ed., *International Politics and Foreign Policy*, revised edition (New York: Free Press, 1969), p. 464.

17. Jones, *op. cit.*

18. James Reston, *The Artillery of the Press: Its Influence on American Foreign Policy* (New York: Harper & Row, 1967), p. 63.

19. Ange Clausen, *How Congressmen Decide: A Policy Focus* (New York: St. Martin's Press, 1973).

20. Cohen, *The Political Process and Foreign Policy.*

21. Raymond Bauer, Ithiel de Sola Pool, Lewis Anthony Dexter, *American Business and Public Policy* (Chicago: Atherton, 1963), p. 210.

22. The balance of testimony before Congress also indicates the greater protectionist strength. See James Walter Lindeen, "Interest Group Attitudes Toward Reciprocal Trade Legislation," *Public Opinion Quarterly*, 34, No. 1 (Spring 1970), pp. 108–112.

23. Bauer, Pool, and Dexter, *op. cit.*, p. 25.

24. Holbert Carroll, *The House of Representatives and Foreign Affairs* (Pittsburgh: University of Pittsburgh Press, 1958), p. 39.

25. Dayton D. McKean, *Party and Pressure Politics* (Boston: Houghton Mifflin, 1949), p. 456.

26. William Chittick, *State Department, Press, and Pressure Groups* (New York: John Wiley-Interscience, 1970), p. 36. Also see Samuel A. Lawrence, *United States Merchant Shipping Policies and Politics* (Washington, DC: Brookings Institution, 1966).

27. One study suggests that among economic groups, not all are equally legitimate in the eyes of the legislators. Bonilla finds much more sympathy for business than for labor—see Bernard Cohen, *The Influence of Non-Governmental Groups on Foreign Policy Making* (Boston: World Peace Foundation, 1959), p. 17.

28. Donald C. Blaisdell, *Economic Power and Political Pressures*, Temporary National Economic Committee, Monograph No. 26 (Washington, DC: U.S. Government Printing Office, 1941).

29. Roscoe Baker, *The American Legion and American Foreign Policy* (New York: Bookman Associates, 1954).

30. Robert Dahl, *Congress and Foreign Policy* (New York: Harcourt Brace Jovanovich, 1950), p. 54.

31. Holbert Carroll, *op. cit.*, p. 254.

32. Bernard Cohen also suggests the importance of these ad hoc groups. See *The Influence of Non-Governmental Groups on Foreign Policy Making.*

33. Morton Berkowitz, P. G. Bock, and Vincent J. Fuccillo, *The Politics of American Foreign Policy: The Social Context of Decisions* (Englewood Cliffs, NJ: Prentice-Hall, 1977).

8

The American Public
and Foreign Policy

The last chapter made a number of relative statements about the importance in the foreign policy process of the attentive and opinion leader publics, the press, parties, and economic and non-economic interest groups. Specifically, it generalized about the issues on which each of these segments of the public wield greatest power in the policy process. The chapter laid the basis for a reexamination of the various foreign policy making models discussed in Chapter 1. We turn now to such a reexamination.

Classical Democratic Theory

Classical democratic theory portrays the general public as controlling the actions of those who make foreign policy by means of rational activist behavior. That is, people act rationally to choose positions on issues, and then are sufficiently activist to vote for decision makers on the basis of that rational choice. This model, like all others, conveys an understanding of part of the decision process but is inappropriate for the majority of people and for the majority of foreign policy issues.

The institutional structure that makes foreign policy works against the general applicability of the classical democratic model. Foreign policy decisions are made by the executive more often than are domestic decisions; this markedly reduces potential for public control over these decisions. The foreign policy interest and information levels of the public also work against general democratic control. Only about 30 percent of the public has fairly consistent interest in and basic knowledge about foreign policy. Another 40 percent or so can be counted on to be aware of the most crucial foreign policy issues. Those who argue normatively that the general public *should not* control foreign policy, given these interest and knowledge levels, are unfortunately as correct as those who argue descriptively that it *does not*. There are only minor differences on foreign policy issues between general public adherents of the two major parties, which makes general public control over foreign policy even more difficult.

We must turn our attention to the minority of the public that does meet the conditions for democratic control of foreign policy, that does have foreign policy knowledge and interest, and that is capable of acting to influence policy. The classical democratic model is appropriate for this group, taken separately. The members of this minority can act to control policy in a number of ways. For instance, they can use elections and the party system; congressmen frequently do vote along partisan lines on foreign policy issues, particularly economic ones.

Thus the classical democratic model really can work on some issues. Party differences are greatest on economic-based foreign policy issues. Since the public attends most to issues that have an economic *and* a security component, it should be those issues, such as the defense budget size, over which the public can theoretically exercise greatest control. For the public to influence policy, the period of decision making also has to be quite long or the issue has to recur. Both of these conditions provide time for public sentiment to form and to be recognized by decision makers. As importantly, these conditions maximize the opportunity for Congress to participate in the decision process. Best suited to public control are thus economic/security issues that recur frequently or allow long decision time, especially those that extend across elections. Examples

TABLE 8.1
IDENTIFICATION OF ISSUE CLUSTERS THAT BEST ILLUSTRATE VARIOUS MODELS OF FOREIGN POLICY DECISION MAKING

ECONOMIC CONSIDERATIONS IMPORTANT				ECONOMIC CONSIDERATIONS RELATIVELY UNIMPORTANT			
Security issue		Nonsecurity issue		Security issue		Nonsecurity issue	
Decision time long (1)	Decision time short (2)	Decision time long (3)	Decision time short (4)	Decision time long (5)	Decision time short (6)	Decision time long (7)	Decision time short (8)
CLASSICAL DEMOCRATIC	Rational actor	Bureaucratic political	Rational actor	Rational actor	RATIONAL ACTOR	ORGANIZATIONAL	ORGANIZATIONAL
or	or	or	or	or	or	or	or
PLURALIST	Classical democratic	Pluralist	Organizational	Power elite	POWER ELITE	Pluralist	Rational actor
or	or	or					
BUREAUCRATIC POLITICAL	Power elite	Organizational					

Note: Capital letters indicate the issues for which the model is most appropriate; lowercase letters indicate issues for which the model also has some explanatory power.

are the size of the defense budget, the deescalation of the Vietnam War, and policy concerning trade with the communists.

Between elections and on issues allowing less decision time, public opinion polls and the press can communicate public sentiment to makers of foreign policy and permit some opinion leader public control over policy. Again, this will be most effective when party positions differ (the issue has an economic component) and when the public is most attentive (the issues combine security and economic concerns). Table 8.1 reproduces Table 7.1 but notes for each issue cluster those foreign policy models that appear most appropriate. The classical democratic model (restricted to a minority of the public) can describe policy making best in Column 1, on economic/security issues with long decision time, and can to a lesser degree describe policy making on issues in Column 2, economic/security issues with shorter decision time. For explanation of the policy process on other issue clusters, we must turn to other models.

The Rational Actor Model

The rational actor model attributes to foreign policy decision making the steps of a rational decision process: deciding on goals and values, laying out alternatives, projecting and evaluating the consequences of alternative actions, and choosing. This model precludes the interactions of various groups with different goals, since not even the first step could be accomplished by such groups.

This model comes closest to describing foreign policy behavior in Column 6 of Table 8.1, on security issues with little time to make decisions. In all such crises, the president and his closest advisors basically follow a rational actor decision model, although they do it with varying degrees of competence. Frequently, the entire crisis is secret from the public, as was the Cuban missile crisis, and no public elements enter into the decision process in any way. At other times, as in 1950 after the North Korean attack on South Korea, the public becomes aware of events but has very marginal opportunities for participation in decisions.

Graham Allison, who first distinguished clearly among the rational actor, organizational, and bureaucratic politics models, would correctly argue that all three of those models help describe decision behavior on issues in the foreign policy crisis category. In fact, he used the Cuban missile crisis to illustrate the explanatory power of all three models. We are not disagreeing here. All of the models discussed in Chapter 1 and in this chapter can help us understand decision making (and public involvement) on *all of the issues* in Table 8.1. Nevertheless, security issues with restricted decision time best illustrate the rational actor model, and that model best describes the public role on those issues.

Decision making on nonsecurity/economic issues for which there is little decision time also can be described fairly well with the rational actor model, although not as well as decision making on security issues can be. The short decision time does not allow significant segments of the population to become involved, although as Chapter 7 noted, economic interest groups frequently become involved in the issue *after* initial decisions have been made. Often, of course, decision makers have made initial decisions on such issues that favor domestic economic groups. This neither means that such groups participated in the decisions nor implies that the decision-making procedure did not follow the rational actor model. If the goals and the values against which alternatives are evaluated prove to be those of such interest groups (for *whatever* reason), the rational actor model still applies.

Organizational-Institutional Models

The standard operating procedures and incremental decision making of the organizational model are relied on most heavily when the security of the organization is *not threatened*. This also appears true for that massive organization, the U.S. government. On largely diplomatic issues, such as those in Columns 7 and 8 of Table 8.1, the government infrequently reviews its standard responses or operating procedures and leaves significant authority for decision making and implementation with the State Department bureaucracy.

On largely economic issues, the organizational model applies to a lesser extent. Tariff policy, weapon system choices, and responses to nationalizations are quite formalized and slowly changing. The interest and influence of various economic groups, however, means that a stimulus to change more frequently surfaces than on diplomatic issues. Moreover, the shift of decision-making locus on those issues with longer decision time from the bureaucracy to the Congress, with its changing personalities and power balances, reduces long-term consistency in policy and the applicability of the organizational model. On the economic issues with little decision time, the organizational model shares descriptive power with the rational actor model. The latter will be especially important when the attention of top governmental officials is available for these relatively low-priority economic foreign matters or when the issue has infrequently arisen before, so that organization routines have not been developed. One study discovered, for instance, that even on a security issue such as the status of Berlin, the frequent repetition of crises threatening Western access to Berlin gradually moved the issue from one dealt with in a crisis atmosphere by small, rational actor-type group to one handled with standard procedures at lower levels.[1]

The Bureaucratic Politics Model

Proper functioning of bureaucratic politics decision-making procedures requires participation in the decision by a large range of bureaucratic groups and of allies for these groups in the wider public. Security/economic issues with considerable decision time are ideal for the model. These are the same issues to which the classical democratic model best applies. There is, in fact, much similarity between the two models. One difference centers on the motivation for participation by the attentive and opinion leader publics. In the bureaucratic politics model, their motivation is largely one of support for bureaucratic or governmental units that broaden the arena of conflict to permit public group participation or actually call on them for assistance. In the classical democratic model, the groups external to government are self-motivated and autonomous, rather than directed and allied. In reality, the truth is frequently a mix of these two motivations. A second difference between the two models concerns the nature of decision makers. The classical democratic model focuses primarily on elected and therefore controllable officials. The bureaucratic politics model directs our attention in addition to the appointed officials of the civilian and military bureaucracies.

The bureaucratic politics model has some but lesser applicability to predominantly economic issues with long decision time. Here again a fairly broad range of governmental and extragovernmental groups generally becomes involved in decisions. Because the range is narrower than with economic/security issues, however, more organizational model behavior can be expected on the part of the government.

The Power Elite Model

Power elite theories stress the convergence of interest among economic, military, and governmental elites. One might therefore conclude that the power elite model could best describe decision making on issues that most strongly affect the interests of that joint elite: economic/security issues. The study of public opinion and interest groups in this book, however, suggests that on such issues a wide variety of competing groups become interested and involved in the policy process. An adherent of the power elite theory would probably not deny such broad interest, but would argue the dominance of the central elite over those other public interests.

This book presents too much evidence of competing interest on economic/security issues and suggests too many opportunities for interests to enter the decision arena, to support a conclusion that a power elite dominates these issues. The absence of competing elites is most obvious on diplomatic and security issues. Diplomatic issues may be dominated by a bureaucratic elite, but a power elite would have relatively little interest in them. That leaves only security issues. In fact, the power elite model becomes a logical competitor with the rational actor model in efforts to explain decision behavior on purely security issues, especially when decision time is short.

The two models, power elite and rational actor, are actually not so different. Power elite theorists have always assumed a basically rational actor mode of decision making in which the values and goals that guide the decision-making process have, of course, been those of the economic/security/governmental elite. It should once again be stressed that the rational actor model of decision making does not imply that the goals and values of the decision makers are "rational" by any objective standard, only that those values, whatever they are, guide the decision process in a rational manner. That rational actor model is, for instance, widely used to interpret Soviet decision behavior, especially by those who feel that the basic values and goals of the Soviet Union are ideological and that the Soviet government is dominated by a power elite.

There is one additional set of issues, not reflected in the categorization of these last two chapters, for which the power elite and rational actor models vie for explanatory power: secret decisions. Many foreign policy decisions are made without public observation of the process. In the post-World War II period, these have included the decision to blockade Cuba during the missile crisis and the decision to invade Cambodia near the end of the Vietnam War. This type of decision, because presidents expect them to eventually be public knowledge, cannot be made as independently of public sentiment as can still another set of decisions—those which are *made and implemented* secretly. The decision to "destabilize" the Chilean government of Allende is a recent example of such action.

The choice between the power elite model and the rational actor model to explain crisis and/or secret decision making thus becomes a choice dependent on a perception of the values that guide the decision process and the decision makers. If the values and goals guiding the decision process are those of a societal elite only, the power elite model is appropriate. If the values underlying the decisions are more widely shared, the decision process can still be described by a rational actor model, but not the power elite variant.

The power elite model has some but less potential applicability on (nonsecret) security issues allowing more time or on economic/security issues with little decision time. It has less applicability because competing interests become more important in both categories. This conclusion assumes, of course, that economic interests are divided among themselves and frequently find themselves opposed by other domestic and governmental interests; if the reader does not accept that assumption, growing out of the analysis in Chapter 6, the power elite model becomes applicable across the entire range of foreign policy issues.

The Pluralist Model

The pluralist model has much in common with both the bureaucratic politics model and the classical democratic model. It differs from the bureaucratic politics model in the same ways that the classical democratic model does: in terms of motivation for participation by public groups and in the nature of the decision makers. It differs from the classical democratic model in its focus on a smaller segment of the population (primarily the opinion leaders), in its emphasis on the division of elites into various interests, and in its perception of competition among those interests.

Not surprisingly, the pluralist model seems best fitted to explain decision behavior on economic/security issues with considerable decision time. A wide variety of competing elites did interact during the debate over the Vietnam War and that over the ABM. The defense budget so clearly affects the interests of everyone in the country that it draws the attention of nearly every organized group. The pluralist model is applicable to a lesser degree on other issues that allow considerable decision time, especially economic and diplomatic issues. In the case of the diplomatic issues, Chapter 7 discussed how ad hoc groups became involved in the issues of U.S. adherence to the World Court and how the Committee of One Million influenced U.S. behavior toward China.

Final Comment

A model is a simplified view of reality. It focuses on and exaggerates some aspects of reality, while deemphasizing or ignoring others. Models are thus never completely accurate and are only more or less useful, depending on their ability to teach us something and to help us organize our understanding of the environment. Each of the models we have discussed has these capabilities. Each clarifies some aspects of the relationship between the American public and American foreign policy. It might be satisfying to end with a simple, definitive statement about the way in which the United States makes foreign policy, rather than with this sketch of a more encompassing model. Fortunately for scholars, practitioners, and observers, the political process remains more complex and exciting than any model we have yet devised.

Note

1. Charles McClelland, "Access to Berlin: The Quantity and Variety of Events, 1948–63," in J. David Singer, ed., *Quantitative International Politics* (New York: Free Press, 1968), pp. 159–186.

Index